BEHIND THE NUMBERS

U.S. Trade in the World Economy

ANNE Y. KESTER, *Editor*

Panel on Foreign Trade Statistics
ROBERT E. BALDWIN, *Chair*

Committee on National Statistics
Commission on Behavioral and Social Sciences and Education
National Research Council

NATIONAL ACADEMY PRESS
Washington, D.C. 1992

AMH 8527-7/2

NATIONAL ACADEMY PRESS 2101 Constitution Ave., N.W. Washington, D.C. 20418

NOTICE: The project that is the subject of this report was approved by the Governing Board of the National Research Council, whose members are drawn from the councils of the National Academy of Sciences, the National Academy of Engineering, and the Institute of Medicine. The members of the committee responsible for the report were chosen for their special competencies and with regard for appropriate balance.

This report has been reviewed by a group other than the authors according to procedures approved by a Report Review Committee consisting of members of the National Academy of Sciences, the National Academy of Engineering, and the Institute of Medicine.

This project was supported by funds from the Bureau of the Census, the Bureau of Economic Analysis, and the International Trade Administration, all of the U.S. Department of Commerce; the Customs Service of the U.S. Department of the Treasury; and a research grant from the Chase Manhattan Bank.

Library of Congress Cataloging-in-Publication Data

National Research Council (U.S.). Panel on Foreign Trade Statistics.
  Behind the numbers : U.S. trade in the world economy / Panel on
Foreign Trade Statistics, Committee on National Statistics,
Commission on Behavioral and Social Sciences and Education, National
Research Council ; Anne Y. Kester, editor.
    p. cm.
  Includes bibliographical references and index.
  ISBN 0-309-04590-8
  1. Exports—United States. 2. United States—Commerce. 3. United
States—Foreign economic relations. I. Kester, Annie Y.
II. Title.
HF3031.N38 1992
382'.0973—dc20   91-42746
                                                            CIP

This book is printed on acid-free recycled stock that is made from 70% de-inked fiber of which 10% is postconsumer waste. ♻

Printed in the United States of America

Contents

PART II

IMPROVING DATA ON MERCHANDISE TRADE,
INTERNATIONAL SERVICES TRANSACTIONS, AND CAPITAL FLOWS

APPENDICES

The National Academy of Sciences is a private, nonprofit, self-perpetuating society of distinguished scholars engaged in scientific and engineering research, dedicated to the furtherance of science and technology and to their use for the general welfare. Upon the authority of the charter granted to it by the Congress in 1863, the Academy has a mandate that requires it to advise the federal government on scientific and technical matters. Dr. Frank Press is president of the National Academy of Sciences.

The National Academy of Engineering was established in 1964, under the charter of the National Academy of Sciences, as a parallel organization of outstanding engineers. It is autonomous in its administration and in the selection of its members, sharing with the National Academy of Sciences the responsibility for advising the federal government. The National Academy of Engineering also sponsors engineering programs aimed at meeting national needs, encourages education and research, and recognizes the superior achievements of engineers. Dr. Robert M. White is president of the National Academy of Engineering.

The Institute of Medicine was established in 1970 by the National Academy of Sciences to secure the services of eminent members of appropriate professions in the examination of policy matters pertaining to the health of the public. The Institute acts under the responsibility given to the National Academy of Sciences by its congressional charter to be an adviser to the federal government and, upon its own initiative, to identify issues of medical care, research, and education. Dr. Stuart Bondurant is acting president of the Institute of Medicine.

The National Research Council was organized by the National Academy of Sciences in 1916 to associate the broad community of science and technology with the Academy's purposes of furthering knowledge and advising the federal government. Functioning in accordance with general policies determined by the Academy, the Council has become the principal operating agency of both the National Academy of Sciences and the National Academy of Engineering in providing services to the government, the public, and the scientific and engineering communities. The Council is administered jointly by both Academies and the Institute of Medicine. Dr. Frank Press and Dr. Robert M. White are chairman and vice chairman, respectively, of the National Research Council.

Acknowledgments

This report covers many major issues and areas concerning the information needed to guide public and private decision making in the increasingly internationalized U.S. economy. In undertaking the study, the panel benefited greatly from the technical assistance provided by the capable staffs of the sponsoring agencies, as well as from the help of numerous experts from other federal agencies, international organizations, businesses, trade associations, and private researchers.

For their invaluable assistance, we are particularly indebted to Charles Waite and Don Adams of the Census Bureau; Samuel Banks of the Customs Service; Allan Young, Carol Carson, Steven Landefeld, and Obie Whichard of the Bureau of Economic Analysis; William Sullivan of the International Trade Administration; Lois Stekler of the staff of the Federal Reserve Board; Fuku Kimura of the State University of New York at Stonybrook; Mark Watson of Northwestern University; and Ruth Judson at the Massachusetts Institute of Technology.

We are also grateful to many others: From the Census Bureau: Bruce Walter, Gerald E. Kotwas, Walter Neece, Francis McCormick, John Govoni, Kathy Puzzilla, Charles Wood, and Michael Farrell. From the Customs Service: Roland Bernier. From the Bureau of Economic Analysis: Betty Barker, Anthony J. Dilullo, Ralph Kozlow, Howard Murad, David Belli, Russell Scholl, and Paula Young. From the International Trade Administration: Victor Bailey, Lester Davis, Bruce Guthrie, Douglas Cleveland, and Roger Palmeroy. From the Office of Business Analysis of the Department of Commerce: John E. Cremeans.

From the Federal Reserve Board: Peter Hooper III, Guy V.G. Stevens, Albert M. Teplin, and Kathryn Morisse. From the Federal Reserve Bank of New York: Akbar Akhtar and Beth Schwartzberg.

From other government agencies: Bernard Ascher and Geza Feketekuty, Office of the U.S. Trade Representative; Paul Bugg, Office of Management and Budget; Henry Kelly, Office of Technology Assessment; Ashby McCown, U.S. Department of the Treasury; Katrina Reut and Brian MacDonald, Bureau of Labor Statistics; and Eugene A. Rosengarden, U.S. International Trade Commission.

From the International Monetary Fund: Jack J. Bame, Mahinder Gill, Keith McAlister, and John McLenoghan. From the World Bank: Michael Finger. From the Organization for Economic Cooperation and Development: Andrew Wyckoff.

Researchers, business executives, and others: Walter Joelson, General Electric; Walter Lederer, private consultant; Clopper Almon, University of Maryland; William Cline, Institute for International Economics; Joseph Duncan, Dun & Bradstreet; Jacob Ryten, Statistics Canada; Nicholas Sargen, Salomon Brothers, Inc.; Robert Mellman, J.P. Morgan; F. Helmut Brammen, the National Trade Facilitation Council; Brian Horrigan, WEFA Group; Alvis Pauga, Foreign Trade Data Users Group; Margaret McCarthy, University of Maryland; and staff of the Committee on International Trade and Foreign Relations, National Governors' Association.

Many data users and data filers participated in our canvass of their views of the existing statistical systems on U.S. international transactions. To each of them, we extend our gratitude for their insightful comments.

The completion of the study would not have been possible without the dedication and expertise of the panel's staff. Under the capable leadership of our study director, Anne Kester, our consultants worked effectively to gather information, analyze it, and develop options. We thank Thomas Jabine for his analyses of the possible uses of sampling in the collection of data and of users' data needs, Samuel Pizer for his reviews of existing data on international services transactions and capital flows, Jacob Deutch for his work on quality control and the need for increased automation, and Ellen Tenenbaum for her assessments of the comparability of trade and domestic economic data.

We could not have undertaken this effort had it not been for Miron Straf, director of the Committee on National Statistics, and Edwin Goldfield, senior associate on the committee staff, who were instrumental in the formation of the panel, sought funding for its work, and freely shared their many insights about the federal statistical systems. We are also grateful to Eugenia Grohman, associate director for reports of the Commission on Behavioral and Social Sciences and Education, for her able and efficient guidance throughout the editing and production of this report. We thank Melissa Marsden and Helen Lopez for their patience in typing various drafts of the report and their capable assistance on a host of administrative matters.

Our special appreciation goes to Anne Kester for her outstanding efforts in directing the study. Anne recruited our consultants. She worked untiringly with panel members to thoroughly investigate the issues and enthusiastically coordinate our work with numerous experts in the United States and abroad. Anne also made significant substantive contributions to the study.

Finally, over the past 2 years, the panel members provided their untiring services despite their busy schedules. I am especially grateful to them for their efforts and achievements on behalf of the study.

Robert E. Baldwin, *Chair*
Panel on Foreign Trade Statistics

BEHIND THE NUMBERS

Summary of Major Conclusions and Recommendations

As the U.S. economy becomes increasingly internationalized, it is essential that public and private decision makers have timely, accurate, and relevant information on U.S. international economic activities. The existing data collection system for U.S. international transactions was developed in a period when the United States was less integrated in the world economy than it is today. Although various federal agencies in recent years have made significant efforts to improve the data, the increasingly complex nature of international economic activities has complicated their tasks, and major shortcomings remain.

To assist public and private decision makers, who increasingly face new economic policy issues and unprecedented business opportunities in a competitive world economic environment, federal statistical agencies must set priorities as they seek to upgrade existing data systems. The goal should be to move toward a flexible and responsive system of data collection that provides timely, accurate, relevant, and cost-effective data. To reach the goal, the Panel on Foreign Trade Statistics concludes that the agencies must undertake three sets of activities:

• Supplementing the existing statistical framework and integrating disparate data sets to accurately reflect the changing structure of the U.S. economy and facilitate more comprehensive analysis of U.S. international economic activities in the emerging global trading environment;

• Enhancing data accuracy, coverage, and usability through increased emphasis on compliance by data filers and through increased productivity in data collection processes; and

• Improving the data collection and data analysis interface to ensure relevant data are compiled.

This overarching conclusion is based on an extensive review of existing systems used to collect data on U.S. merchandise trade and international services transactions, and, to a more limited extent, capital flows.

This summary presents the panel's specific conclusions and high-priority recommendations, which are in the order of the chapters of the report. Detailed analyses and additional recommendations are in each chapter.

The panel's recommendations have taken into account the budgetary constraints faced by statistical agencies. The panel supports the economic statistics initiative of the President's Council of Economic Advisers that calls for increases in several agency budgets to improve the quality of federal economic statistics, particularly those on U.S. international transactions. The panel's emphasis is on increasing the operational efficiency and cost-effectiveness of statistical programs and the importance of producing useful information relevant to the new global trading environment, rather than on correcting old problems that may not be worth attention in the internationalized U.S. economy.

SUPPLEMENTING THE EXISTING STATISTICAL FRAMEWORK AND INTEGRATING DISPARATE DATA SETS

Two major economic forces have been shaping the international trading environment over the past several decades: rapid technological changes and the liberalization and deregulation of domestic and international markets. These forces have accelerated the movement of goods, services, labor, capital, and information across national boundaries, which in turn have increased globalization of production, integration of financial markets, and proliferation of transnational investment activities. These developments have altered the nature and extent of international transactions. They have also significantly transformed the U.S. economy and made it considerably more interdependent with those of other countries.

As the U.S. economy has become more internationalized, policy makers increasingly have had to deal with new economic policy issues, including coordinating U.S. economic policies with those of other nations; negotiating bilateral, regional, and multinational trade agreements to enhance market access for U.S. goods and services abroad; formulating domestic programs to improve the nation's ability to compete internationally; and assessing the impact of international trade and financial transactions on the domestic economy and its various sectors. Businesses increasingly have to weigh the opportunities of selling at home and abroad; evaluate the cost-effectiveness of producing domestically and overseas; and consider the merits of engaging in various collaborative activities with foreign counterparts to maximize market opportunities. The new economic policy issues arising from the growing interdependence of national economies and increasingly complex commercial relations of business enterprises call for a broadened statistical framework that relates explicitly to the emerging international trading environment.

A Supplemental Framework

Underlying the compilation of existing data on U.S. international transactions is the concept of cross-border transactions—of residents versus nonresidents—as well as the separation of domestic and international economic activities. International transactions are defined as involving the transfer of ownership of goods, services, and capital flows between U.S. residents and those of foreign states, with national boundaries establishing the distinction between residents and nonresidents. These concepts are used because a common purpose of these statistics is to provide data for the nation's balance-of-payments accounts, a summary statistical statement of transactions in goods, services, and capital flows between U.S. residents and those of the rest of the world during a given period.

Although the balance-of-payments framework is useful for understanding changes in the nation's general price level and domestic output and employment, it is inadequate for analyzing new economic issues arising from the emerging international economic order. Most important, it does not capture the sales and purchases of goods and services by foreign affiliates of U.S. firms abroad and U.S. affiliates of foreign firms in the United States; those transactions are several times larger than the combined value of U.S. imports and exports.

A supplemental statistical framework that integrates data on cross-border goods and services activities compiled under the balance-of-payments accounts and those on sales and purchases by affiliates' operations collected outside the balance-of-payments framework is needed (1) to improve understanding of the transformation of the U.S. economy; (2) to assess the international competitiveness of U.S. firms; (3) to examine the impact of foreign direct investment in the United States on the U.S. economy and that of U.S. direct investment abroad on foreign economies; and (4) to facilitate multilateral, regional, and bilateral negotiations on improved market access for U.S. firms in foreign countries and for such purposes as developing local-content rules in free trade areas.

One convenient way of developing such a framework is to organize data on U.S. international economic activities by national ownership (that is, U.S. owned versus foreign owned) of the firms selling the goods and services, rather than the country of residency of the firms selling the goods and services. Using such a framework to report on U.S. international economic activities provides a different perspective on the performance of the U.S. internationalized economy from that depicted under the balance-of-payments accounts. For example, the balance-of-payments account for 1987 shows a U.S. trade deficit of goods and services of $148 billion, but the supplemental framework shows that the sales of goods and services by U.S.-owned firms (located either in the United States or abroad) were only $64 billion less than purchases from foreign-owned firms (located either in the United States and abroad.

The figures derived under the supplemental framework do not mean that the usual macroeconomic concerns about the U.S. trade deficit should be modified, but one can infer from the framework that U.S.-owned business is competing in the world economy better than is often inferred from the trade statistics. The supplemental framework also provides additional perspectives on the impact of foreign-owned enterprises on the economic performance of the internationalized U.S. economy.

COMPARABLE DATA

As domestic and international economic activities are increasingly linked, improving the comparability of domestic production and other economic data with data on international economic activities will enhance the analytical usefulness of existing data. Moreover, as the world economy becomes increasingly interdependent, international economic activities will require more comparable economic data across countries.

At present, there is limited comparability between data on U.S. international economic activities and those on domestic production.

Different classification systems, collection methods, and levels of detail are currently used to compile data on U.S. trade in goods and services and capital flows. Still other classifications, collection methods, and levels of detail are used to monitor domestic production, employment, services, and financial activities. Although comparisons of data on trade in goods and domestic production are possible through the use of concordances that artificially bridge the data sets, it remains extremely difficult to make such comparisons for services and financial transactions. The disparateness of data sets has limited the analytical usefulness of existing data, especially for assessing the impact of international economic activities on the domestic economy and its various sectors.

Cross-border trade in services, for example, is grouped in only about 25 categories, as compared with 125 for domestic services, while sales of services by foreign affiliates of U.S. firms are classified into still fewer categories. Meanwhile, some types of services—for example, transportation, communications, finance, and insurance—are not even covered in the domestic quinquennial economic censuses, but they are included in international services data. Other categories of transactions are classified at different levels of detail of the Standard Industrial Classification (SIC), a classification system that is unique to the United States. Because of these differences in the level of detail at which disparate data are compiled, different sectors of the internationalized U.S. economy can be related to each other only at a fairly aggregate level.

Comparable data on international transactions at disaggregated detailed levels across countries are not available because of differences among countries in their coverage, definitions, concepts, and methodologies. As a result, international comparisons of production, trade, and financial activities are at best tenuous. Several efforts are currently under way by international organizations to harmonize data across countries. U.S. efforts to improve the nation's statistical systems for international transactions can fit into that ongoing work.

RECOMMENDATIONS

Recommendation 1-1   A supplemental statistical framework that integrates balance-of-payments data and data on affiliates' operations at home and abroad should be developed to better reflect the link between trade and foreign direct investment.

Recommendation 2-1 The United States should take the lead in international cooperative efforts to build coherent comparable worldwide accounts through standardizing data concepts and methodologies on production, trade, employment, and investment and establishing a statistical framework that captures changing international commercial relations.

Recommendation 2-2 As part of the quinquennial surveys, the Census Bureau should collect data on purchases of imported goods and services. The Bureau of Economic Analysis should use the data to strengthen its program on the compilation of the U.S. input-output tables.

Recommendation 2-3 Data at the four-digit SIC industry level, compiled in most cases on a four-digit SIC product basis, should be collected not only on the domestic production of goods, but also on the domestic production of services, the production of goods and services by foreign affiliates, and foreign direct investment so that data on international trade in goods and services can be related to these data. Quantitative and qualitative information about the use of labor, capital, and intermediate inputs in producing goods and services should also be collected at the four-digit SIC level. Data on the trade of affiliates should also be collected in greater detail.

ENHANCING DATA QUALITY

There are major data gaps and quality problems with existing data on U.S. international transactions. One indication of the seriousness of the data gap problem is the growing statistical discrepancy in the U.S. balance-of-payments accounts, which, in 1990 alone, surged to an unprecedented $63.5 billion, or about 70 percent of the current account deficit. Underreporting of exports of goods and inadequate coverage of U.S. international services and portfolio transactions are among the key sources of such discrepancies. Among factors contributing to these errors and omissions are deficiencies in the existing data collection systems. They include lax enforcement of compliance requirements, inadequate data base management by statistical agencies, and reliance on archaic methods of data collection.

Adequate data are also lacking on foreign goods and services used as intermediate inputs in domestic production activities. To date, analysts have only been able to make a rough estimate for the input-output table of the value of intermediate inputs that are imported and used by any industry. Yet having accurate information about the foreign content of any product is becoming increasingly important not only as indicators of the rising trend of intracompany trade and guides to setting standards in bilateral, regional, and multilateral negotiations involving customs unions and free trade areas, but also as indicators of the changing structure of U.S. industry.

There are also problems with the timeliness and usability of existing data. Although there is often a tradeoff between data accuracy and timeliness, we believe that enhancing the quality and the productivity of processes for producing existing statistics will improve both accuracy and timeliness.

Existing data could also be made more useful. Users of data on U.S. international transactions often report difficulties using the data in their current forms, formats, and distribution media. Changes in processing procedures or definitions have made data comparisons over time difficult or impossible, and limited data comparability has diminished the analytic usefulness of the data.

There is almost no evidence of modern process quality management in the statistical agencies that produce the data on U.S. international transactions. Although some inspection-based quality-control measures exist, these appear largely focused on controlling human processing errors. Yet improvements in process quality and productivity are essential for significant gains in the efficiency, accuracy, and timeliness of U.S. international trade and financial statistics.

MERCHANDISE TRADE

Enhanced coordination between the Customs Service and the Census Bureau and a substantial rise in electronic filing of import data have significantly reduced processing delays and lowered carryovers on merchandise trade data in recent years. Nonetheless, the underreporting of exports remains a problem, and other operational improvements are needed. Underreporting of exports is related to the de facto voluntary compliance by filers. Although import documents are reviewed in connection with tariff collection, export documents are subject to minimal scrutiny by Customs. In addition, in an effort to promote U.S. exports, Customs avoids creating obstacles to export shipments. One result is that there are few incentives for exporters to file promptly and accurately. The well-documented underreporting of U.S. exports to Canada, port audits conducted by Customs and Census, and comparisons of U.S. export data with corresponding ones on imports from the United States reported by major trading partners all indicate that U.S. exports have been persistently undercounted. The underreporting of U.S. exports to Canada has been addressed through data reconciliations and data exchanges with Canada, but the same basic reporting system that led to the undercount of U.S. exports to Canada is still in use for U.S. exports to the rest of the world, although the magnitude of undercounts in vessel and air shipments to these other countries may be lower because document controls (for example, manifests, entrance and clearance documents) exist for those cargoes. Underreporting of exports can be attributed to a failure to file as well as to inaccurate filing to avoid high shipping costs, circumvent export controls, and reduce tariffs and duties in importing countries. Lax enforcement efforts perpetuate the underreporting.

Other common errors in merchandise trade data include commodity misclassifications and inaccuracies in data on quantity, weight, and country of destination or origin. Such errors are frequently detected by users.

Although Customs and Census are aware of the shortcomings of the data collection system, they do not have a formal data management framework to guide the collection, processing, storage, and dissemination of merchandise trade data. This lack makes it difficult for the agencies to monitor and evaluate their own performance and identify areas for improvement. There is also little interaction between data filers and the two agencies, yet data filers hold the key to the accuracy and timeliness of the incoming data.

INTERNATIONAL SERVICES TRANSACTIONS

Primarily by improving surveys on travel and adding new surveys on education and selected business, professional, and technical services for 1985-1987, Bureau of Economic Analysis (BEA) in 1989 uncovered an additional $20 billion of net receipts of U.S. international services transactions previously unaccounted for in the data for those years. Such improvement was possible with minimal additional resources. Similar efforts directed at other services undoubtedly would yield similar results, especially for financial services.

Nonetheless, several difficulties will persist and complicate the collection of U.S. international services data, making them vulnerable to inaccuracies and inadequate coverage. These obstacles stem largely from the diversity of the various service activities and the manner in which transactions occur. To determine data to be collected requires a basic understanding of the nature and scope of services and what constitutes international transactions in services. In addition, rapid technological and organizational changes in the service industries impede efforts to define, classify, and measure the activities. Full coverage of transactions is also difficult because it is not easy to locate all possible respondents to surveys, including newly established companies. In addition, similar transactions may not be reported consistently by different companies.

It is difficult to delineate boundaries between individual sectors when service activities overlap. Telecommunications, for example, may cover the same ground as data processing and information transmission; tourism may encompass transportation. In addition, goods and services sold or provided jointly in a package present enormous problems of classification, which is an increasingly important feature of a variety of products. For several types of services, the minimum values of individual transactions for which reports are requested are so high that some types of transactions (for example, legal services) are substantially underreported or simply not represented at all, and the total value of such omitted transactions may be substantial.

CAPITAL FLOWS

One recent development that will improve the quality of direct investment data is the enactment of the Foreign Direct Investment and International Financial Data Improvement Act of 1990. This act allows BEA access to the Census Bureau's Standard Statistical Establishment List (SSEL) data, enabling BEA to produce more disaggregated data on foreign direct investment in the United States. This, in turn, will facilitate the analysis of the impact of foreign direct investment on the domestic economy at detailed, industry-by-industry establishment level. Nonetheless, in improving the coverage and accuracy of capital flow data, BEA, Treasury, and the Federal Reserve Bank of New York have to contend with the less than satisfactory compliance by filers. Sizable revisions of these data do occur when late reports are received and errors detected.

More important, Treasury and the Federal Reserve Bank of New

York have to deal with the increasingly complex nature of financial portfolio transactions. The existing reporting system for these transactions is designed to collect the bulk of the information from a panel of large financial intermediaries and corporations. Yet the integration of financial markets and innovations in electronic and communications technology have greatly increased the number of financial transactions, led to a proliferation of new financial instruments, and facilitated new modes of transactions, bypassing traditional financial intermediaries and channels. These changes have made it increasingly difficult and costly to capture comprehensive and accurate data on portfolio transactions under the existing system, rendering the data inaccurate and incomplete.

The low number of filers on securities transactions, which totaled only 350 in 1990, raises doubt that the data fairly represent the volume of transactions. In addition, sizable discrepancies and undercounts exist, for example, in data on Eurodollar deposits by U.S. residents and nonbank financial assets and liabilities abroad as recorded by Treasury, when compared with those reported by the Bank for International Settlements (BIS) and the International Monetary Fund (IMF). Such discrepancies are estimated to have amounted to about $80-180 billion for Eurodollar deposits in 1988 and $155-190 billion for nonbank assets and liabilities in 1990. Although there are differences in definitions and, in particular, in coverage between the Treasury reporting systems and the BIS and IMF statistical frameworks, such sizable discrepancies suggest the need for an examination of the possibility of underreporting in the U.S. data.

RECOMMENDATIONS

Merchandise Trade

Recommendation 4-1   The Customs Service and the Census Bureau should strengthen their enforcement efforts to assure accurate and timely reporting of exports to correct the problem of export underreporting. The Census Bureau should no longer allow carriers to report exports as late as 4 days after departures of shipments. Incentives should be provided to exporters to file promptly and accurately. Increased efforts should be made to exchange and reconcile data with major trading partners and to perform port audits. In order to guide the allocation of resources devoted to data quality improve-

ment, the Census Bureau should identify the characteristics of those filers prone to incomplete or inaccurate reporting.

Recommendation 4-2   The Customs Service and the Census Bureau, in order to guide those responsible for data collection, analysis, and dissemination, should identify and develop measures of the quality of merchandise trade statistics. The quality measures should permit overall estimates of the quality of the published merchandise trade data and estimates of the quality of specific key processes, such as data collection, coding, editing, imputation, error correction, and revision procedures.

Recommendation 4-3   The Census Bureau and the Customs Service should work closely with data filers to evaluate and improve the quality of the incoming trade data. They should also work closely with merchandise trade statistics users to monitor continuously the users' perceptions of the quality of trade statistics and to improve continuously their production processes and the quality of the data.

Recommendation 4-4   The Census Bureau should establish a continuous independent review system (CIRS), in which the incoming information for a small sample of import and export transactions would be independently reviewed by professional staff and the results would be used to determine the sources and causes of errors and to develop procedures to improve data quality.

Recommendation 4-5   In addition to coordinating with the Customs Service, the Census Bureau should develop mechanisms for comparing Census data with monthly agricultural export data compiled by the Department of Agriculture directly from firms and with monthly oil import data gathered by the Energy Information Administration (EIA) of the Department of Energy directly from oil companies. Agricultural exports and oil imports not only represent two large components of U.S. trade, but also are subject to large seasonal changes. Cross-checking of monthly data with Agriculture and EIA should enhance the ability of the Census Bureau to detect error-prone data and work toward improving their accuracy. Furthermore, comparisons of Census's Foreign Trade Division annual export data on manufactured goods with data on manufactured exports recorded in the Annual Survey of Manufactures (ASM) conducted by Census's Industry Division should yield similar payoffs.

Recommendation 4-10 The Census Bureau should accelerate its efforts to improve its processes for collecting, processing, and disseminating trade data through increased automation. The Census Bureau should initiate a joint effort with other appropriate agencies to develop a simplified universal electronic shipping and trade document.

Recommendation 4-11 The Census Bureau and the Bureau of Economic Analysis should consider initiating a substantial multiyear effort to develop and test concepts, content, design, and procedures for surveys to collect integrated merchandise and services trade data from establishments. Initially, the goal of such surveys might be to supplement existing sources of data, but the Census Bureau should give serious consideration to the long-run objective of replacing the compilation of merchandise trade data from official documents. Common data sources will enhance comparability of data.

International Services Transactions

Recommendation 5-1 Among the international services categories, improvements in data on international financial services should be accorded a high priority. The Bureau of Economic Analysis, the Treasury Department, and the Federal Reserve should work together to develop a clear conceptual framework, as well as effective statistical methods and procedures for collecting the information.

Recommendation 5-2 The Bureau of Economic Analysis should place greater emphasis on increasing the response rates of the mandatory surveys.

Recommendation 5-3 For the travel accounts, a study should be made of the feasibility of introducing methods other than the current questionnaire card surveys or of obtaining improved responses from the present method.

Recommendation 5-4 For information on international sales and purchases of services by affiliates, beyond that required for the balance-of-payments tabulations, the Bureau of Economic Analysis should develop separate and expressly designed surveys, in coordination with the service sectors concerned, to obtain the additional data. Burdening the existing system with additional details would increase time lags in reporting, reduce the quality of responses, and weaken the basic data requirements of the balance-of-payments accounts.

Capital Flows

Recommendation 6-1 Because the existing system for collecting data on international portfolio transactions was developed before the advent of modern electronic and telecommunications technology currently used by growing numbers of transactors, research is needed to explore alternative methods of data collection. Over the long term, the clearing systems for securities, the payments systems for banking transactions, and other clearing channels for nonbanking transactions should be explored as alternative sources of information. Increased automation in trading and clearing systems would facilitate the compilation of data from such sources.

Recommendation 6-2 Research should be performed to develop ways to broaden coverage and to enforce compliance of reporting by filers. For securities transactions, improvements in coverage of U.S. outward investment in foreign securities and transactions by nonfinancial entities are of particular importance. For reporting by banks, the principal research effort should focus on enhancing the timely and accurate reporting of U.S. affiliates of foreign banks. For transactions on nonbanking concerns, improvements in the coverage of activities of the U.S. nonfinancial population, both corporate and personal, are needed. A broadening of the filing of TIC C forms, perhaps through lowering exemption levels for reporting, should also be considered.

Recommendation 6-3 The adequacy of data on official U.S. government international capital transactions should be examined. Official U.S. government international capital transactions are of growing importance, but the myriad forms of transactions in U.S. official reserve assets and other government assets and the involvement of numerous government agencies make them susceptible to inadequate reporting. There have also been few evaluations of government agencies' compliance with reporting requirements.

Recommendation 6-4 The methodology of estimating portfolio investment incomes should be improved, including new methods to measure current values of U.S. securities holdings abroad, as well as other forms of U.S. international financial assets and liabilities. Appropriate rates of return can be developed through close consultations with financial institutions at home and abroad.

Recommendation 6-5 In view of the difficulties of obtaining data on residents' direct purchases or sales of foreign securities, research should be undertaken to explore the feasibility of exchanging data with partner countries. This would require, among other things, the development of universal codes for identifying securities and uniform standards for reporting, as well as common definitions of the residence of the immediate transactor and of the ultimate owner.

IMPROVING THE DATA COLLECTION AND DATA ANALYSIS INTERFACE

The major function of federal statistics is to inform public policy making. To this end, data must be responsive to policy and program needs. To best accomplish the task, data collection agencies must understand the basic purposes of the data and build appropriate concepts and definitions into the design and development of the statistical framework. To ensure that the data collected are suitable for the purposes intended, statistical agencies must also be able to analyze and interpret them. In addition, since users understand the need for the data and are knowledgeable about the policies and programs for which the data are collected, data collection agencies need to work closely with users to ensure that relevant data are compiled. Such collaboration also makes users more aware of the availability of data and data limitations and enables them to make maximum use of the data for their purposes. Until now, the absence of a strong nexus between data collection and data analysis has resulted in the production of data of limited analytic usefulness or, in other cases, not fully utilized.

An important symptom of the communications failure between data users and data collectors is the absence of clear measures of uncertainty accompanying the data provided by the federal government. In our judgment, those who collect data and those who use data need to be cognizant that these are not perfect measures, but only estimates. Currently, collectors of data report statistics as if they were perfect measures, and users generally use them as if they were perfect; major misinterpretations can easily occur. There is strong demand for more data, but little demand for more accurate data. Because the international trading environment will continue to evolve, continuing interaction between statistical agencies and users is essential to ensure that relevant data will be collected and irrelevant data will not. Such interface will promote flexibility in the data collection system. Moving toward a responsive system of data collection is critical to enhance cost-effectiveness in compiling the massive international trade and financial data.

MERCHANDISE TRADE

The quality of the merchandise trade data and their limitations are inadequately communicated to users. The published merchandise trade balance data also routinely fluctuate widely from month to month. Users at times have interpreted a large fluctuation in the monthly change as indicative of shifts in the underlying trend or other basic properties of the data. This, in turn, has sent inappropriate signals to financial and foreign exchange markets.

Our analysis shows the monthly changes in the U.S. merchandise trade balance over the period from February 1987 through February 1991, corrected for trend and for correlation over time, have a mean value which is *small*, $249 million, and a *large* standard error, $1.4 billion. Moreover, monthly changes tend to alternate in sign from positive to negative to positive. These results show that large monthly changes in the merchandise trade balance can exist without any change occurring in the underlying trend. Our analysis also suggests that fluctuations in the reported monthly changes in the merchandise trade balance can be induced by the seasonal adjustments procedure used by the Bureau of the Census. Alternative methods of seasonal adjustments could model seasonal movements as well or better than current methods and reduce the volatility of the monthly trade balance data.

The monthly merchandise trade statistics also lack a long-term orientation, limiting their usefulness for policy analysis and research. As a statistical agency, the Census Bureau's objective is to collect, process, and disseminate the monthly data on a timely basis. From a data collector's perspective, each batch of the monthly figures is largely a product in itself, rather than part of an ongoing time series. As a result, consistent time series of merchandise trade data are lacking.

INTERNATIONAL SERVICES TRANSACTIONS

The development of data to cover new services has been hampered by BEA's limited analytic resources. Such constraints have kept BEA from improving concepts and methodologies, especially to determine how different types of services should be measured, and from refining survey questionnaires. Data compiled in large sector aggregates mask major changes in particular components; lack of detailed U.S. international services data limits analytic uses. At present, BEA does not analyze extensively the data it collects nor present its own analyses and interpretations widely to the public. Users' access to data on U.S. international services transactions is also limited.

CAPITAL FLOWS

Data on capital flows are also not well synthesized and organized in usable formats, limiting their usefulness. BEA and Treasury have yet to exploit fully the analytic potential of the data and to disseminate them broadly to users. Existing data are not regularly reviewed by BEA and Treasury to determine if additions, deletions, or other modifications are necessary.

RECOMMENDATIONS

Recommendation 3-1   The Bureau of Economic Analysis, the Treasury Department, and, especially, the Census Bureau should strengthen their research and analytic capabilities so that they can develop proper concepts and methods to measure the U.S. international economic activities. The Census Bureau and the Bureau of Economic Analysis should work jointly to develop concepts, definitions, measures, and strategies for capturing in more detail the rapidly growing intracompany trade and trade in intermediate inputs. The Treasury Department and the Federal Reserve should jointly explore similar improvements to cover portfolio transactions and the flow-

of-funds accounts. In addition, efforts should also be made to measure more accurately prices of international transactions and other dimensions of competitiveness, including taxes, costs, and rates of return, as well as to improve constant-price measures of exports and imports. These agencies should seek outside professional advice from analytic users and other experts in these efforts.

Recommendation 3-2   Sufficient information in the form of data quality profiles should be provided to users to help them evaluate the quality of the data.

Recommendation 3-3   An advisory body should be established to guide long-term developments, as the international trade environment continues to evolve and transactions become increasingly complex. This advisory body should be composed of experts from industry, academia, and government; it should include research and analytic data users, data filers, and respondents to government surveys, as well as user agency officials. Priority should be given to the development of timely, accurate, relevant, and cost-effective data for public policy making.

Recommendation 3-4   For data that primarily benefit specialized groups that can be clearly defined, market mechanisms should be developed to coordinate the supply of and demand for the data. When the benefits of the data accrue largely to specialized groups but also to public policy makers, cost sharing should be the rule.

Recommendation 4-6   Measures of uncertainty about the accuracy of trade data should be published. In particular, attention should be given to establishing normally acceptable ranges for the fluctuations displayed in monthly trade balance figures. In addition, the Census Bureau should assess the feasibility of applying alternative seasonal adjustment procedures to produce data more indicative of underlying trends.

Introduction

The United States economy is becoming increasingly integrated with the world economy. The nation's trade deficit and foreigners' investment in the United States have generated newspaper headlines, affected financial markets, and become an issue in U.S. domestic and foreign affairs. In the face of this new global economic environment, several questions become critical: How complete is the available picture of U.S. international economic activities? How accurately do the data depict U.S. international trade and finance? How useful are they for public and private decision making, especially since most of the data collection systems were devised decades ago in a different economic environment? How efficiently does the United States manage the collection, analysis, and dissemination of these data?

Although U.S. systems for collecting data on international transactions are probably the most advanced in the world, rapid changes in the global economic environment have outpaced improvements to them. In a recent report, the Working Group on the Quality of Economic Statistics (1987) of the President's Economic Policy Council recommended that a panel of experts be convened to study the adequacy of existing systems for the collection, processing, and dissemination of U.S. merchandise and services trade data, and to recommend data that will most usefully and accurately represent U.S. international trade in coming decades.

With the support of the Bureau of the Census, the Bureau of Economic Analysis, and the International Trade Administration of the U.S. Department of Commerce and the Customs Service of the U.S. Department of the Treasury, the Panel on Foreign Trade Statistics was convened under the aegis of the Committee on National Statistics at the National Research Council in June 1989. A subsequent research grant from the Chase Manhattan Bank also supported the panel's work.

At the time the panel was formed, its charge was much narrower than the one it subsequently assumed. The original mandate was to examine the adequacy of the system for the collection of merchandise trade statistics and, to the extent possible, that for services. The panel soon recognized, however, that the key issue to be addressed was much broader: to provide useful economic data to better inform public and private decision makers at a time when the U.S. economy is becoming increasingly integrated with the world economy. The panel thus undertook a more comprehensive study to address both narrow and broad questions about international merchandise trade and services transactions. In addition, in view of the growing linkages among transactions in goods, services, and capital flows, the panel believes that it is also necessary to consider data on international capital flows.

By evaluating existing data on U.S. international transactions in goods, services, and capital flows, the panel hopes to emphasize the importance of examining these disparate data in more unified ways and integrating the results into a broad statistical framework that can be used to better understand the changing nature and extent of U.S. international economic activities. A comprehensive review of all three types of data also highlights what data gaps exist and what possible changes yield the highest payoffs. The panel hopes that this approach will spur additional efforts to enhance the usefulness of data on U.S. international economic activities.

Recent studies on the adequacy of existing data on U.S. international transactions are few: most separately address data on merchandise trade, international services transactions, and capital flows; some examine only certain aspects of them. For example, two recent studies undertaken by the International Monetary Fund (1986a, 1992) on the statistical discrepancies of the world current accounts and the world capital accounts discuss the possible sources of errors and omissions in the balance-of-payments transactions of major industrialized countries, including the United States. To the panel's knowledge, no comprehensive reviews of all three major types of data on U.S. international transactions have been undertaken in recent years. Thus, although this study benefits from the existing literature, we hope it also breaks new ground by taking a comprehensive approach and gathering information from many sources and experts. Our study focuses on the emerging global trading environment, how it has increased the demand for international economic data, in what respects the existing data are inadequate for meeting current and future data needs, and what correctives can be introduced.

THE INTERNATIONAL ECONOMIC ENVIRONMENT

Even the most cursory review of major international economic trends over the past two decades shows that there has been a dramatic expansion in the volume of world trade in goods, accompanied by even more rapid growth in services transactions and capital flows across national boundaries. U.S. statistics (adjusted for inflation) show that over the decade of the 1980s, while U.S. gross national product (GNP) rose 30 percent, U.S. imports and exports of goods and services increased 72 percent, and combined capital inflows and outflows jumped 60 percent. These developments have significantly transformed the U.S. economy and made it considerably more interdependent with those of other countries.

Underlying these trends have been quantum changes in technology and major institutional developments. Innovations in transportation technology, especially in aviation industries, have facilitated the movement of goods and people. Changes in computer and telecommunications technologies have revolutionized the gathering, transmission, and processing of information, facilitating a dramatic expansion in financial and other business services transactions across national borders. Technological developments have reduced the costs of managing operations around the globe, further spurring cross-border direct investment.

At the same time, successive rounds of multilateral trade negotiations and a new emphasis on free trade areas have significantly lowered trade barriers for goods and services. Deregulation and removal of restrictions on capital flows in major industrial countries have liberalized international financial transactions. More recently, developments around the globe—such as the progress made toward the economic unification of the European Community, the rapid growth of East Asian economies, the implementation of the United States-Canada Free Trade Agreement and its possible expansion to include Mexico, and emerging efforts to integrate Eastern Europe into the world economy—have expanded business opportunities globally. Coupled with new and improved managerial techniques, these developments have accelerated the multinationalization of enterprises.

Several factors in the United States—including significant economic growth over the past decade, a strengthening of the technology-driven and information-based service sector, deregulation of the telecommunications and finance industries, and a strong dollar in the early 1980s—further boosted U.S. merchandise imports, expanded U.S. services exports, and attracted considerable foreign direct and portfolio investment to this country.

Globalization of markets will continue throughout the 1990s because it offers many benefits to the world economy. Larger markets tend to lower unit costs by enabling producers to take advantage of economies of scale. Increased international competition is likely to prod inefficient firms and promote productivity. Rising transnational activities will accelerate technological diffusion.

In this new international economic environment, the United States faces enormous challenges and opportunities. As cross-border movement of goods, services, labor, capital, and technology have spawned rising numbers of production and financial centers, international trade and finance have become more competitive. Meanwhile, enlarged regional markets and the economic strengths of a number of developing nations have provided immense opportunities for international commerce. To deal effectively with these challenges and to take full advantage of the opportunities they present, both the public and the private sectors need timely, accurate, and relevant information on the new global economy.

DATA NEEDS

In the internationalized U.S. economy, many new economic issues and increasingly complex traditional concerns face public officials:

• Coordinating U.S. macroeconomic policies with those of other countries to reduce global external imbalances, stabilize exchange rates, promote full employment, and foster strong economic growth with low rates of inflation;
• Negotiating bilaterally, regionally, and multilaterally to enhance market access for U.S. goods and services abroad, reduce foreign restrictions on U.S. direct investment activities abroad, and protect U.S. intellectual property rights;
• Assessing the impact of international transactions in goods

and services, as well as foreign direct and portfolio investment, on domestic production, employment, and overall economic growth; and

• Determining appropriate adjustment measures to assist domestic industries to meet foreign competition, such as policies to strengthen the U.S. technological edge, raise workers' skill levels, and improve research and development capabilities.

Similarly, to remain competitive as multilateral trading opportunities increase, business decision makers face a range of increasingly complex new and old issues:

• Weighing the opportunities of selling their products at home and abroad;

• Evaluating the alternatives of producing their goods and services domestically for export or of undertaking direct foreign investment and producing the goods and services abroad;

• Considering the opportunities for importing various components of a final product rather than purchasing supplies and parts from domestic sources;

• Determining what combination of local and host-country personnel to employ and whether they should be permanent or transient;

• Identifying the most cost-effective sources of financing of both domestic and foreign operations, taking into account differences among countries in capital costs, exchange-rate risks, and political conditions; and

• Considering the appropriate forms of cross-national commercial activities including joint ventures, coproduction, partnerships, mergers and acquisitions, and other collaborative arrangements with foreign counterparts.

In this global environment, informed public and private decision making requires a wide range of data, including:

• The international trade of the United States and other countries in goods and services;

• The intracompany trade of U.S. firms and their foreign affiliates and their use of traded intermediate inputs;

• The production and sales of goods and services abroad by foreign affiliates of U.S. multinational companies;

• The production and sales of goods and services in the United States by U.S. affiliates of foreign multinational companies;

• U.S. direct investment abroad and foreign direct investment in the United States;

• U.S. portfolio investment abroad and foreign portfolio investment in the United States;
• The employment and economic contributions of foreign firms in the United States and the employment and economic contributions of U.S. firms abroad;
• Expenditures on research and development by U.S. multinational firms abroad and those by foreign firms in the United States;
• The financing arrangements for affiliates' operations at home and abroad; and
• The availability of technological innovations and their diffusion.

In addition, to assist public policy deliberations and business analyses, the growing interrelationships between domestic and international economic activities necessitate that data on international economic activities be comparable to domestic economic data and that international trade and finance data be comparable among countries.

FOCUS OF ANALYSIS

How well do existing data serve public and private users' needs? How can the data be improved? Our review shows that an enormous quantity of data is collected by different federal statistical agencies on U.S. international transactions, but their adequacy for informing public and private decision making has been called into question by the myriad of new demands, as well as by clear gaps. Many new economic issues have risen from the emerging international trading environment, and the existing statistical framework is inadequate for analyzing them. This report discusses the need for a broadened statistical framework to supplement the existing balance-of-payments accounts—one that will reflect emerging international economic relations. The supplemental framework should be conducive to analysis of such issues as the extent of the internationalization of the U.S. economy and how well U.S. institutions (public and private) have responded to it; the international competitiveness of U.S. firms; the impact of foreign direct investment on the domestic economy; and bilateral, regional, and multilateral negotiations on market access for trade and investment and the enforcement of the negotiated rules. It should also improve estimates of components in the foreign sector of the national accounts.

Our review also shows that there is limited comparability between U.S. international trade data and domestic production and other domestic economic data. This limited comparability has detracted from the analytical usefulness of the data for assessing the impact of international transactions on domestic economic output and employment, which is a greater problem now than in the past because of the increasing linkage between domestic and international economic activities. There is also limited comparability of international economic data across countries, and the report notes that there are several efforts being undertaken by international organizations to harmonize international economic data. The report also considers the quality of U.S. domestic data in relation to prospective improvements in U.S. international data.

A third general topic discussed in the report is the lack of connection between statistical agencies and data users in evaluating the usefulness of the data collected. Growing demand for data and the changing international economic environment—all in a period of tight federal budgetary constraints—require that statistical programs be made more cost-effective.

Among the data gaps addressed in our review are shortcomings in coverage and accuracy of existing data on merchandise trade, international services transactions, and capital flows. These are evident in the rise in the magnitude, as well as in the direction, of the statistical discrepancies shown in the U.S. balance-of-payments accounts. Under the double-entry accounting concept, the balance in the current account—which records transactions in goods and services and investment incomes, as well as unilateral transfers—should mirror that in the capital account, but with opposite signs. The latter shows capital flows, consisting of changes in U.S. assets abroad and foreign assets in the United States. In fact, however, discrepancies in the two accounts in the U.S. balance of payments have grown significantly in the past decade. As reported in the U.S. balance-of-payments accounts over the years, cumulated errors and omissions, for example, surged from –$5.5 billion for the decade of 1960-1969 to +$36.4 billion for 1970-1979 and to +$151.74 billion for 1980-1989. In 1990 alone, such errors and omissions rose to an unprecendented high of +$63.5 billion, or about 70 percent of the current account deficit. Our review shows that these persistently rising statistical discrepancies are more a result of increasingly inaccurate valuations, growing inadequacies in coverage, and errors in estimation procedures than of time lags between offseting transactions in the current and capital accounts. Large errors and omissions have diminshed the meaningfulness of individual trade balance figures and compounded the difficulty of assessing the economic standing of the United States in the international economy.

Other topics considered in our analyses include measurements of merchandise trade, affiliates' transactions, services trade, and direct and portfolio investment, which have been complicated by frequent foreign currency conversions related to fluctuations in exchange rates, arbitrary intracompany pricing practices, and outdated assumptions used in estimation methods and asset valuations. Growing numbers of financial intermediaries and product innovations that facilitate capital transfers through nontraditional channels have also made it more difficult to capture capital transactions under existing data systems. They also have compounded the difficulty of identifying the location of residents and nonresidents and rendered geographic breakdowns of data less meaningful and less useful. In addition, our review points out that although information on U.S. merchandise trade is collected in great detail, data on the rapidly growing U.S. services trade, foreign direct and portfolio investment, and sales of goods and services of U.S. and foreign affiliates are much less complete.

The panel recognizes that federal statistical agencies have been confronted with tight budgetary constraints over the past decade. On the basis of information provided by the Office of Management and Budget (OMB), we computed in real dollar terms (that is, adjusted for inflation) the budgets for the two agencies with major responsibility for the compilation of data on merchandise trade and international economic accounts, the Bureau of the Census for merchandise trade statistics and the Bureau of Economic Analysis (BEA) for international economic accounts:[1]

	1977	1991
	$ Millions	
Census	13.8	12.6
BEA	4.3	8.1
Total	18.1	20.7

---

[1]The Customs Service, which is responsible for the collection of trade documents, does not in its budget separate its data collection functions from its other commercial operations; hence, no budget figures covering Customs' data collection functions are available. Similarly, for the U.S. Department of the Treasury, which uses the Federal Reserve banks as agents in the collection of data on U.S. portfolio transactions, with the Federal Reserve banks bearing the costs, no separate budget figures for statistical programs are available.

Between 1977 and 1991, the combined budget for the two agencies grew less than 1 percent a year over the 15-year period.

The panel is aware that the President's Council of Economic Advisers has proposed an economic statistics initiative that calls for increases in several agency budgets to improve the quality of federal economic statistics, including those on U.S. international transactions. The panel supports the initiative. Our recommendations have taken into account budget constraints and rising costs and problems associated with capturing growing arrays of U.S. international economic activities. In setting priorities for improving data to meet current and future data needs, our emphasis is on enhancing the analytic capabilities of federal statistical agencies and strengthening the coordination and cooperation among them, especially in developing a conceptual framework that will integrate the disparate data sets to elucidate the complex linkages of the economy; increasing productivity of the data collection systems to improve accuracy and timeliness of existing data; and filling data gaps that will yield the highest payoffs, such as those of international services transactions and capital flows. In recommending improvements in data collection systems, the panel also focuses on specific areas requested by the sponsoring agencies, including: the feasibility of using sampling techniques to collect merchandise trade data; the need for increased automation in the collection, processing, and dissemination of data; and quality-control procedures for merchandise trade data.

Most of the panel's recommendations will not add significant costs for statistical agencies. They emphasize in what ways productivity can and should be raised, how cost-saving techniques can and should be used, and how cost-sharing with users can and should be applied. The panel's recommendations also stress the importance of producing useful information relevant to the new global economic environment, rather than correcting old problems or "improving" old data that may not be worth attention. If statistical agencies receive increased funding for their programs, the panel stresses the need to allocate those resources to strengthen agencies' analytic capabilities to produce relevant and meaningful data.

Because significant changes in international trade and finance continue and at an accelerating pace, our work is by no means the last word on the subjects addressed. At a minimum, we believe we have done spadework that will encourage more exhaustive efforts by experts in both the public and private sectors. We hope their goal will be, as ours has been, to develop useful information on international transactions that can be used to guide decisions affecting U.S. and global economic developments in the coming years.

METHODOLOGY AND REPORT STRUCTURE

Our analysis is based on an extensive review of the existing systems used to collect data on U.S. international transactions in goods, services, and capital flows. It has also drawn on the insights and expertise of many individuals in federal and state agencies, international organizations, foreign government agencies, businesses, trade associations, and research institutions. The panel interviewed numerous officials and experts in the United States and abroad, including those from international organizations such as the International Monetary Fund, the World Bank, the Bank for International Settlements, the United Nations, the Statistical Office of the European Communities, the General Agreement on Tariffs and Trade, and the Organization for Economic Cooperation and Development. We also have heard expert testimony and reviewed written comments from more than 100 government, academic, and industry users. Our activities also included canvassing the views of data filers and visiting data collection and processing centers. Because there has been great interest in the nation's merchandise trade balance, we have also performed quantitative analyses to examine its trend and volatility, to show how an alternative procedure might better seasonally adjust the trade balance data to reflect the underlying trend, and to compare the accuracy of U.S. export data with those of U.S. major trading partners.

This report is organized into two parts and a set of appendices. Part I focuses on the need for enhancing the usability of the data; it includes Chapters 1-3. Chapter 1 addresses the increasing internationalization of the U.S. economy and the need for supplementing the existing statistical framework to encompass both balance-of-payments transactions and other multinational operations in analyzing the nation's international economic activities. Chapter 2 examines the comparability of U.S. trade and domestic production and other economic data, as well as the comparability of international data among countries. Chapter 3 considers the need to move toward a flexible data system on U.S. international economic activities so useful, relevant, and cost-effective data are collected to guide public and private decision making in a changing international trading environment.

Part II presents specific reviews of the adequacy of existing data and recommendations for their improvement; it includes Chapters 4-6. Chapter 4 assesses the adequacy of existing merchandise trade statistics and considers how greater automation, use of sampling techniques, and effective database management can enhance the timeliness and accuracy of the data. Chapter 5 reviews existing data on U.S. international services transactions and develops recommendations to improve the data. Chapter 6 examines capital flow statistics and sets forth areas for further research. In this report, investment incomes are covered in the discussion of capital flows. Unilateral transfers are not separately discussed but are indirectly reviewed in the transfer of goods, services, and financial assets. The detailed information provided in Part II on the ways these data are currently collected is meant both to alert readers to the vulnerabilities of the systems that affect the quality of the data and to provide the background for our analysis and recommendations for improvement.

The appendices contain detailed examinations and background material. Appendix A develops the concept of estimating sales and purchases of goods and services by and between U.S.-owned and foreign-owned firms as identified by national ownership of firms. Appendix B contains results from our canvass of users of existing data. Appendix C compares the accuracy of U.S. export data and those of U.S. major trading partners. Appendix D contains an analysis of the volatility of the monthly merchandise trade balance figures. Appendix E demonstrates how the application of an alternative seasonal adjustment procedure can better reflect the seasonal influences on the trade balance and reduce the volatility in the monthly merchandise trade balance figures. Appendix F discusses the feasibility of using sampling techniques in the collection and processing of merchandise trade data. Appendix G presents biographical sketches of panel members and staff.

PART I

*Enhancing the Usability of Data on
U.S. International Transactions*

1

Supplementing the Balance-of-Payments Framework

Data on U.S. international transactions are currently grouped into three major categories: merchandise trade, international services transactions, and capital flows. Merchandise trade statistics, which cover U.S. imports and exports of goods, are assembled by the Bureau of the Census of the U.S. Department of Commerce on the basis of information contained in import and export documents. Those documents are collected primarily by the Customs Service of the U.S. Department of the Treasury as goods enter and leave the United States. Merchandise trade data are tabulated in detailed commodity categories and geographical breakdowns and are published monthly by the Census Bureau.

Data on U.S. international services transactions cover travel, transportation, and other services (royalties and fees; reinsurance and direct insurance; construction, engineering, architectural, and mining; and business, financial, medical, and educational services). Most of the data presently available on U.S. international services transactions are collected and compiled by the Bureau of Economic Analysis (BEA) of the Department of Commerce on the basis of periodic surveys of establishments engaged in those services. U.S. international services transactions are published by BEA in broad categories and include limited country breakdowns on a quarterly basis.

Data on capital flows cover transactions on direct investment and portfolio investment, as well as on incomes and earnings generated from them. BEA collects information on both U.S. direct investment abroad and foreign direct investment in the United States on the basis of periodic surveys of U.S. firms investing abroad and U.S. affiliates of foreign corporations in the United States. BEA publishes quarterly estimates of these activities.

The Department of the Treasury, using the Federal Reserve banks as agents, collects information on portfolio investment. Treasury International Capital (TIC) forms capture sales and purchases of long-term securities and amounts of outstanding claims and liabilities reported by banks and nonbanking concerns. Banks, financial institutions, brokers, dealers, corporations, and other entities in the United States that engage in portfolio transactions are required to file TIC forms. The Federal Reserve Bank of New York consolidates the data and makes them available to the Treasury Department, which publishes the data on a quarterly basis.

BEA compiles data on incomes and earnings on direct investment from its surveys of direct investment. It also estimates incomes and earnings on portfolio investment, using its calculations of selected rates of return and information on portfolio investment provided by the Treasury Department.

EXISTING STATISTICAL FRAMEWORK

These enormous quantities of data are compiled largely under the balance-of-payments framework. Underlying these compilations of data on U.S. international transactions are the concepts of residents and nonresidents and the separation of domestic and international economic activities. International transactions are defined to involve the transfer of ownership of goods, services, and capital flows between U.S. and foreign residents, with national boundaries establishing the distinction between residents and nonresidents. Under this framework, U.S. residents are persons residing and pursuing economic interests in the United States, and nonresidents are those residing and pursuing economic interests outside the United States. (Exceptions include members of the U.S. armed forces serving abroad, who are considered U.S. residents). The term "residents" is broadly defined to include individuals, business enterprises, and governments and international organizations.

These concepts are used because one common purpose of these statistics compiled by Census, BEA, and Treasury is to provide data for the nation's balance-of-payments accounts. The accounts represent a summary statistical statement during a given period of transactions in goods, services, and capital flows between U.S. residents and those of the rest of the world. Components of the balance-of-payments accounts, in turn, are incorporated into the national income and products accounts (NIPA), which measure the production, distribution, and use of output in the United States by four economic groups: persons, businesses, government, and "the rest of the world." BEA estimates both the U.S. balance-of-payments accounts and the NIPA on a quarterly basis. (For a detailed description of the concepts, data sources, and estimation procedures used in the balance of payments, see Bureau of Economic Analysis, 1990c.)

A country's economic transactions with the rest of the world are believed to be a function of fundamental economic conditions—such as relative levels of domestic and foreign prices, incomes, exchange rates, interest rates, and savings rates, and rates of economic growth between the country and the rest of the world. The balance-of-payments framework is valuable, therefore, for understanding changes in the nation's general price level, and domestic output and employment. (The extensive use of the dollar abroad, however, has reduced the direct link between the U.S. balance of payments and the exchange rates of the dollar.)

The balance-of-payments framework was developed when the world economy was much less integrated. It reflects the economic conditions at that time, when sales and purchases by multinationals and their affiliates were much less significant relative to cross-border transactions than they are now. Under this framework, the scope of statistics on international transactions was developed primarily to cover cross-border movement of goods and selected services, the income earned on U.S. investments abroad and foreign investments in the United States, and the volume of capital flows. The balance-of-payments framework is not intended to account for sales of goods and services by affiliates or to distinguish intracompany trade from trade between unrelated parties. Yet key features of the internationalized economy are the significance of foreign direct investment and the close relationship between this investment and trade. As Julius (1990) has stressed, trade and foreign direct investment are twins in the sense that both enable firms in one country to reach markets for outputs or sources for inputs in other countries. Firms have found that they can exploit their own technological and managerial knowledge most profitably by establishing production units in foreign countries rather than just exporting to (or importing from) foreign markets or by permitting foreign firms to use their specialized knowledge for royalties and fees.

BEA estimated U.S. direct investment abroad and foreign direct investment in the United States in 1989 at $536 billion and $458 billion, respectively, on a current-cost basis (see Landefeld and Lawson, 1991); on a market-value basis, the estimates are $804 billion and $544 billion, respectively. (Earnings on U.S. direct investment abroad and on foreign direct investment in the United States in 1987, which are recorded in the balance-of-payments accounts, were $55 billion and $10 billion, respectively.) The sales of goods and services by these foreign affiliates of U.S. firms and U.S. affiliates of foreign firms in 1987 were $815 billion and $731 billion, respectively. These transactions contrast with U.S. goods and services exported and imported in that year of $336 billion and $484 billion, respectively. The close connection between foreign direct investment and trade is further evidenced by other statistics. In 1987, goods and services exported by U.S. firms to their affiliates abroad accounted for 26 percent of total U.S. exports of goods and services, and goods and services shipped by foreign firms to their U.S. affiliates in the United States accounted for 30 percent of U.S. imports.

The increase in foreign direct investment and its link to trade has created a new set of policy issues among nations that did not exist when direct investment and intracompany trade were less important (see Cooper [1968:Chap. 4] for an early discussion of the new policy issues created by foreign direct investment). Concerns are often raised in host countries, for example, that affiliates of foreign firms give preference to suppliers from their home countries over local suppliers of intermediate goods and nonfactor services (such as insurance). Even though there is little evidence, it is also said that they neither export as much nor treat workers as well as domestically owned firms and that they stifle scientific research and development in host countries. There is also a fear that the cultural heritage of the country may be undermined. In contrast, concerns are often expressed in home countries that foreign direct investment abroad results in significant losses of jobs domestically and a decrease of tax revenues for the government. In addition, direct investors are concerned about being discriminated against in their economic activities in the host country.

Traditional international economic issues have also been modified by the increased importance of foreign direct investment. The competitiveness of a country's firms in world markets, for example, is no longer just a matter of their ability to export; it is also determined by their ability to sell through their affiliates abroad. New issues of macroeconomic policy, antitrust policy, and tax evasion also arise with the mergers and acquisitions of U.S. firms by foreign companies, their establishment of domestic production facilities to circumvent import restrictions, and their transfer-pricing activities.

To analyze these issues, a framework that links direct investment and trade is needed: the existing balance-of-payments framework does not do since only earnings of foreign investment are included, and the trade balances do not differentiate the export and import activities of U.S. and foreign firms in the United States.

A SUPPLEMENTAL FRAMEWORK

One way to develop a supplemental framework to analyze the new economic issues and the increasingly complex traditional ones is to integrate data on cross-border trade flows (as reported in the balance-of-payments accounts) with those on sales and purchases of goods and services of U.S. direct investors abroad and foreign direct investors in the United States, which are currently collected outside the balance-of-payments framework. Figure 1-1 shows the balance-of-payments framework and the panel's proposed framework.

The set of accounts being proposed measures the sales and purchases of goods and services by U.S.-owned firms (whether located in the United States or abroad), the U.S. government (but excluding military sales), and the households of U.S. residents to and from foreign-owned firms (whether located abroad or in the United States), foreign governments, and the households of foreign residents. (In estimating the set of accounts, no attempt is made to distinguish either between households of U.S. citizens and foreigners residing abroad or between households of U.S. and foreigners residing in the United States.) Since sales of goods and services are mainly undertaken by firms, for simplicity, the following description ignores sales by governments and households: see Appendix A for a complete description of the selling and buying activities between U.S.-owned firms, the U.S. government, and U.S. households and foreign-owned firms, foreign governments, and foreign households. To show the essential difference between the proposed framework and the balance-of-payments framework, Figure 1-1 is further simplified by assuming that purchases, as well as sales, are undertaken entirely by firms.

Under the proposed framework, total sales of U.S.-owned firms to foreign firms, foreign governments, and foreign households (referred to hereafter as "foreigners") are computed in three steps.

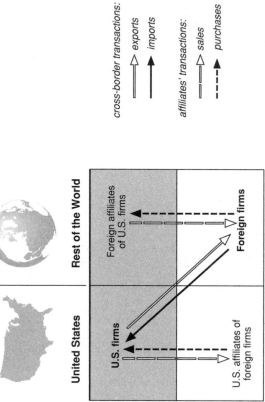

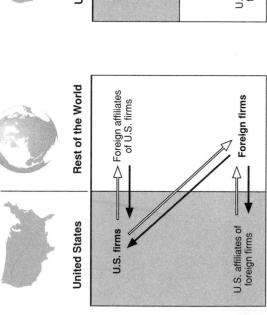

FIGURE 1-1 The balance-of-payments framework and a proposed supplemental framework.

First, exports of U.S.-owned firms to their foreign affiliates abroad and exports of U.S. affiliates of foreign firms in the United States to foreigners are subtracted from the total U.S. export figure, since they represent within-firm transactions between U.S.-owned firms and between foreign-owned firms, respectively.[1] The net figure represents cross-border sales of U.S.-owned firms to foreigners. Second, to this figure are added sales to foreigners by foreign affiliates of U.S. firms abroad. Third, sales by U.S.-owned firms to U.S. affiliates of foreign firms in the United States are added.[2] The sum, combining the three sources of sales, represents the total sales of U.S.-owned firms to foreigners.

Purchases of U.S.-owned firms, the U.S. government, and U.S. households (referred to hereafter as "Americans") from foreign-owned firms are computed in three comparable steps. First, from total U.S. imports are subtracted imports from foreign affiliates of U.S. firms abroad and imports by U.S. affiliates of foreign firms located in the United States. The net figure represents cross-border purchases by Americans from foreign-owned firms. Second, to this figure are added purchases by Americans from U.S. affiliates of foreign firms in the United States. Third, purchases by foreign affiliates of U.S. firms abroad from foreign-owned firms are added.[3] The sum of all three sources of purchases represents total purchases by Americans from foreign-owned firms.[4]

Components of the proposed set of accounts can be rearranged to yield related concepts that are of interest to policy makers.

---

[1]A foreign (U.S.) firm is one that is organized, operated, or incorporated abroad (in the United States). An affiliate is a business enterprise located in one country that is owned or controlled by a single person or firm of another country to the extent of 10 percent or more of its voting stock. An unaffiliated firm is one that neither owns nor is owned by other firms in the 10 percent voting-stock sense.

[2]The data needed to obtain the latter figure are unavailable; it is only possible to obtain sales by all firms located in the United States to U.S. affiliates of foreign firms in the United States.

[3]The data needed to obtain the latter figure are not available; it is only possible to obtain sales by unaffiliated firms abroad to foreign affiliates of U.S. firms.

[4]After we developed our broadened framework, we discovered the work of DeAnne Julius, who developed a somewhat similar set of accounts; see Julius (1990, 1991). An important difference between her set of accounts and the one discussed here is that she includes payments to direct productive factors, for example, wages and capital costs, in her estimates of purchases of U.S. affiliates of foreign firms within the United States and purchases of foreign affiliates of U.S. firms abroad. As Guy V.G. Stevens of the staff of the Board of Governors of the Federal Reserve points out in an internal memo (July 25, 1990), this methodology leads to the result that the Julius measure reduces to the sum of the trade balance, other services (net), and net direct investment income (exclusive of capital gains). These figures can be obtained directly from the balance of payments.

The value added in the United States by U.S. affiliates of foreign firms (that is, the gross domestic product of U.S. affiliates of foreign companies) can be calculated from their sales and purchases data. Similarly, the value added abroad by foreign affiliates of U.S. firms can be calculated from the data on the sales and purchases of those firms. The percentage of the local content of sales of U.S. affiliates of foreign firms in the United States (that is, the sum of value added and purchases from local firms divided by total sales of U.S. affiliates of foreign firms in the United States, expressed in percentage terms) can also be calculated, as can the foreign-content percentage of sales by foreign affiliates of U.S. firms. Appendix A discusses in detail the various components of this supplemental framework and presents estimates of sales and purchases of goods and services by U.S. firms to and from foreign firms for 1987.

Table 1-1 summarizes the difference in U.S. international economic performance under the balance-of-payments framework and the supplemental framework and also presents value-added and local-content estimates. The balance-of-payments framework in 1987 shows a U.S. trade deficit of goods and services of $148 billion; the supplemental framework shows that the sales of goods and services by U.S.-owned firms (located either in the United

TABLE 1-1   A Comparison of U.S. International Economic Performance Under Two Frameworks, 1987 (in billions of dollars)

Balance-of-Payments Framework		Supplemental Framework	
Cross-border sales to foreign countries (exports)	336	Total sales to foreigners	1,239
Cross-border purchases from foreign countries (imports)	484	Total purchases from foreigners	1,303
Difference	−148	Difference	−64

Value added in the U.S. by U.S. affiliates of foreign firms	152
Value added abroad by foreign affiliates of U.S. firms	244
Domestic content of sales of U.S. affiliates of foreign firms	592 (81%)
Foreign content of sales of foreign affiliates of U.S. firms	728 (89%)

NOTE: The balance-of-payments framework is based on country of residency of firms selling and purchasing goods and services. The supplemental framework is based on national ownership of firms selling and purchasing goods and services; see text for details of the supplemental framework.

States or abroad) are only $64 billion less than purchases from foreign-owned firms (located either in the United States or abroad). The value added in the United States by U.S. affiliates of foreign firms was $152 billion in 1987; in contrast, the value added abroad by foreign affiliates of U.S. companies was $244 billion. The local-content percentage was also higher for these latter firms (89 percent) than for U.S. affiliates of foreign firms (81 percent).

It should be emphasized that the figures derived from the supplemental framework do not mean that the usual macroeconomic concerns about the U.S. balance-of-payments accounts should be discounted. However, the supplemental framework provides additional perspectives on the impact of both foreign direct investment and trade on the economic performance of the U.S. economy; it should be used to supplement the balance-of-payments accounts. For some purposes, especially analyses of contributions to national output and employment, the resident-based statistics are appropriate. For other purposes, however, statistics based on ownership will be more useful to policy makers.

Uses for Public and Private Decisions

The supplemental framework can lead to improved decision making in several specific policy areas. Consider the issue of market access, for example. Today, managers of international firms are interested not only in improving the opportunities for their exports to enter foreign markets, but also in ensuring that the foreign sales of goods and services produced by their affiliates abroad are free of discriminatory rules and regulations within foreign markets. In the ongoing Uruguay Round of negotiations under the auspices of the General Agreement on Tariffs and Trade, the negotiators are seeking to liberalize trade-related investment issues (TRIMS) and sales of services. The issues are likely to become more important in future negotiations. The supplemental framework, in measuring sales from home and abroad by both U.S. firms and foreign firms, would enable policy makers to assess the extent of market access of U.S. and foreign firms in the United States and in foreign markets.[5] (Of course, for bilateral negotiations, sales information by country would be needed.)

---

[5]BEA recently has presented a set of accounts for nonfactor services that provides such a picture by presenting data on the delivery of services to foreign and U.S. markets through cross-border transactions and through sales by affiliates; see DiLullo and Whichard (1990).

Another key aspect of market access concerns the extent to which the sales of U.S. affiliates of foreign firms increase total wages and other forms of income and employment in the United States, in contrast to simply increasing wages, profits, and employment in foreign countries where their parent firms are located. In other words, what is the value added or gross domestic product contribution of U.S. affiliates of foreign companies to the total gross domestic product of the United States?[6] In addition, policy makers may want to know the extent to which these firms purchase intermediate goods and services from producers in the United States rather than importing these goods and services. More specifically, they are interested in knowing the domestic content of the sales of U.S. affiliates of foreign firms, which consist of the gross domestic product of these firms and their purchases of U.S.-produced goods and services from other firms. (An accurate measure of the domestic content, however, would require the collection of data on imported immediate goods by U.S. firms and related improvement in the U.S. input-output tables; see Recommendation 2-2 in Chapter 2.) The contribution of foreign affiliates of U.S. firms to the gross domestic product of foreign countries and the foreign content of the sales of these companies are also of interest and can be obtained from the proposed supplemental framework.

The proposed framework also sheds light on the international competitiveness of U.S. firms, a topic that has received considerable attention since the early 1980s. Because indicators of a country's international competitiveness have commonly involved only measures of cross-border trade, the decline in the U.S. share of world exports from the 1960s through the mid-1980s signaled to many that the United States was faring poorly relative to many other countries. One popular explanation for this loss in competitiveness stresses that U.S. firms have lost their lead in technology and managerial skills. The Omnibus Trade and Competitiveness Act of 1988 states, for example, that there has been inadequate growth in the productivity and competitiveness of U.S. firms and industries relative to their overseas competitors. This legislation contains various provisions aimed at increasing U.S. international competitiveness, including changes in trade policy, measures to promote technology competitiveness, and steps to encourage better education and training for American workers. But the international performance of U.S.-owned firms relative to foreign-owned firms is indicated better by comparing the total cross-border and

---

[6]BEA has recently estimated this figure as a separate exercise; see Lowe (1990).

affiliates' sales by U.S. firms with those of their foreign counterparts—and noting the relative growth rates of the various sources of sales—than by just comparing exports and imports.

The growth of intracompany trade, which is directly related to the rise in U.S. direct investment abroad and the increase in foreign direct investment in the United States, has also raised new issues concerning macroeconomic policy, the arbitrary valuation of exports and imports, evasion of taxes, and dumping practices. For example, a tighter monetary policy in the United States to curtail inflationary pressures is likely to restrain the investment activities of U.S. affiliates of foreign firms less than those of U.S. firms, since the former firms generally have easier access to foreign capital markets than U.S. firms. In intrafirm trade, there is a tendency to price traded goods to minimize a firm's tax liabilities, which yields misleading trade statistics and creates tax evasion problems for public authorities. For example, as of July 1991, some 30 corporations, including Apple Computer, BASF, Bausch & Lomb, Exxon, Hitachi, Nestlé, and Yamaha, had cases before the U.S. Tax Court that involved improper valuations by the companies to reduce their profits subject to U.S. taxes. It is also possible to carry out dumping under the guise of transfer pricing practices. The supplemental framework, which indicates the relative importance of intrafirm trade, informs public policy making in these areas.

The increased willingness of the United States to enter into special regional agreements with other countries is still another example of the value of the supplemental framework. In regional trade arrangements, such as the North American Free Trade Area, minimum regional content percentages for goods traded among members are established to minimize problems associated with differences in tariffs among member and nonmember countries. The supplemental framework facilitates such calculations for affiliates of foreign firms operating within the free trade area, as well as the enforcement of the negotiated rules.

IMPLICATIONS FOR EXISTING DATA SYSTEMS

Much of the data required for the supplemental framework are readily available from the balance-of-payments data, BEA's benchmark and annual surveys on U.S. direct investment abroad and foreign direct investment in the United States, and BEA surveys on trade in services. Development of the supplemental framework requires that the disparate data sets be integrated.

A key matter that arises in constructing the supplemental framework is how to define an affiliate. In compiling the balance-of-payments accounts, BEA regards a foreign affiliate as a foreign firm in which one person (in the legal sense that includes a firm) in the home country owns or controls 10 percent or more of the enterprise's voting securities. Consequently, under current practices, two or more countries can treat the same firm as a foreign affiliate. This will lead to double counting of the total sales and purchases if an affiliate is assigned to each country with a 10 percent or more ownership interest. One approach would be to allocate the sales and purchases of affiliates in proportion to the ownership interests of the different countries. Another approach is to include only those affiliates that are majority owned: that is, affiliates in which the combined ownership of those persons individually owning 10 percent or more of the voting stock from a particular country exceeds 50 percent. One could assign all sales and purchases of affiliates to countries with majority-ownership interests or only the proportions equal to the ownership interests. The increasing diversification of portfolios by pension funds and other institutional investors raises similar issues. Although these funds sometimes acquire 10 percent or more of the voting stocks of firms, they often do not attempt to exert control by proposing candidates for the firms' boards of directors. According to existing rules for determining foreign affiliates, if a U.S. firm owns 100 percent of a foreign firm, but the U.S. firm is, in turn, wholly owned by another foreign firm, the first foreign firm will be counted as a foreign affiliate by the U.S. firm, and again, indirectly, by the second foreign firm that owns the U.S. firm. These and other related issues should be considered in implementing the supplemental framework to avoid double counting.

Integration of disparate data sets under the proposed framework would parallel ongoing efforts undertaken by the United States and international organizations in improving existing statistical systems to better reflect changing global realities. Work is currently under way in the United States to move its national accounts to the U.N. system of national accounts (SNA) by the end of the 1990s. A central feature of the SNA is that it integrates the recording of the different types of market transactions in an economy. In addition to the income and product accounts, it includes consumption, investment, and saving measures, as well as input-output accounts, flow of funds accounts, and balance sheets (Carson and Honsa, 1990). The SNA is presently being revised to reflect improvements in economic accounting over the past two decades and the changes in the international economic environment. The U.N. task force is working toward developing concepts, definitions, and statistical methods in the SNA that reflect the growing importance of foreign direct investment and the rise in intracompany trade of multinational corporations, among others. The purpose is to facilitate meaningful economic analysis and forecasting, as well as policy formulations. Other major objectives of the current revisions of the SNA and those of the revisions of the *Balance of Payments Manual* presently undertaken by the International Monetary Fund are to harmonize concepts and classifications of international transactions; their goals are to facilitate international comparisons, a topic that is further discussed in Chapter 2.

RECOMMENDATION

Recommendation 1-1   A supplemental statistical framework that integrates balance-of-payments data and data on affiliates' operations at home and abroad should be developed to better reflect the link between trade and foreign direct investment.

2

Extending the Comparability
of International and Domestic
Economic Data

Different classification systems, collection methods, and levels of detail are currently used to compile data on U.S. international trade in goods and services and capital flows. Still other classifications, collection methods, and levels of detail are applied to collect data on domestic production, employment, services, and financial activities. The disparateness of data sets has limited the analytical usefulness of existing data, especially for assessing the impact of international transactions on the domestic economy and its various sectors (Maskus, 1992). Comparability of domestic and international data is essential for maximal usability, particularly now that domestic and international economic activities have become increasingly connected.

COMPARABLE DATA: NEEDED BUT LACKING

Although detailed data on U.S. exports and imports are of considerable interest in themselves, business decision makers, government officials, and researchers often want to relate international trade data to domestic economic data. Domestic producers of a given product, for example, want to know not only the quantities of competing products that are imported, but also what share of the total domestic consumption of that product is represented by those imports. They also want to know what share of the total consumption of comparable products in various foreign countries are represented by their exports. And they are interested in the changes in these import and export shares over time. Similarly, in considering whether to reduce tariffs and nontariff measures that protect a particular industry or whether to grant increased protection to an import-injured industry, public officials need to know both the volume of imports in the industry and its level of employment and production.

Private-sector and government researchers trying to understand the reasons for the competitive strengths and weaknesses of various industries need economic data that are classified on the same sectoral basis. They need information, for example, about physical capital, human capital and skills, and educational levels of labor in import-competing and export-oriented product industries, as well as information about such market features as the degree of concentration among firms and the importance of scale economies in different economic sectors. Furthermore, as the globalization of production continues, there is an increasing need for such comparable national and international information as the extent of trade in services, the value of U.S. direct investment abroad and of foreign direct investment in the United States, and volume of goods and services production by affiliates.

In the changing world economic environment, policy makers also need to know the extent to which the structure of U.S. industry has been affected by increased internationalization of the economy. How widespread is "the global factory"? How much has the mix of goods and services supplied by the United States to the world changed over time? To what degree has specialization shifted in today's markets? How well have U.S. industries adapted to the increased internationalization? What has been the impact on employment and occupational patterns by industry and regions of the country? Are there new or changed educational or skill requirements for U.S. workers? How well have public and private U.S. institutions met and responded to changes? Obtaining answers to these and to other questions about the performance of the U.S. economy requires that U.S. foreign trade and domestic data be comparable over time; comparable data among countries are also vital to understanding the increasingly global world economy.

U.S. FOREIGN AND DOMESTIC DATA

In contrast to the clear need for comparable domestic and international U.S. economic data is the reality of different classification systems for almost every data set. For example, data on U.S.

merchandise trade are currently classified under the international Harmonized Commodity Description and Coding System (HS), while domestic production is classified by the Standard Industrial Classification (SIC) codes, which are unique to the United States. One major difference is that data on merchandise trade are classified by *product*, and many data series on domestic economic activity are classified by *industry* of establishment. Although comparisons of data on trade in goods and domestic production are possible through the use of concordances that artificially bridge the data sets, there are still significant differences between merchandise trade data and domestic economic data.

For services and financial transactions, it is extremely difficult to make any comparisons. Cross-border trade in services, for example, is broken down into only about 25 service categories, compared with 125 for domestic services. And sales of services by foreign affiliates of U.S. firms are classified by the industry of the affiliate: there is no detail by type of service. Meanwhile, some types of services—for example, transportation, communications, finance, and insurance—that are covered in international services data are not even covered in domestic data.

Other differences exist at almost every level of data collection and classification. For example, domestic production data are collected on an establishment basis, but direct investment data are obtained from enterprises. Also, data on sales of goods by foreign affiliates of U.S. firms and U.S. affiliates of foreign firms, on U.S. direct investment abroad, and on foreign direct investment in this country are recorded at one level (two- and three-digit) of the SIC, while data on merchandise trade and most domestic activities (such as production and employment) are available at a different level (four-digit) of the SIC. Moreover, although some direct investment data are classified by "industry of sales," most data are available only by the primary industry of the affiliate. These differences in the level of detail and classification schemes at which disparate data are compiled mean that different sectors of the internationalized U.S. economy can be related to one another only at a fairly aggregate level, not at the level most needed by public and private decision makers.

Adequate data are also lacking on the trade in goods and services used as intermediate inputs in domestic production activities. Analysts to date have only been able to make imprecise estimates from the current input-output table of the value of intermediate inputs used by any industry that are not produced domestically. The input-output tables do not distinguish between imported products and domestically produced products used as intermediate inputs. Yet having accurate information about the foreign content of any product is becoming increasingly important not only as an indicator of the rising trend in affiliated transactions and a guide in bilateral and multilateral trade negotiations, but also in understanding the transformation of the economy.

INTERNATIONAL DATA

The situation regarding international comparability of data has improved significantly since January 1989, when the United States adopted the international HS for classifying U.S. merchandise trade. More than 80 other countries have now adopted the HS, making it easier to compare merchandise trade among countries. But comparisons of other U.S. international economic activities with those of other nations remain difficult. International comparability of services data is hampered by differences in definitions, classifications, and coverage among countries. Historically, worldwide compilation of balance-of-payments statistics has focused on certain major categories of services, such as trade and transportation. Data on other services are fragmentary, with little uniformity among countries in the range of services covered. Few countries collect international services data in the same detail as the United States, and no other country currently conducts regular surveys of services sold through affiliates of multinational firms (establishment transactions) (Ascher and Whichard, 1992). These obstacles also apply to international comparisons of data on capital transactions, for which differences in concepts, definitions, and coverage among countries are significant.

Although the United Nations, the International Monetary Fund, the World Bank, the Organization for Economic Cooperation and Development (OECD), and the Bank for International Settlements have established various statistical frameworks to compile data on international trade and finance from different countries, such compilations are often developed only at aggregate levels. Comparable international data at greater levels of detail are not available due to differences in coverage, definitions, concepts, and methodologies.

Work is currently under way to further harmonize the concepts and classifications for international transactions contained in the International Monetary Fund's *Balance of Payments Manual* and in the U.N. system of national accounts (SNA). This effort at further harmonization, which began in the 1980s and is now in the final stages of revisions for both systems of accounts, is seen as promoting the consistency and enhancing the analytic potential of both systems. Among major issues that are being addressed are the delineation of resident entities; the distinction among commodities, nonfactor services, factor and property income, and current transfers; the treatment of certain imputed flows, such as reinvested earnings on direct investment; and valuation. Because the United States intends to move its national accounts closer to the SNA and to revise its international accounts in light of the forthcoming new edition of the *Balance of Payments Manual*, the harmonization of the two sets of international guidelines moves work on the U.S. national and international accounts in the same direction. For the international accounts, it is envisaged that the United States will have considerable work to do to introduce a fully integrated system of stocks and flows, which is a theme of the SNA that is being carried into the new *Balance of Payments Manual*, and to introduce a more detailed set of accounts for travel, transportation, construction, insurance, finance, other business services, and other personal services.

Meanwhile, attempts to establish a standardized format or classification system for international services, similar to the HS for merchandise trade, are currently being made at the United Nations, where the central product classification (CPC) system is being developed for this purpose. Other efforts to refine concepts and definitions of international services and direct investment are being undertaken by the OECD, the Statistical Office of the European Communities, and the Voorburg Group (organized informally under the auspices of the U.N. Statistical Office to establish a new services unit to coordinate the work on services statistics within the OECD and with other international organizations). OECD also has recently completed a detailed compilation of services trade statistics of member countries covering 1970 to 1987, attempting to put them on a comparable basis.

It will be valuable for U.S. public and private decision makers if current international efforts to harmonize economic data among countries are matched by similar pursuits to improve domestic data and make them comparable to data on international transactions. The next sections of this chapter describe data sets that warrant particular attention; their different classification schemes are discussed below and shown in Figure 2-1.

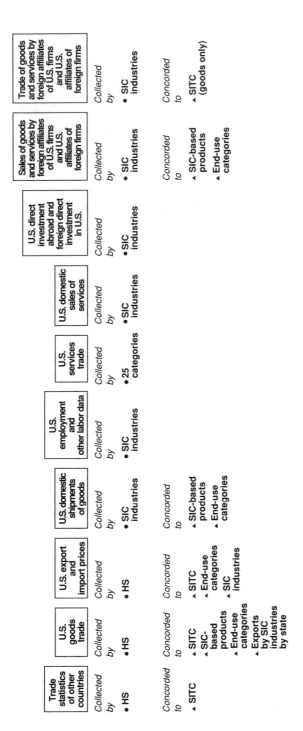

FIGURE 2-1 Classification systems for selected U.S. foreign trade, direct investment, and domestic economic data.

MERCHANDISE DATA

U.S. AND OTHER COUNTRIES DATA

One obvious requirement for an adequate trade data system is the ability to compare a country's own merchandise trade with that of other countries by product and industry categories. Until recently, such comparisons required the use of concordances between the unique U.S. import and export classification systems and a trade classification system developed under United Nations auspices, the Standard International Trade Classification (SITC). The situation changed on January 1, 1989, when the United States adopted a new classification system, the Harmonized Commodity Description and Coding System (HS), developed by an international group of customs and statistical experts.[1] Because many countries also now use the HS, it is possible to directly compare trade among countries in about 5,500 product groups.

The changeover has created problems, however, for those who want internationally comparable trade figures over a long period of time. While trade on an HS basis has been estimated by the Census Bureau and the International Trade Commission for the period 1983-1988, this series is only a rough estimate of actual trade during these years classified according to the new system. For example, in allocating shares when goods within a former product group are distributed among more than one product group under the HS system, the allocation weights based on the world trade in the products are applied to each individual country.

PRICE INDEXES FOR IMPORTS AND EXPORTS

Users of time series of merchandise import and export data invariably want price indexes for traded goods in order to compare real changes in trade over time. Other users are interested in price data for analyzing changes in a country's terms of trade. For imports, price indexes have been available only since September 1982; for exports, price indexes have been available since September 1983 (for details, see Alterman, 1992). The Bureau of Labor Statistics (BLS) now collects quarterly import and export price data on about 22,000 products from more than 8,300 companies.

---

[1]The pre-1989 import classification system was the Tariff Schedule of the United States Annotated (TSUSA), while the export system was the Statistical Classification of Domestic and Foreign Commodities Exported from the United States (Schedule B).

Since January 1989 it has published import and export price indexes on a monthly basis.

Before monthly import and export price indexes became available, time series of trade in real terms were usually constructed by deflating figures using unit-value indexes produced by the Census Bureau as a by-product of the collection of U.S. merchandise trade data. The problem of shifts in the composition of industry products over time and the differences among the sets of goods produced, exported, and imported in an industry made this an unsatisfactory procedure. Many years ago, the Interagency Committee on Measurement of Real Output (1973) recommended that price data from the BLS wholesale and industrial price index programs be used more for deflation in the absence of import and export price indexes than the export and import unit-value indexes.

The BLS publishes import and export price indexes by three classification structures: SITC, SIC, and BEA end-use categories.

Domestic Production and Import and Export Data

Another basic requirement for an adequate trade data system is the classification of imports and exports on the same basis as the classification of information on domestic production. In the United States, this is accomplished by rearranging the classification system on which production data are collected and reclassifying trade data by that system.

The basic unit for collecting production data is an establishment, an economic unit located at a single physical site. The Standard Industrial Classification (SIC), which is used by the United States to classify establishments by industry, classifies largely on the basis of two factors: the specific activity performed by the establishment and the nature of the customers served. The general objective is to establish industries that are relatively homogeneous in both their inputs and outputs. The latest classification system (1987) divides economic activities by agriculture, mining, manufacturing, and various service sectors (the first digit of the code) and then into more detailed breakdowns, ending with 1,005 four-digit industries. Since a particular establishment assigned to a specific four-digit industry may produce more than one product—for example, a plant producing mainly aluminum castings may produce some copper castings—the Census Bureau has developed an SIC-based system (up to eight digits) that classifies by product. Unlike the four-digit SIC industry data, the four-digit SIC-based product data consist only of shipments of the primary products of the industry, including sales of these products by establishments classified in other industries, but excluding secondary products of establishments in the industry.

Since import and export data are classified by product under the HS, trade data can be related to the product codes of the expanded SIC system. Nonetheless, trade codes frequently lump together products that bridge two or more of the five-digit SIC product codes. When it appears that assigning the entire amount of the traded good to a single product code would significantly distort the import or export data, five-digit product codes are combined, and trade in the good is assigned to the more comprehensive code. The resulting combination of one or more five-digit SIC product codes yields the "SIC-based trade classification system." Obviously, classifying import and export data by this system produces a far from perfect match with domestic output data.

The Census Bureau's periodical *U.S. Commodity Exports and Imports as Related to Output* presents the results of classifying trade and output data by the SlC-based trade system at the four- and five-digit level. The latest edition, issued in June 1990, covers 1985 and 1986. For some import-sensitive industries, however, the Census Bureau publishes comparisons of exports, imports, and production at the seven-digit level of SIC-based detail in its perodical *Current Industrial Reports*, and these reports appear monthly, quarterly, and annually, depending on the industry. The International Trade Administration (ITA) of the Department of Commerce also constructs series of imports, exports, and domestic shipments at the four-digit SIC-based level and has calculated ratios of imports to new supply (domestic shipments plus imports) and exports to shipments back to 1972. These data are published in part in its annual *U.S. Industrial Outlook*.

Using COMPRO, a computerized database on U.S. foreign trade maintained by ITA, federal government analysts could obtain SIC-based import and export data at up to the eight-digit level for the period 1978-1988. From 1989 onward, however, data in this bank are available only on a four-digit SIC-based level. The Census Bureau stopped supplying post-1988 SIC-based import and export data at up to the eight-digit level because of problems in data quality associated with the conversion to the HS. COMPRO also provides time-series trade data classified on the basis of the HS, TSUSA, SITC, and end-use categories.

Nongovernment officials and researchers have had difficulty in recent years in matching imports, exports, and production at the four-digit SIC-based level. Through 1984, the Census Bureau provided import and export data at a detailed SIC-based level in two volumes, but they were discontinued for budgetary reasons; the data are available on microfiche. Some users report it is so difficult to read the data on microfiche that they cannot be used for developing comprehensive time series. The Census Bureau plans to provide trade data at the four-digit SIC-based level on CD-ROMs (compact disk-read only memory).

In the Annual Survey of Manufactures, the Census Bureau has asked establishments since the 1960s to report a single figure for the value of products shipped for export during the year. These data are then adjusted for underreported exports by using the trade data collected directly by the Customs Service and the Census Bureau to derive establishment exports of manufactured goods by three-digit SIC industry codes. The data are also reported by state on a two-digit SIC industry basis. Efforts to obtain export data by state have also been facilitated by including a question relating to state of origin on the shippers' export declarations (SEDs) collected by the Census Bureau. A similar question was included for the state of imports, but, because the state of the importer or broker office responsible for the paperwork was being listed rather than the state for which the merchandise was destined, the reporting of this information was suspended pending improvements in collection methodology. Since July 1991 the Customs Bureau has required that import documents report the state to which imported merchandise is destined.

IMPORT AND EXPORT DATA AND EMPLOYMENT, CAPITAL, AND OTHER ESTABLISHMENT DATA

When BLS collects data on employment in its monthly survey, it does not ask establishments in a particular SIC four-digit industry code to list the number of employees by product or product type, probably because employers usually do not keep employment records on this basis. The same is true with respect to figures on capital stock. Thus, it is not possible to relate trade data (classified on a four-digit SIC-based level) to data on such economic variables as employment, skill levels, wages, hours of work, earnings, turnover rates, productivity, unemployment, investment, and capital stock.

Other rich sources of data on the economic and social characteristics of the labor force by SIC industries are the Current Population Survey (annual) and the decennial census. These data provide a variety of information on characteristics of employees, such as educational level, age, occupation, income, sex, race, and marital status. But the level of industry detail has changed considerably over time. Even today, data for agriculture, mining, and construction are presented only at the two-digit SIC level. Information for other sectors are generally given at the three-digit level.

CLASSIFICATION OF INTERMEDIATE INPUTS

As national economies become increasingly internationalized, a greater proportion of imported goods are used as intermediate inputs in the production of other goods and services rather than as final goods and services by consumers, investors, or governments. Unlike a number of industrial countries, however, the United States does not collect information on the extent to which industries use as intermediate inputs imported goods that are substitutable for domestically produced goods. Imports are not distinguished from domestically produced substitutes in the input-output tables constructed by the Department of Commerce that indicate the intermediate and final uses of the primary products of more than 500 SIC industries. Consequently, it is possible neither to determine exactly the domestic content of any product nor to estimate the direct and indirect increase in imports associated with a given increase in demand for that product.

Such information is important not only for determining the extent of the internationalization of domestic production, but also for the successful implementation of policies aimed at protecting domestic industries subject to injurious import competition and at helping domestic industries become more competitive. Although it is not feasible to determine the country source of every intermediate input, a significant share of the imports used as intermediate inputs could be allocated to the proper industry by relying on the import records of major industry producers and their main suppliers. These companies could report these allocations as part of the 5-year economic censuses and their annual updates.

SERVICES DATA

Until 1987, information on cross-border transactions in services was limited to a comparatively small number of categories, such as royalties and licenses fees, travel, passenger fares, freight, port services, reinsurance, telecommunications, and film rentals. As of 1987, however, data on trade in services are available for about 25 separate categories, covering various types of business, professional, and technical services in particular detail. As discussed in

Chapter 5, continued efforts are needed to develop more detailed descriptions of traded services codes. Additional work is also needed in the ongoing efforts to develop price indexes for internationally traded services.

Benchmark data on domestically produced services by 174 four-digit SIC service industries are provided in the quinquennial economic censuses, which cover retail trade, wholesale trade, and selected other services. Yet some major services are excluded from these economic censuses, such as transportation, communications, finance, and insurance.[2] Data collected in the economic censuses cover employment, value of output, capital stock, investment, and cost of materials used.

Employment and payroll data for service sectors are available on an annual basis from the BLS monthly survey of establishments, as are data on the value of services provided, based on records of the Internal Revenue Service and the Annual Survey of Selected Service Industries. BEA also annually estimates real GNP originating in selected two-digit service sectors.

The classification system for collecting data on traded services does not directly match the SIC industry basis on which information on domestically produced services is assembled. For some traded services categories, such as royalties and license fees, matching would not be appropriate. For many traded services, however—especially business, professional, and technical services—it would be valuable to compare the volume of international trade in services with the domestic output of those services, just as trade in goods is compared with the domestic production of these goods.

At present, the relatively small number of traded services categories does not make it too difficult to compare these with broad SIC domestic service groups, but as more and more traded services are distinguished, the comparability issue will become more important. In particular, data on the production of domestic services should be classified by SIC-based product codes so that they can be easily compared with data collected on traded services.

To improve domestic services data, the Census Bureau has expanded its quinquennial economic censuses and its annual sample surveys to cover a greater number of services. In addition, the Federal Reserve Board has recently developed experimental output indexes for services, similar to its indexes of industrial production. Extension of these efforts to cover U.S. international

---

[2]The Committee on National Statistics of the National Research Council has recommended that benchmark data for these services be developed; see Helfand et al. (1984).

services transactions would enhance comparability of domestic and international data on services.

OTHER DATA

SALES OF GOODS AND SERVICES BY FOREIGN AFFILIATES

In its surveys of U.S. direct investment abroad and foreign investment in the United States, BEA collects data on the sale of goods and services by foreign affiliates of U.S. firms abroad by two- and three-digit SIC industries and also the sales by U.S. affiliates of foreign firms in the United States by two- and three-digit industries. Data on employment, capital stock, investment, etc. are also collected on affiliates. Detailed information is provided every 5 years, with annual surveys being used to augment the benchmark surveys. Data on merchandise (but not services) trade between affiliates and the home country of the parent are collected only at the level of one-digit SITC codes in benchmark surveys. Although trade between foreign affiliates and their home countries at this level can thus be compared with total U.S. imports and exports of these products, trade data at a much more detailed level are needed in view of the economic importance of foreign affiliates (30 percent of U.S. exports are to foreign affiliates of U.S. firms). Of course, U.S. merchandise trade must be reclassified on an SITC basis, too. The HS rather than SITC would be a better basis for collecting trade data. The Census Bureau currently collects information on merchandise exports between related parties on the SEDs, but funds have not been appropriated for tabulation or analysis of the data.

DIRECT INVESTMENT

Data on U.S. direct investment abroad and foreign direct investment in the United States are collected by BEA in detailed quinquennial surveys and in less detailed annual and quarterly surveys. Such information as the total value of foreign investments, annual investment, and employment by foreign affiliates is available for both U.S. direct investment abroad and foreign direct investment in the United States from these surveys on a two- and three-digit SIC industry basis that covers both goods and services sectors. These data, together with data on domestic investment, can be used to measure the extent to which the capital stock of the United States is being internationalized as well as the extent to which the United States is penetrating foreign markets through investment activities.

Comparing growth rates of direct investment and goods and services trade is also useful in understanding the internationalization of national economies. To obtain more information, the data on investment need to be collected on a four-digit SIC industry basis. The possibility of reclassifying those data to four-digit SIC product basis should also be explored.

NATIONAL TRADE DATA BANK

The National Trade Data Bank (NTDB) is a depository database containing trade and export promotion information from 15 federal agencies. Established by the Omnibus Trade and Competitiveness Act of 1988, the NTDB assembles economic, demographic, social, and other statistics of the United States and other countries that are of use to promote U.S. exports. In addition to the Census Bureau's merchandise trade data, the NTDB provides data on international transactions and the quarterly NIPA compiled by BEA; data on exchange rates and foreign interest rates gathered by the Federal Reserve Board; international labor and price statistics prepared by BLS; and other data series on the U.S. industrial outlook. Figure 2-2 shows the information programs accessible through

FIGURE 2-2   National Trade Data Bank (NTDB) Information
Programs

Central Intelligence Agency
  Handbook on Economic Statistics
  The World Factbook
Department of Agriculture, Foreign Agricultural Services
  Foreign Production Supply and Distribution of Agriculture Commodities
Department of Commerce, Economics and Statistics Administration (ESA),
    Bureau of the Census
  Exports from Manufacturing Establishments
  Merchandise Trade—Imports (Country-Commodity)
  Merchandise Trade—Exports (Country-Commodity)
  Merchandise Trade—Imports (Commodity-Country)
  Merchandise Trade—Exports (Commodity-Country)
  Total Mid-Year Populations and Projections through 2050
  Trade and Employment
Department of Commerce, ESA, Bureau of Economic Analysis
  Fixed Reproducible Tangible Wealth Estimates
  Foreign Direct Investment in the U.S.: Position, Capital, Income
  International Service
  National Income and Product Accounts, Annual Series
  National Income and Product Accounts, Quarterly Series
  Operations of U.S. Affiliates of Foreign Companies

continued on next page

FIGURE 2-2 *Continued*

Department of Commerce, ESA, Bureau of Economic Analysis—*continued*
  Operations of U.S. Parent Companies and Their Foreign Affiliates
  U.S. Assets Abroad and Foreign Assets in the U.S.
  U.S. Business Acquired and Established by Foreign Direct Investors
  U.S. Direct Investment Abroad: Position, Capital, Income
  U.S. Expenditures for Pollution Abatement and Control (PAC)
  U.S. International Transactions (Balance of Payments)
  U.S. Merchandise Trade (Balance of Payments Basis)
Department of Commerce, ESA, Office of Business Analysis
  NTDB BROWSE Manual
  Sources of Trade Information and Contacts
Department of Commerce, International Trade Administration (ITA)
  Business America
  A Basic Guide to Exporting
  Domestic and International Coal Issues and Markets
  EC 1992: A Commerce Department Analysis of EC Directives, Volumes I–III
  Foreign Traders Index
  Market Research Reports
    Country Marketing Plans
    Industry Sector Analyses
    Foreign Economic Trends
  North American Free Trade Agreement (NAFTA) Information
  Understanding U.S. Foreign Trade Data
  U.S. Industrial Outlook
Department of Commerce, National Institute for Standards and Technology (NIST)
  GATT Standards Code Activities of NIST
  Organizations Conducting Standards-Related Activities
  Standards, Certification and Metric Information Program
Department of Energy
  International Energy Database
Department of Labor, Bureau of Labor Statistics
  International Labor Statistics
  International Price Indexes
Department of State
  Reference Guide to Doing Business in Central and Eastern Europe
Export-Import Bank of the United States
  Export-Import Bank of the United States, Quarterly Report
Board of Governors of the Federal Reserve System
  Foreign Spot Exchange Rates
  Foreign 3-Month Interest Rates
  Stock Price Indices for the G-10 Countries
  U.S. 3-Month CD Interest Rates
  Weighted Average Exchange Value of the Dollar
U.S. International Trade Commission
  Trade Between the U.S. and Non-Market Economy Countries
Overseas Private Investment Corporation
  OPIC Program Summaries
Office of the U.S. Trade Representative
  National Trade Estimate Report on Foreign Trade Barriers
  Trade Projections Report to the Congress
University of Massachusetts, MISER
  State of Origins Exports

the NTDB. Although this data bank has undoubtedly eased problems of data access for trade analysts, other data are needed to gauge the international positon of the U.S. economy and its various sectors. Such data include measures of productivity, costs, profit rates, capital costs, and overall competitiveness and measures of tariffs and other trade barriers. The data are particularly needed to facilitate valid international comparisons.

RECOMMENDATIONS

Recommendation 2-1 The United States should take the lead in international cooperative efforts to build coherent comparable worldwide accounts through standardizing data concepts and methodologies on production, trade, employment, and investment and establishing a statistical framework that captures changing international commercial relations.

Recommendation 2-2 As part of the quinquennial surveys, the Census Bureau should collect data on purchases of imported goods and services. The Bureau of Economic Analysis should use the data to strengthen its program on the compilation of the U.S. input-output tables.

Recommendation 2-3 Data at the four-digit SIC industry level, compiled in most cases on a four-digit SIC product basis, should be collected not only on the domestic production of goods, but also on the domestic production of services, the production of goods and services by foreign affiliates, and foreign direct investment so that data on international trade in goods and services can be related to these data. Quantitative and qualitative information about the use of labor, capital, and intermediate inputs in producing goods and services should also be collected at the four-digit SIC level. Data on the trade of affiliates should also be collected in greater detail.

Recommendation 2-4 COMPRO should be made available to all users through its inclusion in the National Trade Data Bank.

Recommendation 2-5 Measures of productivity, costs, profit rates, capital costs, and overall competitiveness and other measures of tariffs and trade barriers should be included in

the National Trade Data Bank to facilitate valid international comparisons.

Recommendation 2-6 Efforts to measure traded services in greater detail should continue along with efforts to develop price indexes for internationally traded services. The United States should participate fully in international efforts to develop a common classification system for traded services for all countries.

3

Developing a Flexible Data System for U.S. International Economic Activities

The major function of federal statistics is to inform public policy making. Thus, data collection agencies must understand the basic purposes of the data and build appropriate concepts and definitions into the design and development of the statistical framework. To ensure that the data collected are suitable for the purposes intended, data collection agencies must also analyze and interpret them.

In addition, since users—both public and private—understand the need for the data and are knowledgeable about the policies and programs for which the data are collected, statistical agencies need to work closely with users in developing the statistical framework and designing data collection and analysis. Such interface would also make users aware of the availability and the limitations of data and make maximum use of the data for their purposes. Until now, the absence of a strong nexus between data collection and data analysis has resulted in the production of data of diminishing analytic usefulness or data that are not fully utilized.

Because the international trade environment will continue to evolve, continual interaction between data collection agencies and public and private users is essential to ensure that relevant data are collected and irrelevant data are not. Such interface will promote flexibility in the data collection system. Moving toward a responsive system of data collection is critical to enhance cost-effectiveness in compiling needed international trade and financial data.

CURRENT DATA

In the early 1980s, when the merchandise trade statistics showed a surge in U.S. imports, there were alarming reports on the impending deindustrialization of the U.S. economy and the displacement of tens of thousands of U.S. workers. Later, when the U.S. merchandise trade deficit reached unprecedented heights, analysts predicted a "hard landing" for the U.S. dollar. At the same time, data on merchandise trade of semiconductors led to great concerns about foreigners' dumping computer chips in the United States to the detriment of the U.S. semiconductor industry and urgent calls for a U.S.-Japan semiconductor agreement to safeguard the U.S. industry. And, on a monthly basis, the U.S. stock market rose and fell with the release of data on the U.S. merchandise trade balance. The huge drop in the stock market in October 1987 was attributed partly to the increasing deficit reported during that period.

Also, in the late 1980s, data on foreign investment in the United States—including foreigners' production of automobiles, electronic products, and other manufacturing, wholesaling, and retailing activities in the domestic economy, as well as purchases of prime real estate—raised fears of foreigners' buying up the United States and of this country's losing control of its production and real estate. More recently, data showing slackening of inflows of foreign capital led analysts to predict a sharp rise in U.S. interest rates at the beginning of the 1990s.

The history of the past decade shows that most of these analyses were off the mark. The United States has not deindustrialized. The number of U.S. jobs has risen since the early 1980s (manufacturing jobs have declined, but service jobs have multiplied). The value of the dollar did decline in the mid-1980s, but it did not have a "hard landing." At the same time, the U.S.-Japanese semiconductor agreement has not achieved many of its proponents' objectives. The stock market has recovered. Foreign direct investment in the United States has not taken over management of the U.S. corporate sector nor have foreign purchases of U.S. real estate come to represent a major proportion of U.S. assets. Moreover, U.S. interest rates have remained lower than those of most industrialized countries in recent years.

This recent history shows that data on U.S. international transactions have at times been wrong, misunderstood, or misused. The data have thus misinformed policy debates.

For merchandise trade (discussed in Chapter 4), the monthly

data are subject to large errors, especially on the export side. U.S. exports have been underreported, which may have overstated the nation's trade deficit. The merchandise trade balance can also fluctuate widely from month to month without any change in the underlying trend. Yet users have often interpreted those fluctuations as shifts in the underlying trend, which, in turn, has sent inappropriate signals to financial and exchange markets. There are also errors in the detailed merchandise trade data. Moreover, the monthly merchandise trade statistics lack a long-term orientation, limiting their usefulness for policy analysis and research.

For services transactions (discussed in Chapter 5), until recently substantial volumes of services trade were not included in the published data, making the U.S. current account balances inaccurate. There are still major international services that are inadequately covered, such as financial services. The development of data to cover new services has been hampered by limited analytic capabilities in the Bureau of Economic Analysis (BEA). Such constraints have kept BEA from improving concepts and methodologies (especially of determining how different types of services should be measured) and from refining survey questionnaires. BEA does not analyze extensively the data it collects and present analyses and interpretations to users, and users' access to data on U.S. international services transactions is limited. In addition, data compiled in large sector aggregates mask major changes in particular components; the lack of detailed data on U.S. international services limits analytic uses.

For capital flows (discussed in Chapter 6), data are marred by gross inadequacy in coverage—especially on new modes of capital transactions and new types of financial instruments—as well as by outdated assumptions on asset valuations and estimation methods. These inadequacies have adversely affected the accuracy of the data. In addition, data on capital flows are not well synthesized and organized in usable formats, further limiting their usefulness. BEA and the Treasury Department have yet to exploit fully the analytic potential of the data they do collect and to disseminate them broadly to users. Existing data are not regularly reviewed by BEA and Treasury to determine if additions, deletions, or other modifications are necessary.

More important, as discussed in Chapter I, the traditional balance-of-payments framework is inadequate for analyzing issues arising from the changing global environment. Closing data gaps, improving data adequacy, and anticipating new data needs call not only for increased research, analysis, and evaluation on the part of data collection agencies, but also for enhanced communications between statistical agencies and data users.

ROLE OF STATISTICAL AGENCIES

STRENGTHENING RESEARCH AND ANALYTIC CAPABILITIES

In analyzing ways to improve the federal statistical systems over the past decade, various experts have all separately come to the same conclusion: to produce relevant economic statistics of high quality, statistical agencies must strengthen their analytic capabilities. The importance of analysis and research in the production of federal statistics is obvious. Schultze (1988) states that since federal statistics generated should primarily serve policy making, the specification of data needs for economic policy must originate from economic and social research agenda. Triplett (1990) expands on this theme, noting that today's research needs often drive tomorrow's analytic efforts. Similarly, the Juster (1988) report on quality of economic statistics, prepared under the auspices of the American Economic Association, concludes that since research points to emerging needs for economic data, the role of analysis and research is the single most important contribution toward making statistical agencies more responsive to emerging needs. Lipsey (1990) observes that BEA's recent improvements in data on international services transactions represent a response to continued academic complaints about deficiencies of the data. In addition, Congress and the administrative agencies became aware of the data shortcomings when services trade was put on the agenda for the Uruguay Round of the General Agreement on Tariffs and Trade negotiations. Similarly, BEA's recent introduction of current-cost and market-value methods in revaluating U.S. net international investment position is a response to researchers' discontent with book-value data of U.S. direct investment abroad and U.S. gold reserves, given inflation over time and significant changes that have occurred in the values of gold and other U.S. assets abroad.

Experts have pointed out that the main reason that statistical agencies respond slowly to users' data needs is that the agencies consider as their main task to produce the monthly or quarterly data on time. There are often few professional analysts in the agencies, and when agencies have such professionals, they are often not closely involved in the agencies' program planning and development. To enhance the quality and relevance of federal statistics calls not only for skilled personnel to staff the research and development function, but also for close linkage between the research output and the ongoing programs of the statistical agencies (Cole, 1990). One area for which such efforts are needed is a thorough review of the scope, concept, and methodology currently used to compile international trade and finance data, as well as to upgrade domestic economic data and the national accounts to reflect the transformation of the U.S. economy.

Determining Data Needs

The panel solicited the views of public and private users on the adequacy of the existing data on international transactions and heard from persons representing more than 100 organizations, covering a wide spectrum of government, business, academic, and other activities (see Appendix B). Although we asked users to identify both currently unmet needs and anticipated future needs for foreign trade data, most of the responses concentrated on the present. A few of the unmet needs described by users referred to data that are currently available, indicating that some users lack complete knowledge of existing data sources. Publication of a broad catalogue of available foreign trade data from all sources, including other countries, international bodies, and private organizations, might lead to better use of existing data.

Most of the comments on unmet needs had to do with new data that could be provided by modifying or expanding the Census Bureau's processing and publication of data based on official trade documents. Areas touched on most often were the level of commodity detail, data on low-value shipments, and data regrouped by states. Manufacturers and their industry associations frequently wanted more commodity detail than is presently provided by the Harmonized System because they would like to be able to monitor their market shares in specific commodities they produce. Several types of users saw a need for greater compatibility between merchandise trade and domestic production commodity data. Interest in low-value shipments, which are presently excluded from the detailed merchandise trade statistics, came from representatives of the transportation industry, especially the airlines. Requests for more detailed data on exports compiled by U.S. state of origin and imports by state of final destination were voiced by the National Governors' Association and state officials charged with promoting exports. Requests for other kinds of data were numerous and varied. Examples include data on affiliated trade, data on trade and domestic production by nationality of ownership, expanded coverage of the Bureau of Labor Statistics foreign trade price indexes to cover more commodity detail and bilateral trade, and information on tariffs and nontariff trade barriers. Most of these suggestions came from the economic research community.

The panel members, many of whom use foreign trade statistics, can understand the desire of users to have numerous new kinds of trade data. Nonetheless, meeting all such requests would be prohibitively expensive. High-cost data initiatives, such as expansion of state data and processing low-value shipments, would require especially strong justification.

The panel also asked users to comment on the costs of obtaining foreign trade data and on how they process the data before using them. The nature of the responses varied greatly, depending on the type of organization and its needs, resources, and awareness of the sources and nature of foreign trade data. Those who use foreign trade information in a more than casual way seldom acquire it in a form suitable for their purposes. The raw data must be processed to convert them into forms appropriate for making decisions, monitoring macroeconomic trends, understanding the determinants of trade flows, and other purposes. Such processing occurs in several ways: by extracting some data cells from a large data set; by calculating derived statistics, such as unit costs; by developing time series and performing seasonal adjustment; by converting from one classification system to another; and by converting the data from hard copy (or microfiche) to electronic format, or the reverse.

Users have a range of options as to how much of the processing they do themselves. At one end of the spectrum, they can purchase raw cross-sectional data from the Census Bureau (and its counterparts in other countries, if needed) and do all of the processing necessary to convert the data to meet their needs. At the other end of the spectrum, a private-sector organization with minimal facilities for processing data might pay a consulting firm to prepare a market analysis of international or bilateral trade in specific commodities of interest, receiving only the finished product. Some type of cost-benefit analysis is implicit in the strategies that users adopt to decide what information they need and how best to acquire it. Since it is in the users' interest to minimize their costs, it is not surprising that many would like the primary and secondary producers in governments and international organizations to add more value to raw data, preferably with no increase in user charges.

To determine the data needs of the private sector and how much information the federal government should provide, there is a need for new mechanisms to guide federal statistical policy. Historically, the division of labor has had extraordinary effects on productivity, partly because a market system is an effective method for the coordination of the specialized activities of producers and consumers. But in the absence of a market or other means of coordination, the productivity gains from specialization can be more than offset by coordination errors. In our judgment, the division of labor between statistical agencies and data users in the private sector has gone far beyond the point at which the gains from specialization exceed the costs of coordination failures. Indeed, there is no organized system by which users communicate their needs to data collection agencies. Loud user complaints do seem to stimulate responses, but volume and value are not necessarily highly correlated. Substantial changes in institutions are needed to coordinate the demand for and supply of data.

Data cannot be supplied by a competitive market system because of the cost advantages of centralization and because use of data by one party does not exclude use by another party. In the language of economics, information is a public good. But when the benefits of a data set accrue primarily to clearly definable specialized groups, it is appropriate that these groups pay for the data. In some cases, these groups should look to private vendors. For example, shippers need detailed information on merchandise shipments between cities of the United States and elsewhere in the world. We do not think there is a compelling argument that the federal government should respond to that need.

When a data set serves the public good and when the federal government has ongoing activities that make it the low-cost provider, then it is the provider of choice. Groups that gain substantial private benefit from the data should contribute to the costs of collection. Moreover, willingness to pay is a clear signal of the value of data. Generally, the benefits will accrue not only to specialized groups, but also to federal decision makers and to the public. In that event, cost sharing should be the rule. For example, data on international transactions of enterprises within individual states serve the needs of state governments, and they also are important for studying the regional consequences of federal commercial and migrant policy: the cost of collecting these data should therefore be borne both by state and federal governments.

The costs of collecting much economic data cannot be passed

on to users because of the public nature of the data. At the same time, willingness to pay (i.e., markets) cannot necessarily direct the federal government to collect data that are valuable. It is not easy to create institutions other than markets that collect data. If willingness to pay is not a sufficient signal, there needs to be substantial, organized, and ongoing communications between those who collect the data and those who use them. One possibility would be an annual conference that brings users together with those who are responsible for collecting the data. Another possibility would be to establish an advisory body to guide the development of data concepts and frameworks and help set priorities for data collection with the highest payoffs. Such a body could also review programs of the statistical agencies and monitor their progress toward accomplishing overall program goals. The function of the advisory body would complement rather than substitute for in-house research and analysis. Whatever the mechanism, it must foster an ongoing interaction between data collection agencies and data users.

Communicating Data Quality to Users

An important symptom of the communications failure between data users and data collectors is the absence of clear measures of uncertainty accompanying the data on international economic activities provided by the federal government. In our judgment, those who collect the data and those who use the data need to be cognizant that they are not perfect measures, but only estimates. An estimate without a standard error or some other measures of uncertainty is not fully satisfactory. Collectors of data currently publish statistics as if they were perfect measures, and users generally rely on them as though they were perfect. There is strong demand for more data, but little demand for more accurate data. Yet major misinterpretations can easily occur because of lack of knowledge about data quality.

Ideally, statistical data should be accompanied by standard errors or other measures of uncertainty in a profile delineating their limitations. The reporting of such limitations might well stimulate evaluations that in turn could substantially improve the allocation of scarce resources for data collection. When the reported standard errors or other measures of uncertainty of particular data are so large that users find the numbers virtually valueless, for example, users would be likely to demand more accurate data. And a perfectly legitimate response of federal data collectors when an acceptable level of accuracy cannot be achieved at reasonable costs would be to cease collecting the data. More generally, data users and data collectors should assess how resources could be properly allocated to reduce uncertainty in the data. Changes in the operating procedures that are costly and likely to have little effect on improving data quality would not be undertaken.

Attaching standard errors or other measures of uncertainty to international economic data is not easy, in part because much of the uncertainty in the data is not due to sampling uncertainty, with which statisticians are used to dealing. The larger source of error is response bias of various forms, the size of which often has to be guessed rather than formally estimated. We believe that those who collect the data do have an understanding of those probable biases. They know that the quality of data on exports of travel services is much more uncertain than that on exports of textiles, for example: they should provide users with the benefit of this wisdom. The fact that these standard errors or other measures of uncertainty are only guesses will be disconcerting to those who think of the data currently reported as perfect measures. But those who understand how the data are compiled will not be unduly disturbed by the guesswork involved in selecting standard errors and other measures of uncertainty.

There are other ways to communicate limitations of data to users. If the data are transmitted in machine readable form, it is possible to attach files that contain the associated standard errors or other measures of uncertainty. The print media offer some more creative ways to communicate the inaccuracy of the data. One possibility is illustrated in Table 3-1, which contains part of the 1989 balance-of-payments data of the United States. The numbers in the tables in which the statistical agency has confidence are reported in boldface; others appear in italics. This print type dramatically makes the point that imports are more accurately measured than exports, and merchandise trade data are more reliable than those for services trade.

Some convention has to be adopted to translate a standard error into a type of print. For example, an integer could be regarded to be accurate if it would not be changed if the overall figure were changed by one standard deviation. If merchandise exports were measured to be $360.465 billion with a standard error of 23, a change of one standard deviation would not affect the first integer, but it would affect all the others. Thus the printed number is $360.465. We do not endorse any particular solution to the problem of communicating the inaccuracy of the data. There are many

TABLE 3-1 Current Account Balance, U.S. Balance of Payments, 1989 (in billions of dollars)

Category	Amount
Merchandise	
Exports	360.465
Imports	–475.329
Merchandise trade balance	–114.864
Services	
Net military transactions	–6.320
Net travel and transportation receipts	0.659
Other services, net	26.123
Investment income	
Receipts on U.S. assets abroad	127.536
Payments on foreign assets in United States	–128.448
Net	–0.913
Unilateral transfers, net	–14.720
Balance on current account	–110.034

NOTE: See text for explanation of numbers.

SOURCE: Data from Council of Economic Advisers (1991:Table B-102).

other schemes that might be adopted that could as well or better communicate the accuracy of the data. In documents printed in color, the colors red, yellow, and green could indicate increasing accuracy. Our point is that it can be done in informative ways, and that it should be done.

There are three ways in which data users can find out more about the behavior of the economy: gather more data; gather more accurate data; or determine the accuracy of the data. In part because the federal data producing agencies do not emphasize the reporting of data limitations, only the first of these ways generally has been considered. But if standard errors or other measures of uncertainty accompanied the data, there would also be a demand for more accurate data. Once users became familiar with the inaccuracy of the data, they would realize that there is a third route to a better understanding of the economy: more accurate knowledge of the inaccuracies in the data.

RECOMMENDATIONS

Recommendation 3-1   The Bureau of Economic Analysis, the Treasury Department, and, especially, the Census Bureau should strengthen their research and analytic capabilities so that

they can develop proper concepts and methods to measure the U.S. international economic activities. The Census Bureau and the Bureau of Economic Analysis should work jointly to develop concepts, definitions, measures, and strategies for capturing in more detail the rapidly growing intracompany trade and trade in intermediate inputs. The Treasury Department and the Federal Reserve should jointly explore similar improvements to cover portfolio transactions and the flow-of-funds accounts. In addition, efforts should also be made to measure more accurately prices of international transactions and other dimensions of competitiveness, including taxes, costs, and rates of return, as well as to improve constant-price measures of exports and imports. These agencies should seek outside professional advice from analytic users and other experts in these efforts.

Recommendation 3-2   Sufficient information in the form of data quality profiles should be provided to users to help them to evaluate the quality of the data.

Recommendation 3-3   An advisory body should be established to guide long-term developments as the international trade environment continues to evolve and transactions become increasingly complex. This advisory body should be composed of experts from industry, academia, and government; it should include research and analytic data users, data filers, and respondents to government surveys, as well as user agency officials. Priority should be given to the development of timely, accurate, relevant, and cost-effective data for public policy making.

Recommendation 3-4   For data that primarily benefit specialized groups that can be clearly defined, market mechanisms should be developed to coordinate the supply of and demand for the data. When the benefits of the data accrue largely to specialized groups but also to public policy makers, cost sharing should be the rule.

Recommendation 3-5   Nongovernment users should be given greater access to trade and other international economic data compiled by the federal government.

PART II

*Improving Data on Merchandise Trade,
International Services Transactions,
and Capital Flows*

4

Merchandise Trade

Of all the data on U.S. international transactions, those on merchandise trade probably have improved most in recent years. Despite having to monitor a volume of merchandise trade that has dramatically increased in the 1980s and despite significant budgetary constraints, the Customs Service and the Bureau of the Census have made significant strides in improving the data. However, several areas warrant further attention: doing so will result in a more accurate picture of U.S. merchandise trade.

This chapter describes the key features of merchandise trade data; delineates the existing collection system for those data; discusses the shortcomings of the system; and makes recommendations for their improvement. The emphasis is on ways to improve the quality of the data through strengthened quality assessment and quality assurance procedures, greater automation, and wider use of sampling techniques.

DATA ON MERCHANDISE TRADE: KEY FEATURES

Unlike other U.S. international economic statistics, which are estimates based on sample surveys of firms or establishments and other entities, merchandise trade data are compiled on the basis of full tabulation of the official import and export documents required by the Customs Service for tariff collection and export administration. Since January 1989, U.S. imports have been classified into 14,000 categories derived from the international Harmonized Commodity Description and Coding System (HS); exports have been classified in terms of 8,000 HS-based codes.[1] The Census Bureau enters these data into computers, tabulates them in various forms, and publishes them every month. Many data are collected at the request of various public and private organizations. Monthly merchandise data record the physical movement of U.S. imports and exports of goods by value, commodity, and country of origin or destination, as well as the dutiable status and tariff rates of imports. They also capture the quantity, shipping weight, Customs Service district of exit or entry, method of transportation, and data by state. These detailed monthly statistics comprise more than 200,000 data cells. Their monthly tabulations and publication are beyond the requirements of federal statutes: Public Law 96-39 only requires reporting of imports by commodity (about 14,000 data cells) and the total for exports (one data cell) on a monthly basis.

The Census Bureau releases to the public highlights of the nation's merchandise imports, exports, and trade balance about 45 days after the end of the reference month. The monthly statistics include transactions of the reference month and transactions of earlier months that arrive too late for inclusion in previous reference months (that is, the carryovers). Data disaggregated at detailed commodity levels are often released later in various printed and machine-readable forms but with no regular publication schedules. Major monthly aggregate data series are seasonally adjusted. Aggregate data are also available on an annual basis. In addition, the Census Bureau tabulates various series of specific data at users' requests on a cost-reimbursable basis. The Census Bureau disseminates merchandise trade statistics in various forms, including printed reports, CD-ROMs (computer disk—read only memory), and magnetic tapes. The agency recently eliminated the production of microfiche reports. The Census Bureau's monthly merchandise trade statistics are also disseminated by the National Trade Data Bank, along with other economic data series. Figure 4-1 lists sets of data on merchandise trade prepared by the Census Bureau.

Merchandise trade statistics are the most widely used data on U.S. international transactions. Federal agencies that closely monitor U.S. international trade include the Federal Reserve Board, the

---

[1]There are more commodity codes for imports than exports because imports are subject to tariffs, and they are classified in greater detail in conformance with U.S. tariff schedules.

Department of Commerce, the Department of Agriculture, the International Trade Commission, and the Office of the U.S. Trade Representative. These agencies use the data to assess the U.S. trade outlook and trends in exchange and interest rates, to develop export promotion activities in international markets, and to formulate policy positions in bilateral and multilateral trade negotiations. Other major users of merchandise trade statistics include state and local government agencies, businesses, academic researchers, and private analysts. They use the data to assess trade patterns, evaluate foreign competition, and identify market opportunities at home and abroad. Also, increasingly, the transportation industry relies on shipment data to plan where and how much to invest in terminals and other facilities (U.S. General Accounting Office, 1989).

In addition to the Census Bureau's merchandise trade statistics, other specialized primary data on U.S. exports and imports of specific commodities—not covered in this study—are collected and compiled by other federal agencies and private organizations. These data include: establishment data on exports of U.S. manufactured products compiled in quinquennial economic censuses and the Annual Survey of Manufactures (ASM) by the Census Bureau; monthly (since 1989) and quarterly export and import price indexes produced by the Bureau of Labor Statistics (BLS), based on BLS surveys of importers and exporters of selected commodities; statistics on imports and exports of crude oil and petroleum products generated by the Energy Information Administration (EIA), based on EIA data collected directly from importers and exporters; information on imports and exports of major agricultural commodities (such as grains, cotton, and oilseeds), gathered directly from corporate entities by the Department of Agriculture; and detailed information on U.S. waterborne cargoes to and from foreign countries for 63 U.S. ports, compiled under the privately owned Piers Import/Export Reporting Service (PIERS) of the Journal of Commerce.

In addition, there are federal agencies, international organizations, and private businesses that take the Census Bureau data and add value to them by making them easier for users to get the specific information—for specific commodities and countries, on a time-series basis, seasonally adjusted, or using different classifications than those provided by the Census Bureau. These secondary sources include U.S. federal agencies like the International Trade Administration, which operates a foreign trade data bank, COMPRO, for government users; the International Trade Com-

FIGURE 4-1   Available Data on Merchandise Trade

Monthly Publications and Hard-Copy Reports
    FT900   U.S. Merchandise Trade
    FT920   U.S. Merchandise Trade: Selected Highlights
    FT925   Exports, General Imports, and Imports for Consumption, SITC-Rev.3 Commodity by Country
    TM985   U.S. Waterborne Exports and General Imports
Monthly Computer Printouts of Selected Foreign Trade Commodities
    IM145   U.S. General Imports, by harmonized TSUSA commodity
    IM146   U.S. Imports for Consumption, by harmonized TSUSA commodity
    EM545   U.S. Exports of Domestic and Foreign Merchandise, by harmonized Schedule B commodity
Annual Publications and Hard-Copy Reports
    FT247   Imports for Consumption, 10-Digit HTSUSA by Country
    FT447   Exports, 10-digit HS Schedule-B Commodity by Country
    FT895   U.S. Trade with Puerto Rico and U.S. Possessions
    FT927   Exports and General Imports, Country by 3-digit SITC-Rev.3 Commodity
    FT947   Exports and General Imports, 6-digit HS Commodity by Country
    TA987   Vessel Entrances and Clearances
Microcomputer Compact Discs
    CDEX(yr-mo)   U.S. Exports of Merchandise
                        Detail Database
                        Commodity Summary Database
                        Country Summary Database
                        District of Export Summary Database
                        Harmonized Commodity Masters, Exports Concordance Database
                        Harmonized Commodity Masters, Commodity Descriptions
                        Harmonized Commodity Masters, SITC Descriptions
                        Country Name Database
                        District Database
    CDIM(yr-mo)   U.S. Imports of Merchandise
                        Detail Database
                        Commodity Summary Database
                        Country Summary Database
                        District of Entry Summary Database
                        District of Unlading Summary Database
                        Harmonized Commodity Masters, Imports Concordance Database
                        Harmonized Commodity Masters, Commodity Descriptions
                        Harmonized Commodity Masters, SITC Descriptions
                        Country Name Database
                        District Database
U.S. Merchandise Trade Magnetic Tape
    IM145 Data Bank   U.S. General Imports and Imports for Consumption
    EM545 Data Bank   U.S. General Exports of Domestic and Foreign Merchandise

FIGURE 4-1 *Continued*

U.S. Merchandise Trade Magnetic Tape—*continued*

EM595	Shipments of Merchandise Between the United States and Puerto Rico and Shipments from the United States to the Virgin Islands

Exports by State/Region/Port Magnetic Tapes

EQ912	U.S. Exports of Domestic and Foreign Merchandise by State
EQ932	U.S. Exports of Domestic and Foreign Merchandise by Region
EQ952	Exports of Domestic and Foreign Merchandise by Port

Transportation Magnetic Tapes

TM380	U.S. Waterborne General Imports and Inbound Intransit Shipments
TM780	U.S. Waterborne Exports and Outbound Intransit Shipments
TM385	Monthly Vessel Entrances
TM785	Monthly Vessel Clearances

Microfiche

IM175	U.S. General Imports and Imports for Consumption
EM575	U.S. Exports by 4-digit SIC-Based Product Code
EM595	Shipments of Merchandise Between the United States and Puerto Rico and Shipments from the United States to the Virgin Islands
TM380	U.S. Waterborne General Imports and Inbound Intransit Shipments
TM780	U.S. Waterborne Exports and Outbound Intransit Shipments
TM385	Monthly Vessel Entrances
TM785	Monthly Vessel Clearances
TM980	Exports and General Imports by Vessel and Air

Other Related Merchandise Trade Data Products and Sources

CENDATA	An on-line data service offering the most current and widely used facts, specializing in press releases and information on ordering the latest data products; includes entire monthly U.S. Merchandise Trade Press Release and Supplement.
EBB	The Economic Bulletin Board of the Department of Commerce provides information on economic growth, inflation, monetary and fiscal policy, and foreign trade subscribers.
National Trade Data Bank	Includes merchandise trade import and export data from the Census Bureau.

Network Access to Compact Discs (CD-ROMs); HTSUSA and Schedule B Data

IM145	U.S. General Imports
IM146	U.S. Imports for Consumption
IM545	U.S. Exports of Domestic and Foreign Merchandise

Standard International Trade Classification (SITC) Databases

> U.S. Exports
> U.S. General Imports

End-Use Commodity Category Classification Databases
U.S. Exports by State Database
U.S. Imports Databank Database (HTSUSA)
International Trade Administration COMPRO System

mission, which develops and maintains time-series data on U.S. foreign trade, now available to the public through the National Trade Data Bank operated by the Department of Commerce; the Bureau of Economic Analysis, which issues quarterly balance-of-payments data; and several others.   International organizations, including the United Nations, the International Monetary Fund, the World Bank, the General Agreement on Tariffs and Trade, and the Organization for Economic Cooperation and Development (OECD), also receive and compile foreign trade data from member countries and produce numerous publications and other data products.

In the private sector, many trade associations, consulting and research firms, and other organizations also act as retailers of the Census Bureau merchandise trade data to their clients or members.   Some specialize in particular groups of commodities; others process a wide range of data from many of the primary and secondary sources and offer on-line access, tailored reports, and other information services.

COLLECTION SYSTEM FOR MERCHANDISE TRADE DATA

Under federal regulations (authorized under U.S. Code, Title XIII and its amendments), the Customs Service is responsible for collecting import and export documents, and the Census Bureau is charged to process them to compile merchandise trade statistics.   The federal regulations stipulate that the Customs Service has overall responsibility for import documents (for example, the Customs Form 7501); the Census Bureau and the Bureau of Export Administration of the Department of Commerce are responsible for export documents (for example, the shippers' export declaration [SED]).   Because of the bifurcation of responsibilities between Customs and Census, different federal regulations, methods, and procedures are applied to collect and process data on exports and imports.   Figure 4-2 provides an overview of the collection and processing system for merchandise trade statistics.

Exporters, importers, and their agents can file export and import documents either in paper form or electronically.   Filing is mandatory except under certain conditions.   SEDs are not required for export shipments when the value of commodities classified under each individual export commodity code is $2,500 or less, but commodities that are covered under export control regulations are not exempted.   Reporting requirements for imports apply to transactions valued at $250 or more for selected commodities for which there are import quotas, and for all transactions

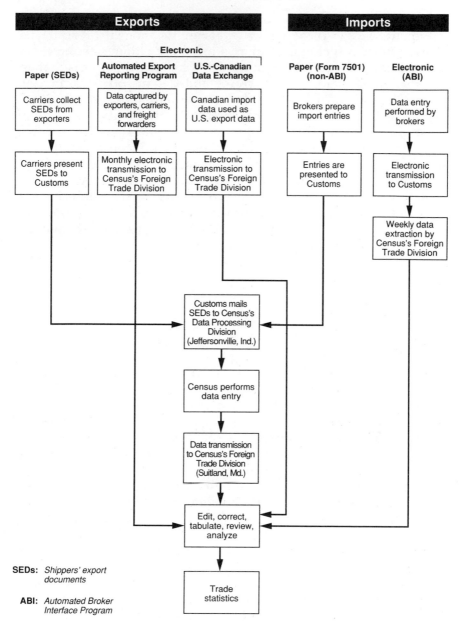

Exports

Imports

Electronic

Paper (SEDs)

Automated Export
Reporting Program

U.S.-Canadian
Data Exchange

Paper (Form 7501)
(non-ABI)

Electronic
(ABI)

Carriers collect
SEDs from
exporters

Data captured by
exporters, carriers,
and freight
forwarders

Canadian import
data used as
U.S. export data

Brokers prepare
import entries

Data entry
performed by
brokers

Carriers present
SEDs to
Customs

Monthly electronic
transmission to
Census's Foreign
Trade Division

Electronic
transmission to
Census's Foreign
Trade Division

Entries are
presented to
Customs

Electronic
transmission
to Customs

Weekly data
extraction by
Census's Foreign
Trade Division

Customs mails
SEDs to Census's
Data Processing
Division
(Jeffersonville, Ind.)

Census performs
data entry

Data transmission
to Census's Foreign
Trade Division
(Suitland, Md.)

Edit, correct,
tabulate, review,
analyze

SEDs: *Shippers' export
documents*

ABI: *Automated Broker
Interface Program*

Trade
statistics

FIGURE 4-2   Merchandise trade data collection process.

valued at $1,250 or more for other commodities. To account for shipments below these cutoff levels in its monthly reports, the Census Bureau includes estimates for these shipments; however, the estimates are derived from outdated historical patterns of these shipments. According to Customs and Census officials, in 1991 about 86 percent of import transactions and about 48 percent of export transactions are being reported electronically. For 1990, a total of approximately 26 million import and export transactions were processed, an increase from about 18 million in 1980. The import and export documents are not protected by the confidentiality provision of Section 9 of Title XIII, U.S. Code. As a matter of policy, when individual companies object to the publication of data that reveal their own activities, Census has sometimes accommodated them by combining data for detailed commodities into larger groups.

EXPORTS

A carrier has 4 working days after the clearance date for departure of a shipment to submit to the Customs Service a manifest consisting of a batch of bills of lading and a summary sheet. The bills of lading contain information on quantities and destinations but not on values. The carrier must also present with each bill of lading a shippers' export declaration (SED) showing the commodity shipped and its value or an explanation why no SED is required (for example, a low-value shipment). If a required SED is not forwarded by the carrier, Customs is supposed to pursue the matter. Small fines are sometimes imposed for failure to comply. The Customs Service ordinarily gives the SEDs little or no review for completeness or accuracy and forwards them daily to the Census Bureau's Data Processing Division at Jeffersonville, Indiana. According to Census, about 500,000 SEDs are currently received monthly by the Jeffersonville center. These account for about 52 percent of the export transactions (60 percent of the value of exports).

SEDs are not required of more than 100 companies participating in the Census Bureau's Automatic Export Reporting Program (AERP). These companies send the required information monthly by modem, computer tapes, floppy disks, or machine-prepared shipment summaries directly to Census's Foreign Trade Division in Suitland, Maryland; 15 percent of export transactions (about 20 percent of the value) is reported through AERP. In addition, since January 1990, under a merchandise data-exchange program between the United States and Canada, SEDs are generally not required for U.S. exports to Canada.[2] The United States uses the import data compiled by Canada to report on U.S. exports to Canada. (Similarly, Canada uses U.S. import data to report Canadian exports to the United States.) These data are electronically transmitted by Statistics Canada (the Canadian government's main statistical agency) to the Census Bureau's Foreign Trade Division; they account for about 32.5 percent of the export transactions (about 20 percent of the value of total U.S. exports). SEDs are also not required for export shipments under U.S. military assistance program aid to foreign countries, which are reported directly to the Census Bureau by the Department of Defense.

IMPORTS

Import data are collected on Customs Form 7501. The forms must be submitted by importers or their brokers to Customs during a period beginning 4 days before and ending 10 days after the arrival of the goods and must be accompanied by commercial documents showing the required tariffs. Because of cash-flow considerations, brokers may delay filing the forms until near the end of the period.

According to Customs, in 1991 about 14 percent of the import transactions (22 percent of the value) were reported on Form 7501, which contains a (yellow) statistical copy. Until recently, Customs ordinarily mailed the statistical copy in daily batches to Jeffersonville without review. This "rip-and-strip" procedure was instituted in 1987 to improve timeliness of data processing. Because of problems with data accuracy, however, Customs started to phase out this procedure in December 1989 and to send the statistical copies to Customs import specialists for review and for necessary corrections before forwarding them by mail to Jeffersonville for processing. As a result, data have been received on a less timely basis, and Customs is working to reduce these delays. Currently, about 100,000 import documents are received by Jeffersonville monthly.

The other 86 percent of import transactions (78 percent of the value) are filed under the Customs Bureau's Automated Broker

---

[2]This exemption applies for general license merchandise; SEDs are required for merchandise transshipped through Canada, for grain shipments exported to Canada (whether or not the country of destination is shown as Canada or a third country), and for shipments exported to Canada that require a validated export license.

Interface (ABI) program, in which brokers transmit information by computer directly to the ABI. The ABI has a computer edit program, which includes statistical edits and parameters jointly developed by Customs and Census. Entries that fail the editing are sent back by computer to the brokers for corrections. Accepted entries are transmitted to the Customs mainframe in Franconia, Virginia. The Customs Service weekly extracts statistical data onto magnetic tapes, which are forwarded also on a weekly basis to Census's Foreign Trade Division at Suitland, Maryland, for further processing. Customs conducts a routine review of accepted entries. A complete review by an import specialist is made of a 2 percent random sample; a 100 percent review is made of certain categories of cases. When changes are needed in the ABI computer edit parameters, they are developed jointly by Customs and Census.

CENSUS BUREAU PROCESSING

When the shipping documents (7501s and SEDs) are received, staff members at Jeffersonville sort out all documents for high-value shipments (those worth more than $2 million for imports and $1 million for exports), which account for 1-2 percent of all documents but represent 40-50 percent of the total value of imports and exports filed manually. They are subjected to close scrutiny by higher level clerical staff. The remaining documents are subjected to various forms of clerical review, which include checking the completeness of the statistical data, identifying nonstatistical documents and separating them, and referring selected documents to higher level clerical staff. About 73 percent of the export documents are entered into the computer system, 24 percent are withdrawn because they are nonstatistical, and 3 percent are referred to higher level clerical staff for review because they contain high-value shipments or lack entries. For imports, the comparable figures are 72 percent entered, 11 percent rejected as nonstatistical, and 17 percent missing data, or, occasionally, of high value. More senior clerks impute missing data either by referring to manuals or, occasionally, by contacting importers or exporters.

After these cursory reviews, serial numbers are affixed to SEDs, and the SEDs are then microfilmed. To minimize processing costs, import documents are no longer microfilmed. (Both the export and import documents are retained in batches for 2-3 months.) The next step is data entry, during which data are subjected to simple computer edits. Computer files of the keyed data are transmitted by telephone daily to the Foreign Trade Division in Suitland for further processing.

At Suitland the data undergo a more complex computer edit called the edit master. It contains commodity codes, permissible parameters and ranges for commodity prices, quantities, and other information. It checks the validity of commodity codes of all transactions. It also examines relationships between commodity value and quantity, commodity and country, and commodity and Customs Service's district. Data that fail this computer edit are either referred back to Jeffersonville for correction or reviewed and reconciled by the professional staff at Suitland. Data that pass are tabulated monthly.

QUALITY CONTROL

Although the Census staff subjects high-value shipments to close scrutiny, there are few formal procedures to ensure timely, accurate, and complete filing of documents (either manually or electronically) by importers and exporters. Computer edits currently represent the major quality-control tool of the data collection system.

As noted above, the Customs Service does not routinely examine export documents. In contrast, it does review import documents as part of the tariff-collection process. In an effort to promote U.S. exports, Customs seeks to avoid creating obstacles to exports. In addition, Census regulations allow a carrier 4 working days after the departure of a shipment to file an SED or an explanation of why none is required. These policies and procedures make export data more vulnerable to inaccurate reporting than import data.

Customs and Census do not systematically coordinate or communicate with importers, exporters, or their agents, except to resolve errors in some documents. Yet data filers directly determine the quality of trade statistics. Unless filers comply with reporting requirements, data will not be timely and accurate. Yet, neither Customs nor Census has systematic controls to ensure that all required 7501s and SEDs are filed and that they are received at the Jeffersonville data processing center. A Census supervisor recalled, for example, a case in which a mail pouch was received with a note from the post office that the pouch had broken in transit. The contents were in disarray. Whether any SED was lost could not be determined.

There is no statistical control in the Jeffersonville mail room where the SEDs and 7501s are sorted and nonstatistical forms are discarded. Whether forms are lost or discarded inadvertently cannot be ascertained. In the early 1980s, a decision was made for budgetary reasons not to institute formal statistical control at this stage in Jeffersonville. According to Census, although there have been no reported instances in which documents on high-value shipments have been accidentally destroyed, there have been cases in which such documents have inadvertently been sent directly to be key-punched rather than to a more intensive review. Similarly, documents on low-value shipments on occasion may not be removed and may be incorrectly routed for keying. These cases are usually identified at the keying or computer-edit stages.

Other vulnerabilities relate to clerical review and imputation procedures. One item most frequently omitted on SEDs is the commodity classification.[3] To impute the missing data, the clerical staff at Jeffersonville use a commodity classification book and edit manual developed by the Foreign Trade Division that contains commodity codes and related price/quantity ratios. The staff also have access to Dun and Bradstreet publications and the Thomas Register, and they can contact exporters to request missing information. Yet even after these clerical edits and imputations are made, computer edits at the data-entry stage reject about 6 percent of the key-punched entries, primarily because of erroneous commodity codes.

Formal quality-control measures are applied at the keying stage. A computer edit program is built in to detect keying and document errors. The edit program at this stage is a simplified version of the edit master used at Suitland. It deals primarily with ranges of acceptable entries within a specified field; it does not test for proper interrelationships or consistencies among fields. When an error is discovered, a green X is placed on the form, and the form is referred to higher level clerical staff for disposition. As noted above, this occurs in 6 percent of the keyed documents.

Another quality-control measure applied at Jeffersonville is the formal statistical sampling program used to control operators' keying errors and to ensure an "average outgoing quality limit" (AOQL) of less than 2 percent errors. The first stage of this effort requires

---

[3]In contrast, according to Customs, this omission generally does not apply to 7501s: import documents are usually scrutinized, and the commodity classification is a required data element that must be reported. An import transaction, whether filed manually or electronically, cannot be processed without this information; an entry without the commodity classification will not be accepted by Customs.

the key-punch operator to key one vessel batch (about 350 forms) and one air or other mode of transportation (MOT) batch with an error rate of under 1.2 percent. During this stage, 100 percent of the operator's work is verified. Operators who qualify by this standard enter the second stage, in which 10 percent of their work is sampled and verified. (Random number tables are used to select the sample, and appropriate tables of acceptance and rejection are provided to the reviewer.) Operators who do not meet the acceptable quality standards of the 10 percent level of review are returned to the first stage, 100 percent review. Operators who qualify move to the third stage, at which 2 percent of their work is sampled and verified. Operators who fail to maintain the required standard return to stage two, that is, 10 percent sample verification. Operators are considered fully qualified when they perform at the 2 percent verification level, stage three. Only fully qualified operators are allowed to key documents for high-value shipments, and all keying for those documents is completely verified.

Nonetheless, according to Census, of the data sent from Jeffersonville to Suitland, the Foreign Trade Division (FTD) rejects about 0.2 percent of the entries containing values of $200,000 or more and about 0.8 percent of the entries of lesser value. FTD sends these data back to Jeffersonville, where the microfilms or original documents are reviewed, and the data are corrected or imputed for reprocessing. At Suitland, FTD relies on its edit master to control data quality. Data forwarded from Jeffersonville, as well as those transmitted electronically under ABI and AERP, are subject to the edit master.

The FTD's commodity analysis branch contains five substantive sections and one classification-system section. The five substantive sections are food, animal and wood section; minerals and metals section; textiles section; chemical and sundries section; and machinery and vehicles section. There are generally four commodity specialists, economists, or statisticians in each section, or a total of about 20 professional staff. With the assistance of about five professionals from the methods research and quality assurance branch, they are primarily responsible for the establishment, conduct, monitoring, and modification of the edit master and imputation program. The systems and programming aspects of the edit and imputations are the responsibilities of system and programming personnel. The edit master recently was redesigned to reflect the new commodity classification system used in reporting the Harmonized Commodity Description and Coding System (HS). Each HS commodity classification has an edit master. The edit master contains approximately 100 fields of information that specify reporting requirements and dictate the applicable edits, edit criteria, and imputation factors.

To develop the edit master, the commodity specialists consider current reporting requirements and examine past shipments to determine price, quantity, and shipping weight parameters and imputations factors. They also consider countries, maximum acceptable reported or imputed quantities, shipping weights, and any known reporting problems. The edit master is used to validate the reported statistical information and to impute missing information and information that is determined to be erroneous.

Imputations on highly improbable or missing entries are made at Suitland for 22 percent of export shipments and about 5 percent of import entries. Most of the imputations involve quantities or shipping weights. The value amounts are accepted as stated. Occasionally, commodity classifications are also imputed. For example, if a value of $50 is attributed to an automobile, the commodity classification may be changed to automotive parts. There is no assurance that the 78 percent of the export transactions and 95 percent of import transactions that pass the edit master provide accurate data, however, because the accuracy of these transactions is not verified.

According to FTD, commodity specialists monitor the patterns of items rejected by the computer and of imputations (as well as the nature of errors pointed out by data users). To resolve problem cases, they may examine past records, and, in the case of high values, they may contact the exporters or importers. If rejects are more numerous than expected, the specialists may review recent price trends. If prices have increased, they may modify the upper limit of the edit parameter accordingly, but FTD staff note that they are more reluctant to modify the lower limits of commodity unit prices. The edit master also may not include current information for all commodities. When commodity prices are volatile—for example, those of oil and major agricultural commodities—they can fall below or rise above the edit ranges, and imputations based on the edit ranges can create errors.

FOREIGN TRADE DIVISION COMPUTER CAPABILITIES

Monthly FTD processing is performed on a UNISYS 1194 mainframe computer. The monthly export and import data are edited on a flow basis in batches, referred to as "cuts." Generally, cuts are made on a weekly basis. At a predetermined time each month, all of the edited data and corrected rejects are combined for tabulations on exports and imports. Various monthly reports, publications, and other special contract tabulations are produced after this monthly "closeout." Currently, the Census Bureau is evaluating the use of microcomputers as potential replacements for selected mainframe activities.

FTD has made increasing use of microcomputers since 1983. According to FTD, as of early 1991 it had 150 microcomputers, 66 printers, on-line storage of 27 billion characters, 4 optical disk systems, 2 CD-ROM servers, 6 tape drives, 12 CD-ROM individual readers, and a 15-cassette backup system. FTD uses microcomputers for 18 statistical applications and 8 administrative functions. Included among statistical applications are maintaining the edit master, performing initial processing, correcting high-value rejects, carrying out analytic work as an interface to the ABI system, and providing access to prior- and current-month export and import databases. However, access to an entire year's data is still lacking due to limited storage capacity.

The FTD analysts need to review and analyze export and import data at the transaction level. More than 2,000,000 export and import transactions are processed each month. Although the storage capacity limits access to detailed data through the use of the microcomputer network to only the month being processed and the prior month, according to FTD, it is now storing data for the past 18 months on optical disks. Summary data for exports and imports by HS code, by country, and by Customs districts for several years are available on CD-ROM disks. FTD plans to install more optical disk systems in the future.

Recent improvements in FTD's computer processing capabilities have resulted in better access to past data by FTD analysts and FTD's ability to respond more quickly to ad hoc requests. Formerly, relying solely on UNISYS processing, FTD lacked the ability to generate special reports quickly and inexpensively. Virtually all historical data were stored on magnetic tape in the UNISYS tape library. It often took 6 months or more for FTD to retrieve the data and to write custom COBOL programs to prepare reports and cost thousands of dollars to process the large volume of data required for the reports. Some of the users' requests were met only through the use of the COMPRO system implemented on the National Institute of Health (NIH) computer network by the International Trade Administration. COMPRO, however, is accessible only to federal agency users and researchers supported by the federal agencies. As a result, FTD could not accommodate all cost-reimbursable requests. Now, according to FTD, using CD-ROM technology, it services ad hoc requests in a few days or weeks at costs usually in the range of $50 to $200.

FTD has recently begun to issue monthly export and import data in compact disk format (CD-ROM). This format provides the most detailed level of summarized data releasable under disclosure rules. Each disk contains supporting files of alphabetical dictionaries and concordances linking one commodity classification to another. Although CD-ROM disks are primarily developed for improving data dissemination, there is an additional benefit for FTD: the disks can be used with standard microcomputers equipped with CD-ROM readers. This capability allows the FTD staff to prepare summary reports from the CD-ROM data, a capability until now available only on the UNISYS mainframe. The availability of data on CD-ROM virtually eliminates the need to print approximately 500,000 pages of tables each month for reference by FTD analysts.

FTD hopes to store an entire year of detailed transactions on the microcomputer network when additional storage is acquired. In order to accomplish this goal, about 6 billion additional characters of on-line storage are estimated to be needed, at a cost of approximately $50,000. Having a year's worth of data on line will provide the capability to revise an earlier month's data. In addition, some of the work using data files on the UNISYS will be shifted to the microcomputer network, resulting in a savings in mainframe computer costs.

FTD is also developing a database of exporters by matching an exporter's employer identification numbers (EIN) reported on the SED to that obtained in the 1987 economic census. This database will provide a profile of exporters. FTD is studying ways to summarize the 9.7 million export shipments for 1987 into a file small enough for use in a microcomputer system. The export database will facilitate analysis of U.S. exports as accounted for by major producers and industries.

FTD has recently converted import and export transportation statistics from batch mainframe processing to an interactive microcomputer-based system. The mainframe systems consisted of 200 COBOL programs, which cost FTD $250,000 a year in computer charges to tabulate the transportation data. The microcomputer system is supported by FTD staff; it involves less than $10,000 a year in mainframe computer charges and shortens processing time. Using this system to tabulate transportation statistics, FTD is able to transfer to Jeffersonville many functions previously performed in Suitland. The microcomputer-based system links the clerical review unit at Jeffersonville to FTD at Suitland. The system also provides on-line analysis and correction capabilities at both Jeffersonville and FTD in Suitland. Similarly, direct transmissions with Statistics Canada are now possible in conjunction with the bilateral data-exchange program.

FTD has outlined four alternatives concerning future development of the data processing system: to perform all work on the UNISYS mainframe, to perform all work on microcomputers, to use a combination of microcomputers and mainframe (the current situation), or to use minicomputers. Each alternative has various advantages and disadvantages in terms of such criteria as staff training, physical and system security, data storage, interactive capabilities, turn-around time, availability of software, and ability to take advantage of latest technology. Recent changes by FTD have moved it from full reliance on mainframe computers toward the mainframe-microcomputer combination.

SHORTCOMINGS OF THE DATA SYSTEM

UNDERREPORTING OF EXPORTS

Until recently there had not been much written about errors in foreign trade statistics. Ryten (1988) attributes the lack of interest in errors to the widespread perception that Customs monitors all merchandise transactions, that it has the power to enforce its writ, and that, as a result, there are few measurable errors left. Discrepancies in data between partner countries are often attributed to differences in definition, timing, and valuation. But with the growing importance of foreign trade to the domestic economy and rising demand for information on foreign trade, there has been increased concern about the quality of the data. Several recent studies show that there is a strong probability that U.S. exports have been underreported, possibly resulting in overstatements of the U.S. merchandise trade deficit (Ott, 1988; U.S. General Accounting Office, 1989).

The underreporting of U.S. exports to Canada prior to 1987 has been well documented. The Census Bureau and Statistics Canada have compared U.S. and Canadian merchandise trade statistics for 20 years. For 1986, the U.S.-Canada data reconciliation studies showed $11 billion in unrecorded U.S. exports to Canada based on Canadian import statistics. In 1987, in an effort to address this undercount, the Census Bureau introduced a monthly summary level adjustment to the total U.S. export figure based on Canada's figure of its total imports from the United States. These adjustments, however, did not correct understatements in detailed product data. By 1989, the value of unreported U.S. exports to Canada rose to $16 billion, about 20 percent of the total value of U.S. exports to that country. Canada was encountering similar, although smaller, undercounts of its export statistics. (In 1990, under an agreement signed 3 years earlier, the United States and Canada dispensed with the collection of export statistics on trade between them. The two countries have since substituted counterpart import data as their own data on exports to each other.) The main factor contributing to the U.S.-Canada export undercounts is the lax enforcement of export reporting requirements along the 3,000-mile U.S.-Canadian border, through which most U.S.-Canadian truck traffic flows.

The same basic reporting system that led to the undercount of U.S. exports to Canada is still in use for U.S. exports to other countries, although the magnitudes of undercounts in vessel and air shipments to these countries may be lower because document controls (for example, manifests, entrance and clearance documents, etc.) exist for these cargoes. In 1988 and 1989, for example, with the aid of the Customs Service, FTD completed a series of audits at four international airports: Seattle-Tacoma, Miami, Los Angeles, and New York-Kennedy. On the basis of these audits, the Census Bureau estimated that undercoverage resulting from the failure of exporters or their agents to file the required information was 7.2 percent of the shipping weight of all air export shipments. Applying this percentage to the 1988 value of all air export shipments would yield $6.7 billion. Since the relationship between weight and value has not been determined, however, Census did not estimate the value of export underreporting. In the audit reports, Census stated that evidence was found, especially in Miami, of deliberate undervaluation of cargo (Puzzilla, 1988).

Comparisons of U.S. export data with data on imports from the United States reported by major trading partners also indicate probable underreporting of U.S. exports (see Appendix C). For example, for the period 1980-1989, such comparisons suggest an undercount of about 7 percent a year of U.S. exports to Japan, Germany, and the United Kingdom. Because of differences in definitions, concepts, and measurements, it is difficult to quantify the magnitudes of the undercounts. According to FTD, a recently completed data reconciliation study with Japan showed a possible 3 percent undercount of U.S. exports to Japan in 1990. FTD is currently engaged in data reconciliation efforts with a number of major trading partners, including the European Community, Korea, and Mexico, to better estimate undercounts of U.S. exports to these countries.

Experts have attributed export underreporting to several factors. The first is that compliance with export reporting is not strictly enforced. Although import documents are reviewed in connection with the process of tariff collection, export documents are subject to minimum scrutiny. There are few incentives for exporters to file timely and accurately except their good will. Second, exporters have incentives to understate sales to reduce their taxable income and to pay lower import duties to importing countries, especially those in Latin America. Third, exporters almost certainly do not report transactions that are restricted or banned under U.S. law, and about 40 percent of all U.S. exports are subject to at least partial restrictions. Lax enforcement efforts obviously contribute to underreporting of exports.

Some of the understatement of exports can be attributed to nonvessel operating commercial carriers (NVOCCs), which are primarily freight consolidators. These carriers consolidate shipments from small exporters into one large shipment. Because of this consolidation, the NVOCCs have greater bargaining power than individual small exporters to negotiate lower freight rates from major carriers, and small exporters save time and effort and reduce shipping costs. The NVOCCs file SEDs for the exporters, and they try not to alienate clients by pressing for information. Their main purpose is to obtain the lowest freight rate for exporters from the major carriers. Thus, if the consolidated shipment consists of different items with different freight rates, the NVOCCs are inclined not to report the higher freight-rate items.

Still another cause of misreporting is that exporters fear that the information reported on the SEDs may be leaked by employees of carriers to competitors.

INADEQUATE REPORTING OF DATA QUALITY

The quality of the merchandise trade data and their limitations are inadequately communicated to users. The published merchandise trade balance data routinely fluctuate widely from month to month; see Figure 4-3. Users at times have interpreted a large monthly change as indicative of shifts in the underlying trend or other basic properties of the data, which, in turn, has sent strong signals to financial and foreign exchange markets. Our analysis

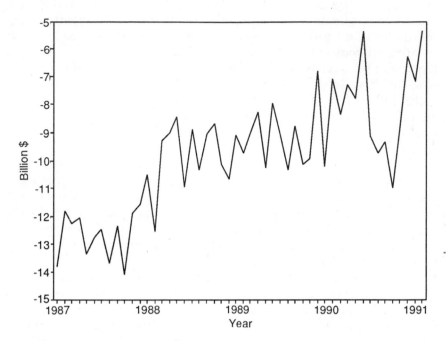

FIGURE 4-3   Seasonally adjusted merchandise trade balance: January 1987-February 1991.

shows that, although the trade balance figures are indicative of underlying trends over time, large month-to-month changes can exist without any change in the trend.   The Census Bureau currently provides no measures of uncertainty to the merchandise trade data.   The statistics are reported as if they were perfect measures, and users often rely on them as if they are.   Major misinterpretations at times can be made.

Appendices D and E address this issue in detail and interpret the data variability.   Appendix D points out that the monthly changes in the trade balance over the period from February 1987 through February 1991, corrected for trend and for correlation across time, have a small mean value, $249 million, and a large standard error, $1.4 billion: that is, the standard error is about six times the mean.   Thus, a monthly change in the trade balance of as much as ±$4.2 billion during this period, for example, would be within three standard errors of the mean (3 × $1.4 billion = $4.2 billion), a kind of band that is widely acceptable in quality-control charts.   Moreover, monthly changes tend to alternate in sign, from positive to negative to positive. These results suggest that large monthly changes can occur without any change in the underlying trend of the trade balance. Appendix E shows that fluctuations in the monthly changes in the trade balance can also be induced by the seasonal adjustment procedure used by the Census Bureau. Alternative methods of seasonal adjustment could model seasonal movements as well or better than current methods and reduce the volatility of the monthly trade balance data.

LACK OF FORMAL DATA MANAGEMENT PROCEDURES

The present processing procedures include several operations designed to detect and correct errors (such as sample verification of data entry, the application of several kinds of automated edit checks, and the imputation of missing and erroneous data) and to subject documents reporting large transactions to close scrutiny. However, there are few established formal data management procedures to guide the collection, processing, storage, and dissemination of merchandise trade data, making it difficult for the Customs Service and the Census Bureau to monitor and evaluate their own performance and pinpoint areas of vulnerability for improvement.

As noted above, there is at present no accounting of export and import documents before they arrive at Census's Jeffersonville data processing center. Imputation of one or more missing or suspect values or codes is required for about 22 percent of export transactions and about 5 percent of import transactions. There is no systematic evaluation of how well these imputations approximate truth or of how accurate the data are that pass the edit master. In addition, the two major quality-control measures applied by Customs and Census, edit checks and imputation procedures, are at times marred by outdated parameter values. Interaction between data filers and Customs and Census staffs is infrequent except when errors are detected in submitted documents.

As a statistical agency, the Census Bureau's mission is to collect, process, and disseminate monthly data on a timely basis. From this perspective, each batch of the monthly figures is largely considered a product itself, a "snapshot" of the current period, rather than an observation of an ongoing time series of which each month is one part in a sequence. Over time, there have been changes in definitions and commodity codes used by Census in compiling the data. As a result, a time series of observations that is consistent across time is lacking, making analysis of trends, seasonality, and other underlying changes difficult.

To gauge the quality of the existing data, we canvassed users' views on the adequacy of U.S. merchandise trade statistics. Appendix B reports in detail their assessments. Among shortcomings cited by users are lack of consistent time series and errors in disaggregated data. Users also point out that different figures of trade balance are reported in trade statistics, in the U.S. balance-of-payments accounts, and in the national income and product accounts. They find the different concepts and definitions of trade balance applied for the various purposes confusing, and it is difficult for them to gauge the accuracy of the different reported figures. Merchandise trade statistics are derived as by-products of administering tariff collection, export control regulations, and other laws governing international commerce. The concepts and definitions applied for several administrative purposes do not coincide with those for analytic objectives. To bring the data into conformity with balance-of-payments concepts, the Bureau of Economic Analysis (BEA) has to make adjustments to the monthly Census merchandise trade data. BEA also makes adjustments to the Census data to relate changes in merchandise trade to domestic production and income data as shown in the national income and product accounts.

The accuracy of foreign trade data clearly concerns many users. Two told us about instances in which data errors have led to incorrect applications of administrative rules developed under U.S. statutes that apply to international merchandise trade. A few others said that errors made specific data series unusable or of questionable value for their purposes. Some of them have informed Census about the errors they have detected and have met with mixed success in resolving specific reporting or processing problems. The quality of detailed data on specific commodities, of estimates of excluded low-value shipments, and of data on exports by state of origin came under particularly heavy attack.

Our interviews with brokers, forwarders, importers, and exporters disclosed that some filers do not understand questions they are required to answer. Under the circumstances, they may supply erroneous data, particularly with regard to the origins and destinations of shipments. In addition, importers and exporters frequently experience considerable personnel turnover; new staff members may lack sufficient training or motivation to provide accurate data. With regard to the origin of exports, the final product may have been manufactured in several stages at different locations. Under such circumstances, attributing the origin to a specific location may be arbitrary. Similarly, individuals who file the import documents may not know the destination of the imports. It is not surprising, therefore, that a disproportionately large percentage of imports show New York as their destination or that Louisiana was shown in trade data to account for 44 percent of U.S. agricultural exports in 1987. In addition, only 75 percent of the SEDs reported the exporter's employer identification number (EIN) in 1987.

In view of the shortcomings of the monthly data and their influence on public and private decision makers, the panel deliberated about a recommendation to end the production of monthly merchandise trade statistics and move to a quarterly reporting basis so merchandise and services trade data could be released at the same time. The panel ultimately decided against the elimination of the monthly data for several reasons:

• The savings of shifting from monthly to quarterly data are minimal, since monthly data are needed to produce quarterly data;
• Significant improvements in existing data are possible with effective enforcement efforts and sound database management;
• When data users are apprised of the data limitations, they will be disabused of many of their false assumptions about the accuracy of the data; and
• When monthly data are made more accurate, they will be more timely and useful than quarterly data.

Instead, the panel considered ways to improve the quality of merchandise trade data.

IMPROVED DATA QUALITY

The need to improve the quality of merchandise trade statistics is well recognized by the Customs Service and the Census Bureau. Given the bifurcation of responsibilities between the two agencies, which can affect the operation of the program, Customs and Census have increased their coordination in recent years. Their efforts have significantly reduced processing delays and lowered the data adjustments for carryovers in recent years. As indicated above, other improvements in the system have included broadening the use of electronic reporting of imports by importers and their agents to Customs, enhancing computer processing capabilities at the Foreign Trade Division at Census, and exchanging data between the United States and Canada to improve the accuracy of U.S. export data. Additional quality measures currently under consideration by Census include: completing postponed sea and border audits; continuing to explore the feasibility of data reconciliations with Japan, Mexico, South Korea, and the European Community; implementing an exporter education program; enhancing editing procedures and augmenting internal computer capacity to facilitate processing, analysis, and publication of data; and developing an integrated multi-agency automated system that would serve a variety of export control and commercial purposes, in addition to facilitating export reporting. In this section we consider these and other methods to improve quality control; the need for enhanced automation; and the feasibility of using sampling techniques to collect merchandise trade data.

IMPROVED QUALITY CONTROL

In determining the adequacy of existing quality-control procedures, one should make a distinction between quality assessment and quality assurance. Quality assessment refers to the use of measures to assess structures, processes, and outcomes and to measure levels of quality over time. Quality assurance refers to adoption of such measures as may be required to improve quality. Most of the proposals by the Census Bureau to improve merchandise data quality pertain to quality assurance rather than quality assessment. With the exception of the proposed data reconciliation efforts and the port audits, there are no new initiatives under consideration for quality assessment.

Below we consider several ways to improve operating procedures of the merchandise trade data system. They are not mutually exclusive. Undoubtedly limited resources will preclude adoption of some of them. They do stress the priority of quality assessment. All of the proposals would improve quality, but only the adoption of the first two—a continuous independent review system and a continual strategic port audit program—in combination with some of the other methods, will quickly achieve the greatest amount of quality improvement.

A Continuous Independent Review System

Under a continuous independent review system (CIRS), a sample of documents received at Jeffersonville would be photocopied and forwarded to the Census's professional staff in Suitland for coding. The sample documents would be replaced in the batch of mail from which they were taken so that they cannot be identified by the operating personnel. On a periodic basis, personnel detailed from Customs would participate in the coding. This independent coding would be entered into a separate database established for CIRS. The results of the independent coding would be matched by computer with the results from the normal processing of the same documents (or transactions, depending on the sampling techniques), reconciliation made, if possible, and causes of differences analyzed. (A slightly different procedure would be required for automated filing.) The small database established for CIRS would thus contain the coding elements of both the independent and ongoing review systems as well as the results and analysis of errors and reconciliations. All of the cases in which reconciliation was not possible and a smaller sample of cases in which no apparent irreconcilable differences were detected would then be used for contacts with the importers or exporters, if possible, or with the brokers or forwarders, to determine what their basic records (not the Form 7501 or SED) show regarding the elements coded. The results of this contact would also be coded and entered into the CIRS database.

As this database built up, a wealth of reliable information would be obtained on the quality of the system, rates of error regarding individual coding and reporting elements, the circumstances under which these errors occur, who or what is responsible for them, and, most important, what changes are needed initially or at Jeffersonville or Suitland in editing or imputation procedures to improve data quality.

A somewhat similar system was introduced at the Social Security Administration, in part in response to a U.S. General Accounting Office (GAO) critique, to obtain unbiased measurements of the validity of policies and procedures for establishing entitlement to old age and survivors insurance benefits and, more important, to determine the necessary modifications to the policies and procedures. This system operated successfully for 15 years.

As an experimental adjunct to the CIRS, reviews could proceed from the other direction. That is, a sample of establishments could be selected and requested to examine their records to determine the value of their exports and imports, and other desired information, during a given period. The data would be coded and compared with the results of the normal system, as above. This approach, even if not fully implemented, would provide valuable information on the feasibility and nature of the data available and on accounting or other record-keeping modifications required to proceed with an establishment survey approach to the collection of some or all of the merchandise trade statistics (see section below, "Use of Sampling Techniques").

The benefits from a CIRS, as indicated above, would be to yield some checks on whether Customs has obtained and forwarded the record, whether Jeffersonville has received and retained the record, and whether the clerical reviews, key punching, and data edits at Jeffersonville conform to established procedures. Most important, it would reveal whether the master edit and imputation procedures at Suitland are valid and what modifications are needed at all stages of the system. A CIRS would not only improve the process, but also provide a measure of the accuracy of the data (except in those cases in which exporters deliberately failed to report transactions or understated their values).

The cost of the system would depend on the scale adopted. Fortunately, a CIRS could be introduced on a small scale and expanded as problems were overcome and the value of the system was ascertained. Designing such a system would require considerable work by the manager of the system, a systems programmer, a clerical employee, and part-time efforts of a statistician and a commodity specialist from each of the five substantive commodity analyses sections. A 4-6 month start-up period would be required.

A Multipurpose Port Audit Program

Although a continuous independent review system would enhance data quality, it would not help for cases in which filers deliberately avoid reporting. In many instances, it also would not detect deliberate understatements of the values of transactions. For these situations, the port audit program should be continued. In addition to the four completed audits, six audits were originally planned but postponed for budgetary reasons. This program should become an integral part of the ongoing process, and the concept and strategy of the program should be expanded to incorporate features of the Internal Revenue Service audits, including parts of its Taxpayer Compliance Measurement Program (TCMP) (see Roth et al., 1989). If funds become available, the prime purpose of the port audit program, which is to measure underreporting, should be expanded also. If the audits are designed to obtain information on commodities, types of exporters, and circumstances contributing a disproportionate share of errors, the results should help to identify process improvements.

In addition, part of the audit should be designed not primarily to permit unbiased estimates, but rather to yield a high-visibility or demonstration effect. Under the leadership of Customs, a particular vessel or a particular forwarder or exporter could be targeted for delay in approval for shipping because of a history of incomplete or inaccurate statistical reporting. Customs may actually select the target because of a drug or other control program but announce and display SED inaccuracy as the cause of such an action. The information from the trading community suggests that word travels fast and such delays would raise concerns about the effects on operating profit and provide an incentive for better compliance with statistical reporting requirements. This strategy is similar to that used by the IRS and other compliance enforcement agencies.

Producer-User Interface

The Foreign Trade Division provides statistical products much needed by federal government agencies, state and local governments, academia, and private industry. User needs are central to any consideration of data quality, and FTD would be better able to decide what to produce if it had more information on user needs. FTD has received some such feedback and has been responsive to some of the demands for data, but there are many users or prospective ones who remain less than completely satisfied with the data now available. Periodic surveys of both public and private current and prospective users should be undertaken.

The panel's survey of data users clearly revealed that different users attach different priorities to having merchandise trade statitsics that are accurate, timely, detailed, or as comprehensive in coverage as possible. In view of resource and other constraints, meeting one user's needs might not fulfill another's. Nonetheless, the panel believes that improvements in process productivity through enhanced data management should enable Customs and Census to improve data accuracy, timeliness, and coverage to better meet the needs of most users.

Producer-Filer Interface

The quality of merchandise trade data depends not only on Custom's and Census's resources, but also on the completeness and accuracy of the original data provided by exporters, importers, brokers, forwarders, and carriers.

Customs and Census should make additional efforts to cultivate and develop a symbiotic relationship with filers. Users should be encouraged to educate the public on the advantages of having reliable trade data and the need to support programs that generate

them. In addition, private industry, through its trade organizations, meetings, and publications, should be urged to take steps to
ensure greater accuracy of the raw data provided to FTD. The
accounting and financial management professions should be asked
to assist in establishing standards for the basic record-keeping
necessary to provide the required information to FTD.

Reporting Data Adjustments for Undercounts and Imputations

Before the commencement of the current U.S.-Canada data exchanges, Census adjusted export totals to account for the undercount
of U.S. exports to Canada on the basis of results of reconciliation
studies. If the completion of several more port audits and the
establishment of a continuous independent review system produce evidence to permit quantification of the extent of undercount
of U.S. merchandise exports to other countries, actual adjustment
of published data to incorporate the undercount should be done.
Relegating mention of undercounts to footnotes or technical publications, while perhaps sufficient for academicians, may not best
serve policy interests. Public perceptions about the U.S. trade
balance and the country's economic well-being, as well as the
reaction of financial markets, may be highly conditioned by newspaper headlines and the 20 seconds of airtime on television and
radio devoted monthly to the release of trade data. In addition,
since little has been published on the methods used in the U.S.-
Canada data reconciliations, such information on future data adjustments should be documented and made available to users.

Moreover, where more than a certain number or percent of the
entries of a given cell are based upon imputations—the criteria
should be statistically determined—data users should be alerted
either by means of a footnote or by use of a different type or size
of print for that cell.

Matrix Organization

Although top Census and Customs officials almost certainly
are highly committed to fulfilling their joint responsibility to provide accurate import and export statistics, this may not always be
the case at working levels. Management attention, incentives,
resources, and rewards in any organizatoin are directed at the
major functions of the organizations and their subcomponents:
Customs is necessarily more concerned with collecting tariffs on

imports and controlling selected imports and exports; Census focuses on processing statistical data.

The preoccupation of organizations with their primary mission to the detriment of secondary or tertiary responsibilities has been addressed in the managerial literature, which is replete with suggestions on how to deal with it. One approach that might have merit for trade statistics would be to create a matrix organization, in which employees of different units or functions are temporarily placed in a unit working on a common problem. Some staff members from Customs and Census have expressed a desire for greater contact and "networking" among employees of the two organizations. Port audits, difficult cases, commodity classification problems, and contact with trade sources are just a few areas for which joint efforts at the working level could be intensified.

Long-Range Planning

Because of the ever-increasing and evolving nature of international trade, fundamental changes in concepts, collection methods, processing procedures, and methods of dissemination will be required to respond adequately to changing data needs. Collecting, tabulating, and disseminating data are arduous tasks requiring attention to immediate problems; those who manage these operations seldom have time to address future concerns.

To permit more detached attention to longer range planning related to trade statistics, consideration should be given to the establishment of a small high-level unit at Census or Commerce. Its principal function would be to deal with long-range problems associated with concepts, computerization, new product development, and organizational adjustments that may be needed in the months and years ahead.

INCREASED AUTOMATION

Although there has recently been a substantial rise in electronic filing of import data under Customs' ABI program, Census has had little success in increasing electronic filing of export data. As a result, there remains a large volume of trade documents that have to be processed manually by Census each month (about 8 million in 1990, in comparison with 13 million in 1985). Indeed, the manual processing of import and export documents consumes about one-third of the $16 million annual budget of Census's Foreign Trade Division. More electronic filing of trade documents by importers and exporters would significantly reduce collection costs. This change, accompanied by a substantial increase in FTD's data processing capabilities, should enhance data accuracy and timeliness. Electronic reporting of imports has increased substantially in recent years, and the prospects are good that additional importers, exporters, brokers, and carriers will automate their operations in the future.

Accuracy

The undercount of exports and erroneous detailed product data are problems relating to accuracy. They result from a failure to file documents and from inaccuracies in information contained in the filed documents. As illustrated by the electronic reporting of imports, greater automation of export reporting could bring benefits. It could facilitate data capture and improve data processing capabilities. It might also reduce costs of implementing improved procedures to detect and correct anomalies in data reported, as well as of following up on missing data. Moreover, it would facilitate the reporting of the apparently growing volume of low-value shipments that are now too costly to capture and tabulate. Each of these changes could increase the accuracy of reported trade data.

Although merely increasing the fraction of documents filed electronically would not necessarily provide more accurate data, an improved database would make it less costly to conduct audits and cross-checks of trade data with other data sources, such as the in-house Census data on manufactured exports reported on the Annual Survey of Manufactures (ASM) questionnaires. Furthermore, a greatly improved data processing capability would enable Census to treat international trade data, domestic production data, and input data as part of a consistent, coherent body of economic information.

Revisions

FTD currently revises monthly import and export statistics in several ways. On a monthly basis, aggregate import, export, and trade balance figures for the prior month are adjusted for carryovers. On a quarterly basis, FTD publishes a list of errata for prior months' statistics. Recently, on an annual basis in May, FTD has been publishing revised merchandise trade statistics for the prior year. With an improved capability to manipulate data, it would be possible for FTD to undertake revisions at the detailed level for the calendar year at minimal costs and on a timely basis.

Timeliness

Increased automation could improve the timeliness not only of the initial trade data releases, which already take place fairly promptly (and which, with improved editing procedures, would be more accurate), but also of the later detailed data that presently have no preassigned schedule for regular release. With both greater processing flexibility and tabulation capability, it would be possible, at little incremental cost, to generate reports that otherwise might have to be delayed or discontinued because of their cost.

Automated Export Reporting

The capture of data can be automated in the paper-handling process by using various available imaging and character recognition or electronic note-pad technologies. It also can be automated by moving toward an all-electronic system of filing trade documents. Two considerations led us to give most attention to the second approach. The first is that many obstacles and disincentives to the electronic filing of export documents have been eliminated or reduced. Until recently, FTD's automated reporting program for exports was perceived to be limited to large exporters. Although the set-up costs had declined markedly since the program was initiated in the early 1970s, it was apparently still considered too costly to be worthwhile for small exporters to participate. The extension of the program to freight forwarders and carriers in recent years has removed a major obstacle, making it feasible for small exporters' shipments to be reported electronically. Our second consideration is that in the not-too-distant future there is likely to be a major effort to standardize international electronic trade and shipping documentation. Simplification and consolidation of export documentation through the development of a universal electronic shipping and trade document should provide an incentive to filers to participate in FTD's automated reported program for exports.

A better understanding is needed of why many exporters are reluctant to file electronically. Our discussions of the program with nonparticipant exporters and forwarders yielded explanations that ranged from "I had not heard of it" to "What's in it for me?" Others noted there is no pressure to participate comparable to that applied by Customs to get importers and brokers to participate in ABI. A forwarder participating in the automated export program for 3 years, who was the only exporter or forwarder in his port to participate, stated that his decision to participate was based on three considerations: his export operations had been computerized 5 or 6 years ago; the trend of all export operations was toward computerization; and steamship companies and exporters were starting to ask for, if not insist on, more computerized handling of data. He suggested that the participation of other forwarders would depend primarily on their current and future use of computers. He also noted that an obstacle to his beginning use of AERP had been that helpful commercial software was not available. As a result, his in-house programmer had to devise a system for his firm. These views may not be representative of the thousands of exporters and forwarders, but they clearly indicate the need for marketing and educational programs.

Customs and Census should consider other measures to advance use of automated reporting in the export clearance process. Such measures might include frequent imposition of penalties for failing to file SEDs or for filing incorrect SEDs and, perhaps, last-in-line handling of nonautomated reporting shipments. More generally, Customs might take more leadership in this area, which would convey the impression that it is Customs, and not Census, that is driving the program.

Customs and Census have developed a joint proposal to expand the Custom's existing Automated Commercial Systems linkage for electronic data interchange with brokers, importers, carriers, and port authorities, which would process data on exports as well as imports. The two agencies tentatively termed this proposal the automated export system (AES). A multiagency committee would be assembled to coordinate development of the system and provide operational guidelines. In addition to Customs and Census, export licensing agencies, including the Departments of Commerce, State, Defense, Agriculture, and Energy, as well as the Office of the U.S. Trade Representative, would be represented on the committee. The proposal anticipates funding largely by Customs. Census would finance its own increase in computer capacity to handle the additional workload. Other participating agencies would underwrite improvements in their own computer systems and the costs of linking to the Customs computer. Initial costs for Custom's share of the export system are projected to be $38 million over a 5-year period. FTD has requested $3 million ($600,000 per year for fiscal 1992-1996) for its portion of development costs.

These costs include capital expenditures as well as four additional full-time employees. It projects that the participating rates of the exporting community will be 10, 20, 40, 50, and 60 percent over the 5 years beginning in fiscal 1992.

FTD summarizes the benefits of AES as follows: reducing the distortions in the trade balance by substantially eliminating the nonreporting and undervaluation of exports; cutting the manual documentation costs to private industry; eliminating the manual data capture of 6 million SEDs annually; facilitating export trade; speeding the export process; assisting in curtailing illegal exports; and providing the potential to release trade statistics earlier. FTD estimates that under AES, it would achieve cost savings of $600,000 in 1994, $900,000 in 1995, and $1.2 million in 1996. In evaluating the proposed development of the AES, one must recognize that securing more accurate merchandise export statistics is only one element. Administration and congressional approval will also depend on the other objectives. Nevertheless, if the projected net benefits can be validated, the proposal should be supported as desirable.

A recent survey by the National Trade Facilitation Council, a large trade association, indicated many current manual reporters would voluntarily consider converting to electronic filing only if convinced that, despite the initial investment of money and time necessary for the conversion, the system would cut their overhead and personnel costs. Our interviews with foreign government officials suggest that importers and exporters have provided the impetus for the automated trade data reporting systems in their countries. Thus, to achieve the desired participation rate, emphasis should be placed on working with exporters and their agents in designing the system so that it is user friendly and economical and advantageous to them. An extensive educational effort should be conducted under the leadership of Customs. In addition, however, since there are incentives for underreporting and nonreporting, concerned agencies should also continue efforts in other areas, such as interchange of data, port audits, and a continuous independent review system.

Use of Sampling Techniques

As described above, export data are currently based on the processing of official documents for all transactions valued at $2,500 or more, and import data are based on all transactions valued at $1,500 or more (plus those valued at $250 or more that are covered by import quotas). The panel was asked to consider whether sampling should be used, primarily in order to reduce the high cost of manual processing of documents; a detailed analysis is presented in Appendix F. We concluded that probability sampling of shipments above the cutoffs (that is, all reported shipments) is not a practical option in the short term because of the large number of cells for which data are published each month. The majority of the cells have fewer than five transactions, and the sampling errors for estimates of these cells would be unacceptably large. The savings for imports would be relatively small because most imports are reported electronically.

For the longer term, the panel sees three options: (1) introducing probability sampling while substantially reducing the level of detail in which monthly data are published; (2) making substantial efforts to increase the proportion of export transactions reported electronically or in another form that will not require manual data entry; and (3) collecting import and export data directly from a sample survey of establishments. Options (1) and (2) should be considered as alternatives. Although several panel members suggested that the present level of monthly detail is unnecessary for public policy-making purposes, the panel decided in favor of option (2), which would preserve the ability to provide the present amount of detailed monthly information on merchandise trade. Option (1) should be considered only as a fallback position if efforts to reduce or at least contain the cost of processing the documents are unsuccessful.

In the longer term, option (3) deserves serious consideration. Future increases in bilateral free trade agreements and regional free trade zones may make it impossible to obtain adequate information from official trade documents. Data on trade in services are already being collected in establishment surveys, and increasing difficulties in distinguishing trade in goods and services may make it desirable to collect information on both types from the same source. In addition, collecting data from establishments and enterprises would make it possible to obtain certain kinds of information not readily available from official trade documents, such as intracompany trade activities and the use of imported intermediate inputs in exported commodities. Another use of sampling techniques would be to collect data on international air shipments (including low-value ones) in surveys of transportation companies, which would include all such large firms; many low-value shipments are currently excluded from coverage by the reporting cutoffs.

RECOMMENDATIONS

Our recommendations for improving merchandise trade statistics are grouped in three major areas: data quality and quality control, automation, and sampling. Within each area, recommendations are listed in order of their relative importance, with the most important one listed first.

DATA QUALITY AND QUALITY CONTROL

Recommendation 4-1   The Customs Service and the Census Bureau should strengthen their enforcement efforts to assure accurate and timely reporting of exports to correct the problem of export underreporting. The Census Bureau should no longer allow carriers to report exports as late as 4 days after departures of shipments. Incentives should be provided to exporters to file promptly and accurately. Increased efforts should be made to exchange and reconcile data with major trading partners and to perform port audits. In order to guide the allocation of resources devoted to data quality improvement, the Census Bureau should identify the characteristics of those filers prone to incomplete or inaccurate reporting.

Recommendation 4-2   The Customs Service and the Census Bureau, in order to guide those responsible for data collection, analysis, and dissemination, should identify and develop measures of the quality of merchandise trade statistics. The quality measures should permit overall estimates of the quality of the published merchandise trade data and estimates of the quality of specific key processes, such as data collection, coding, editing, imputation, error correction, and revision procedures.

Recommendation 4-3   The Census Bureau and the Customs Service should work closely with data filers to evaluate and improve the quality of the incoming trade data. They should also work closely with merchandise trade statistics users to monitor continuously the users' perceptions of the quality of trade statistics and to improve continuously their production processes and the quality of the data.

Recommendation 4-4   The Census Bureau should establish a continuous independent review system (CIRS), in which the incoming information for a small sample of import and export transactions would be independently reviewed by professional staff and the results would be used to determine

the sources and causes of errors and to develop procedures to improve data quality.

Recommendation 4-5 In addition to coordinating with the Customs Service, the Census Bureau should develop mechanisms for comparing Census data with monthly agricultural export data compiled by the Department of Agriculture directly from firms and with monthly oil import data gathered by the Energy Information Administration (EIA) of the Department of Energy directly from oil companies. Agricultural exports and oil imports not only represent two large components of U.S. trade, but also are subject to large seasonal changes. Cross-checking of monthly data with Agriculture and EIA should enhance the ability of the Census Bureau to detect error-prone data and work toward improving their accuracy. Furthermore, comparisons of Census's Foreign Trade Division annual export data on manufactured goods with data on manufactured exports recorded in the Annual Survey of Manufactures (ASM) conducted by Census's Industry Division should yield similar payoffs.

Recommendation 4-6 Measures of uncertainty about the accuracy of trade data should be published. In particular, attention should be given to establishing normally acceptable ranges for the fluctuations displayed in monthly trade balance figures. In addition, the Census Bureau should assess the feasibility of applying alternative seasonal adjustment procedures to produce data more indicative of underlying trends.

Recommendation 4-7 The Customs Service and the Census Bureau should develop a continuing port audit program.

Recommendation 4-8 The Census Bureau should strengthen its research and analytic capabilities so that it can develop a consistent concept to measure the trade balance and derive consistent time-series data on U.S. imports and exports. It should also work with the Bureau of Economic Analysis to develop concepts, definitions, and measures to capture the fast-growing intracompany trade and trade in intermediate inputs. The Census Bureau and the Bureau of Economic Analysis should seek outside professional advice from analytic users and other experts in these efforts.

Recommendation 4-9 Users should be actively encouraged, in meetings of user groups and by other means, to inform the

Census Bureau about suspected errors in the data cells that are of particular interest to them. Census should make a commitment to use such feedback, not just to correct any errors that may be identified, but to look for improvements in processes to reduce future errors.

AUTOMATION

Recommendation 4-10 The Census Bureau should accelerate its efforts to improve its processes for collecting, processing, and disseminating trade data through increased automation. The Census Bureau should initiate a joint effort with other appropriate agencies to develop a simplified universal electronic shipping and trade document.

SAMPLING

Recommendation 4-11 The Census Bureau and the Bureau of Economic Analysis should consider initiating a substantial multiyear effort to develop and test concepts, content, design, and procedures for surveys to collect integrated merchandise and services trade data from establishments. Initially, the goal of such surveys might be to supplement existing sources of data, but the Census Bureau should give serious consideration to the long-run objective of replacing the compilation of merchandise trade data from official documents. Common data sources will enhance comparability of data.

Recommendation 4-12 The Census Bureau should stop including estimates for low-value shipments by country because of the questionable quality of these monthly estimates in the official monthly figures. Available information about the effects of excluding transactions below the cutoffs should be included in statements that describe the sources and limitations of the data. An independent establishment-based survey of international air shipments should be considered as a way of filling one of the significant gaps resulting from the exclusion of low-value transactions, especially if interested user groups are willing to provide partial funding.

Recommendation 4-13 Probability sampling procedures should be used to the greatest extent possible in the Census Bureau's effort to control and improve the quality of its foreign trade data.

5

International Services Transactions

Along with improvements in transportation, communications, information technology, and expansion in domestic services in the past decade, there has been a rapid growth in U.S. international services transactions, both in cross-border delivery of services and in the sales of services abroad by foreign affiliates of U.S. firms. As a consequence, the demand for international services data has greatly increased. The federal government needs such data to better measure economic activities and to formulate and evaluate domestic and international trade policies. The private sector needs such data to monitor trends and assess market opportunities. In addition, for the first time, services are a subject for negotiation in the current Uruguay Round of the General Agreement on Tariffs and Trade (GATT). More specific data on U.S. international services transactions will be needed in the future when the United States begins negotiations on individual services.

Two pieces of U.S. legislation during the 1980s—the Trade and Tariff Act of 1984 and the Omnibus Trade and Competitiveness Act of 1988—have mandated enhancements of statistical programs for international transactions in services. Over the past 5 years, the Bureau of Economic Analysis (BEA) has made great strides in improving the coverage and accuracy of data on U.S. cross-border trade in services and sales of services by majority-owned foreign affiliates of U.S. firms. Nonetheless, there remains a considerable range in the quality of the data now available, and much more needs to be done.

This chapter describes the key features of international services trade data; delineates the existing methods of data collection; analyzes the adequacy of the data; and makes recommendations for their improvement.

DATA ON INTERNATIONAL SERVICES TRANSACTIONS: KEY FEATURES

International sales of services differ from sales of goods: goods can usually be consumed in a different country from the one in which they are produced, but services often must be produced and consumed in the same country. Services sales to foreigners can involve many different forms of delivery: the cross-border movement of a producer, such as the provision of professional and business services to foreigners; the cross-border movement of a consumer, such as services provided to foreign tourists, students, and medical patients; information, including electronic transmission of voice, video, or data; legal instruments, such as contractual arrangements to use intellectual property, including patents, trademarks, and broadcast rights; the movement of services themselves, including transportation of goods and passengers. Unlike the collection of merchandise trade data, the various forms of delivery of international services require the use of different data sources to gather information on transactions.

Also unlike merchandise trade statistics, data on U.S. international services cover two kinds of transactions: (1) cross-border ones, in which services move across national boundaries or are purchased or produced by temporary visitors who cross borders (for example, transportation services for passengers and cargoes and communications and information services); and (2) establishment transactions, which involve the delivery of services through foreign affiliates located in the consuming country (for example, banking, accounting, engineering, and advertising).

Statistics on U.S. international services transactions are compiled and estimated by BEA largely on the basis of periodic surveys of companies engaged in international services transactions. This method is used because international services transactions do not usually generate official records or customs documentations. Some data on international services transactions are based on benchmark surveys conducted at 5-year intervals; others are compiled from annual or quarterly surveys. In developing its estimates for different services categories, BEA often refers to data from other government agencies, private organizations, foreign governments, and international organizations. When only annual data are available, quarterly estimates are interpolations of annual estimates. BEA relies on various sources to update its mailing lists of respondents for its surveys. It also has obtained legal authority to gain access to the Census Bureau's Standard Statistical Establishment List (SSEL), a comprehensive list of business establishments used in Census Bureau's surveys, to enhance the completeness and accuracy of its sampling frames.

Prior to the mid-1980s, data on sales of services to foreigners consisted largely of cross-border transactions of traditional services (such as royalties and fees on the use or sale of U.S. intangible properties, travel, transportation, telecommunications, construction, reinsurance, and film rentals). Separate sales and purchases data on establishment transactions were not available.

Since the mid-1980s, several major developments have improved the coverage and quality of U.S. international services data. Mandatory reporting, as required under the Trade and Tariff Act of 1984, has increased response rates of surveys, improving the quality of the data. In addition to the traditional service categories, new surveys have been conducted by BEA to collect sales and purchases data not previously gathered on business, professional, and technical services, including: advertising; computer and data processing; database and other information services; telecommunications; research, development, and testing services; industrial engineering; management, consulting, and public relations services; legal services; installation, maintenance, and repair of equipment; agricultural services; management of health care facilities; accounting, auditing and bookkeeping services; mailing, reproduction, and commercial art; personnel supply services; sports and performing arts; primary insurance; and construction, engineering, architectural, and mining services. Estimates of medical services sales have been available since 1987 and of educational services sales and purchases since 1989. Noninterest income of U.S. banks, which had been commingled with interest income, was reclassified to services in 1989. Although data on establishment transactions (sales of services through affiliates) have been available since 1982 for foreign affiliates of U.S. companies, corresponding data for U.S. affiliates of foreign firms have been available only since 1987. Since June 1989, incomes paid and received on investments, which had been included in "services" broadly defined, have been labeled separately from services in the U.S. balance of payments.

In addition, the Omnibus Trade and Competitiveness Act of

1988 has provided for U.S. international services data to be included in the National Trade Data Bank and for the improvement of eight specified groups of services: banking services; information services, including computer software services; brokerage services; transportation services; travel services; engineering services; construction services; and health services. Most of the eight services are already covered by surveys. For the two major uncovered services—banking and brokerage transactions—BEA is actively studying ways to improve the data, including investigating the feasibility of instituting a new survey for financial services transactions.

Due to budgetary constraints and for reasons of efficiency, BEA limits its surveys of purchases and sales of services to companies believed to have large transactions, except for travel data, which are collected from individual travelers. Information reported to BEA is confidential. Numbers of responses on which estimates are based vary with different surveys. In 1988 about 35,000 responses were used for the travel estimates; 14 to 130 for different transportation sectors; 900 for business, professional, and technical services; 500 for royalties and fees; 200 for insurance surveys; and 130 for construction, engineering, architectural, and mining services. The differences reflect the degree of industry concentration in the various services categories: for example, there are fewer than 10 U.S. airlines that provide international flights. They also partly reflect the concentration of international service transactions undertaken by firms in certain industries: for example, there are only a small number of firms that do international business in the construction industry.

Unlike merchandise trade statistics, which are published in 14,000 import and 8,000 export commodity categories covering 212 countries and regions, international services transactions statistics are collected in aggregate values in approximately 25 broad categories, and country breakdowns are available only for major services. These statistics on a highly aggregated basis are reported in the quarterly release of the U.S. balance-of-payments accounts. BEA publishes annually the more detailed tables on international services in its September issues of *Survey of Current Business*.

Several difficulties complicate the collection of international services data, making them vulnerable to inaccuracy and inadequate coverage, primarily the diversity of the various service activities and the manner in which transactions occur. Even determining what data should be collected requires a clear understanding of the nature and scope of services and their international dimensions. In addition, rapid technological and organiza-

tional changes in service industries further complicate definition, classification, and measurement of services transactions. It
is also not easy to delineate boundaries between individual service sectors because some service activities overlap one another.
Telecommunications, for example, may cover the same ground
as data processing and information transmission; tourism involves
transportation. In addition, goods and services sold or provided
jointly in a package (such as turnkey manufacturing facilities
and major office and computing equipment) present problems of
classification; there is no standard for allocating value to services
associated with production of goods (this problem also applies to
domestic services).

Full coverage of transactions is difficult, in part because it would
not be easy to locate all possible respondents to surveys, including newly established companies. In addition, similar transactions may not be reported consistently by different companies.
Surveys on services transactions are also subject to sampling and
nonsampling errors and errors in the gathering and processing of
data. The reporting burden on respondents can limit the volume
of data that can be gathered, and the complexity of surveys can
affect response rates and quality of data reported. Data compiled
in large sector aggregates also mask major changes in particular
components.

METHODS OF ESTIMATING INTERNATIONAL
SERVICES TRANSACTIONS

Our discussion on sources and methods used in estimating U.S.
data on international services transactions focuses on procedures
that have been used since 1986, when a program of major improvements was initiated. The improvements resulted in a small
upward revision of net receipts for 1985 (from +$10.5 billion to
+$13.1 billion), followed by a net increase of $6.9 billion in the
revised 1986 data and an upward revision of $6.0 billion in the
previously published 1987 data; see Table 5-1. Nearly all of the
changes represent revisions of transactions with nonaffiliated foreign parties; there is comparatively little change in the data on
transactions between U.S. enterprises and their foreign affiliates
or parent corporations.

Sources and methods differ for the collection of data on services transactions between affiliated parties of multinational corporations; data on "other" private services transactions with

TABLE 5-1 Revisions in Data for U.S. International Services Transactions (in billions of dollars)

Service	Revised Data								
	1987		1988			1989			
	1985	1986	1985	1986	1987	1985	1986	1987	1988
Private service receipts, total	16.8	19.0	16.7	19.7	22.3	19.9	29.4	32.1	35.1
Royalties and fees from affiliates	4.2	4.7	4.1	5.4	6.9	—	5.4	6.9	8.3
Royalties and fees from other nonresidents	1.9	2.1	1.9	1.9	2.1	6.0	1.8	2.2	2.4
Other service receipts from affiliates	2.5	3.1	2.5	3.0	2.4	—	3.0	2.2	2.9
Other service receipts from other nonresidents	8.2	9.1	8.2	9.4	10.9	13.9	19.2	20.8	21.5
Private service payments, total	-6.2	-6.7	-6.2	-7.0	-8.9	-6.8	-9.8	-12.7	-13.5
Royalties and fees to affiliates	-0.5	-0.6	-0.5	-0.6	-0.8	—	-0.6	-0.8	-1.0
Royalties and fees to other nonresidents	-0.4	-0.5	-0.4	-0.4	-0.6	-0.9	-0.5	-0.5	-1.1
Other service payments to affiliates	0.7	1.3	0.7	1.3	1.9	—	1.3	0.6	0.7
Other service payments to nonresidents	-6.0	-6.9	-6.0	-7.3	-8.4	-5.9	-10.0	-12.0	-12.1
Net private services	10.6	12.3	10.5	12.7	13.4	13.1	19.6	19.4	21.6
With affiliates	6.9	8.5	6.8	9.1	9.4	—	9.1	8.9	10.9
Other[a]	3.7	3.8	3.7	3.6	4.0	—	10.5	10.5	10.7

[a]This category does not include shipping or travel; it does include the services enumerated in Tables 5-2, 5-3, and 5-4.

SOURCE: *Survey of Current Business*, various June issues.

unaffiliated parties, including those covering royalties, fees, and payments for intangible rights, reinsurance and direct insurance, and construction and engineering services; data on the two major traditional service sectors, international shipping and tourism; and data on financial, educational, and medical services transactions. For some of the data, BEA uses various surveys; see Figure 5-1.

TRANSACTIONS BETWEEN AFFILIATED PARTIES OF
MULTINATIONAL CORPORATIONS

Services between affiliated parties of multinational corporations primarily include intracorporate receipts and payments of royalties, fees, and other service items between foreign affiliates and their parent companies. Data on services transactions between U.S. corporations and their foreign affiliates, as well as those between foreign corporations and their U.S. affiliates, are compiled from a portion of the information collected in direct investment surveys. Separate surveys are used to cover U.S. direct investment abroad and foreign direct investment in the United States.

Services Transactions Related to U.S. Direct Investment Abroad

A hierarchy of BEA surveys are used to collect information on U.S. direct investment abroad. First are the benchmark surveys of U.S. direct investments abroad, the BE-10 series, which are generally scheduled at 5-year intervals; second are the annual surveys of these investments, the BE-11 series; and third are the quarterly series (BE-577).

The most recent benchmark covers 1989. The benchmark surveys are intended to be all-inclusive: a direct mailing is made by BEA to all U.S. firms identified as being a parent of a foreign affiliate (that is, a U.S. person, or affiliated group, owning a 10 percent or greater voting interest in a foreign corporation, or a comparable interest in an unincorporated foreign business). The BEA mailing list is comprehensive, having been built up over many successive surveys, and it is updated daily on the basis of a wide variety of public and other sources reporting on the establishment of a direct-investment relationship. The exemption level for reporting for individual foreign affiliates is fairly low: a foreign affiliate whose assets, sales, or net income fall between $3 million and $15 million is required to be reported on the short form (BE-10B(SF)); one whose assets, sales, or net income are in excess of $15 million is required to be reported on the long form

FIGURE 5-1 BEA Surveys (Forms Used) on Direct Investment and International Services Transactions

Direct Investment
  Direct Transactions of U.S. Reporter With Foreign Affiliate (BE-577)
  Transactions of U.S. Affiliate, Except an Unincorporated Bank, With Foreign
    Parent (BE-605); Transactions of U.S. Banking Branch or Agency With
    Foreign Parent (BE-606B)
  Benchmark Survey of U.S. Direct Investment Abroad (BE-10A, BE-10A Bank,
    BE-10B, BE-10B Bank)
  Benchmark Survey of Foreign Direct Investment in the U.S. (BE-12)
  Annual Survey of U.S. Direct Investment Abroad (BE-11)
  Annual Survey of Foreign Direct Investment in the United States (BE-15)
  Initial Report on a Foreign Person's Direct or Indirect Acquisition,
    Establishment, or Purchase of the Operating Assets of a U.S. Business
    Enterprise, Including Real Estate (BE-13)
Travel
  Survey of U.S. Travelers Visiting Canada (BE-536)
  Expenditures of United States Travelers in Mexico (BE-575)
Transportation
  Ocean Freight Revenues and Foreign Expenses of U.S. Carriers (BE-30)
  U.S. Airline Operators' Foreign Revenues and Expenses (BE-37)
  Foreign Ocean Carriers' Expenses in the United States (BE-29)
  Foreign Airline Operators' Revenues and Expenses in the United States (BE-36)
Other Services
  Benchmark Survey of Selected Services Transactions With Unaffiliated Foreign
    Persons (BE-20)
  Annual Survey of Selected Services Transactions With Unaffiliated Foreign
    Persons (BE-22)
  Annual Survey of Royalties, License Fees, and Other Receipts and Payments
    for Intangible Rights Between U.S. and Unaffiliated Foreign Persons (BE-93)
  Annual Survey of Construction, Engineering, Architectural, and Mining
    Services Provided by U.S. Firms to Unaffiliated Foreign Persons (BE-47)
  Annual Survey of Reinsurance and Other Insurance Transactions by U.S.
    Insurance Companies With Foreign Persons (BE-48)

(BE-10B(LF)); even if there is no reportable foreign affiliate, a parent company must reply to that effect. There are also specialized reports for banks. In these surveys, more detailed data are collected for majority-owned affiliates than for those that are minority owned.

The annual surveys (BE-11A, B, and C) are not primarily intended to amplify the data used in the balance-of-payments accounts, but rather to keep current other aspects of the operations of the multinational enterprises—such as sales or revenues, employment, details of the balance sheets and profit-and-loss accounts, and trade with parent companies in the United States. Consequently, the data derived from these surveys has no significant bearing on the magnitude of international services transactions in the U.S. balance of payments, but they can be used as a partial measure of the sale of services by U.S. companies in foreign markets.

In contrast, the quarterly survey (BE-577) is used to generate data for the balance-of-payments accounts. Data obtained from the quarterly survey are directly linked back to the coverage of the benchmark surveys. Filing is required for each foreign affiliate with assets, sales, or net income exceeding $20 million. The relative scopes of the benchmark and the quarterly surveys are reflected in the number of reporters and affiliates covered by each. In the benchmark census of 1982, 2,245 reports were filed by U.S. parent companies, covering 33,650 foreign affiliates, of whom 18,339 were required to report detailed information. Recent reporting on the BE-577 has covered 1,200 U.S. parent companies and 9,160 foreign affiliates. Another measure of coverage is given by the percentage of statistical features of the benchmark that is also covered by the quarterly BE-577. On that basis, it is estimated by BEA that almost 90 percent of the current income and service transactions of the universe of direct investors is covered by the quarterly reports, and that percentage, within narrow margins, is used to expand the data cells derived from the quarterly survey to yield universe estimates.

An indication of the magnitude of services transactions between U.S. companies and their foreign affiliates is given in Table 5-1 (above). The net receipts by U.S. parent companies of royalties, fees, and earnings from the use of intangible property rose very rapidly from 1985 through 1988, while receipts from affiliates for other service items, including intracorporate charges for management services, were relatively flat over that period. Table 5-1 also shows that receipts of royalties, fees, and other service items from foreign affiliates of U.S. companies account for almost one-third of all receipts from these types of private services.

These data can be extracted from the various direct investment surveys. In the benchmark report (BE-10B(LF)) filed for each sizable foreign affiliate, items 101-107 provide a set of data on service transactions between an affiliate and its U.S. parent, covering royalties, fees, and payments for the use of intangible property, as well as allocated expenses and service transactions between the affiliate and the U.S. parent. For smaller foreign affiliates reporting on the short form (BE-10B(SF)), service transactions with the parent are covered in items 67-69, with some breakdown by type. In addition, data for royalties, fees, and the like are given in items 82 and 83, but these yield operating rather than balance-of-payments data. As a rough generalization, the coverage of current-account entries in the balance of payments expected to be provided by the short form is estimated at less than 10 percent of the combined coverage of the long and short forms.

There are specialized benchmark reports for banks (BE-10A Bank and BE-10B Bank). Items 70-72 on the BE-10 Bank form parallel the other forms in covering certain service transactions between an affiliate and a U.S. parent company. These entries provide a basis for the entries in the balance-of-payments accounts, but they cover only a small part of the overall entries for international banking services in the accounts.

The annual surveys covering parent companies contain no balance-of-payments type of data on services transactions; the form covering majority-owned foreign affiliates (BE-11B) contains some entries (items 47-50) that cover sales of services abroad by their foreign affiliates, but not by type.

The quarterly reporting system (BE-577) provides the continuing basis for the regular quarterly revisions of the balance-of-payments accounts. This form is limited to entries directly pertinent to the balance-of-payments accounts. For the royalties, fees, and other intracorporate services relevant to this discussion, the data are given in items 17, 18, 19.1, and 19.2. These items follow the comparable items in the benchmark reports; they cover only transactions with the parent company, and some types of transactions or charges for services are not required in detail. In processing these incoming quarterly reports, BEA "blows up" the sample data for each industry/country cell to yield universe estimates. As the incoming reports accumulate, the amount of blow-up required is reduced; when the full sample is in, the amount of blow-up across cells averages about 10 percent. It should be noted that this is not a random sample: essentially all known significant direct investors are required to report quarterly.

Services Transactions Related to Foreign Direct Investment in the United States

For foreign direct investments in the United States, a similar reporting structure has evolved. For these transactions, the most recent benchmark survey (BE-12) covered 1987; the preliminary results were published in the July 1989 issue of the *Survey of Current Business*, and the final results in the July 1990 issue.

More detailed results were published in separate data publications. To speed the tabulation process, the larger returns are tabulated first. The final count of such affiliates for 1987 was 8,577. Given the mandatory filing requirement and the extensive efforts by BEA to search out all potential respondents, it is reasonable to consider the benchmark totals as effectively complete. BEA estimates that more than 80 percent of the balance-of-payments entries or assets of foreign direct investments in the United States is accounted for by majority-owned affiliates.

The basic benchmark form (BE-12(LF)) is filed by each U.S. affiliate with $20 million or more of assets, sales, or net income. Information on international services transactions is rather limited. Lines 75-79 give data on sales of services, not differentiated by type, separately for sales to foreign parents and affiliates and sales to unrelated foreign persons. These data can serve in part to check other data collected on overall sales of services to nonresidents. Lines 253-257 provide greater detail on transactions in services between a reporting U.S. affiliate and its foreign parent, covering all types of services. Moreover, there is an extensive section (Part IV) devoted to gathering information on transactions of a U.S. affiliate with foreign affiliates of the foreign parent company, which yields considerable amounts of information. It appears that in the benchmark years there is complete coverage of services transactions with nonresidents carried out by U.S. affiliates of foreign firms.

The annual report form (BE-15) has two reporting levels: for sales, assets, or net income exceeding $20 million, a long form is required; between $10-20 million, a short form must be filed. At these levels, the annual long form would cover about 95 percent of the benchmark level of assets. The information collected on services only partly parallels the coverage of the benchmark surveys: lines 70-73 cover all sales of services by the U.S. affiliate, but not in detail, although the industry classification of the affiliate may indicate the nature of the services sold. However, no information on services is collected that is relevant to the balance-of-payments accounts. This form is intended primarily to compile data on operational aspects of the U.S. affiliates of foreign firms in the United States.

The quarterly report forms (BE-605 and BE-606B for branch banks) provide basic information for the ongoing entries on services in the balance-of-payments accounts. The reporting requirement (over $20 million) is the same as for the benchmark long form. On average, the coverage of current-account transactions, including services, is estimated at about 90 percent. Blow-ups by BEA are carried out at the level of industry/country cells. On form BE-605, the relevant information on services transactions with foreign parents is given in Part III, lines 19-23, although the breakdown by type is limited. There is also an extended section in Part VII for reporting service and other transactions with foreign affiliates of the parent company. On form BE-606B, there is information (lines 16-19) on services transactions performed between affiliates and parents, but it does not cover the much larger category of service charges to nonaffiliated customers.

As shown in Table 5-1 (above), U.S. affiliates of foreign firms are net recipients of charges from their foreign parent organizations. This partly results from the operations of U.S. affiliates of Japanese firms, which carry out extensive marketing and other functions in the United States on behalf of their parent organizations. Another major source of U.S. receipts from foreign parents for services performed is reimbursement for warranty work.

Other Private Services, Unaffiliated

Under the BEA category of "other private services, unaffiliated" appear all the services between U.S. residents and unaffiliated foreign persons other than tourism and international shipping. Tables 5-2, 5-3, and 5-4 present detailed information on receipts and payments for these services. They show how inadequate the coverage was before later surveys were undertaken and the significant revisions for some of the services (see below). For some years there had been dissatisfaction with the coverage and quality of data for these other private services, and there were widespread estimates of their "true" levels. Responding to its own concerns about these data, as well as to competing estimates that were circulating, BEA used the International Investment and Trade in Services Survey Act (through the Trade and Tariff Act of 1984), a broadened and redesigned version of the International Investment Survey Act of 1976, to revise forms and enlarge mailing lists. Also under that act, reporting of services transactions became mandatory.

The main instrument for improving the data was the introduction in 1986 of a new mandatory reporting system (using form BE-20, and, subsequently, BE-22) that calls for much greater detail by type of service. At the direction of the Office of Management and Budget to work with the respondent community and through consultations with the Business Council on the Reduction of Paper-

TABLE 5-2a   Receipts, Other Private Services, Unaffiliated, 1986 (in millions of dollars)

Service	Original	Revised
Total	9,393	19,150
Education	—	3,480
Financial services	1,656	3,301
Insurance[a]	479	2,041
Primary insurance, net	—	1,600
Reinsurance, net	479	441
Telecommunications	1,628	1,827
Business, professional, and technical services	1,614	4,368
Accounting, auditing, and bookkeeping	—	21
Advertising	—	94
Computer and data processing	—	985
Database and other information services	—	124
Engineering, architectural, construction, and mining, net[b]	1,124	857
Installation, maintenance, and repair of equipment	—	973
Legal services	—	97
Management, consulting, and public relations	—	306
Medical services	490	490
Research and development, commercial testing, and laboratory services	—	282
Other	—	139
Other	4,016	4,133
Wages of temporary workers	104	104
Film rentals	550	656
Expenditures of foreign governments and international organizations	3,006	3,015
Other	356	357
Amount of change (current less previous)	—	9,757
New information	—	7,478
Transferred from other accounts	—	2,394
Revisions	—	–115

NOTES: The original figures are those reported based on earlier surveys; the revised figures are based on later BEA surveys. A dash indicates the data are not available.

[a]Insurance receipts are published net of losses paid, and payments are published net of losses recovered.

[b]Engineering, architectural, construction, and mining receipts are published net of merchandise exports, which are included in the merchandise trade account, and net of outlays abroad for wages, services, materials, and other expenses.

SOURCE: *Survey of Current Business* (1989:57).

TABLE 5-2b Payments, Other Private Services, Unaffiliated, 1986 (in millions of dollars)

Service	Original	Revised
Total	7,252	10,014
Education	—	461
Financial services	1,874	1,769
Insurance[a]	1,406	2,201
Primary insurance, net	—	477
Reinsurance, net	1,406	1,724
Telecommunications	3,027	3,252
Business, professional, and technical services	—	1,252
Accounting, auditing, and bookkeeping	—	29
Advertising	—	77
Computer and data processing	—	32
Database and other information services	—	23
Engineering, architectural, construction, and mining, net[b]	—	379
Installation, maintenance, and repair of equipment	—	466
Legal services	—	40
Management, consulting, and public relations	—	60
Medical services	—	—
Research and development, commercial testing, and laboratory services	—	76
Other	—	70
Other	945	1,079
Wages of temporary workers	698	833
Film rentals	77	73
Expenditures of foreign governments and international organizations	—	—
Other	170	173
Amount of change (current less previous)	—	2,762
New information	—	2,094
Transferred from other accounts	—	321
Revisions	—	347

NOTES: The original figures are those reported based on earlier surveys; the revised figures are based on later BEA surveys. A dash indicates the data are not available.

[a]Insurance receipts are published net of losses paid, and payments are published net of losses recovered.

[b]Engineering, architectural, construction, and mining receipts are published net of merchandise exports, which are included in the merchandise trade account, and net of outlays abroad for wages, services, materials, and other expenses.

SOURCE: *Survey of Current Business* (1989:57).

TABLE 5-3a Receipts, Other Private Services, Unaffiliated, 1987 (in millions of dollars)

Service	Original	Revised
Total	10,851	20,763
Education	—	3,804
Financial services	2,232	3,731
Insurance[a]	690	2,285
Primary insurance, net	—	1,596
Reinsurance, net	690	689
Telecommunications	1,791	2,105
Business, professional, and technical services	1,690	4,270
Accounting, auditing, and bookkeeping	—	27
Advertising	—	108
Computer and data processing	—	629
Database and other information services	—	138
Engineering, architectural, construction, and mining, net[b]	1,174	936
Installation, maintenance, and repair of equipment	—	1,023
Legal services	—	148
Management, consulting, and public relations	—	379
Medical services	516	516
Research and development, commercial testing, and laboratory services	—	182
Other	—	184
Other	4,448	4,568
Wages of temporary workers	120	120
Film rentals	658	740
Expenditures of foreign governments and international organizations	3,293	3,332
Other	377	376
Amount of change (current less previous)	—	9,912
New information	—	7,763
Transferred from other accounts	—	2,266
Revisions	—	–117

NOTES: The original figures are those reported based on earlier surveys; the revised figures are based on later BEA surveys. A dash indicates the data are not available.

[a]Insurance receipts are published net of losses paid, and payments are published net of losses recovered.

[b]Engineering, architectural, construction, and mining receipts are published net of merchandise exports, which are included in the merchandise trade account, and net of outlays abroad for wages, services, materials, and other expenses.

SOURCE: *Survey of Current Business* (1989:57).

TABLE 5-3b Payments, Other Private Services, Unaffiliated, 1987 (in millions of dollars)

Service	Original	Revised
Total	8,406	12,006
Education	—	513
Financial services	—	2,077
Insurance[a]	2,443	3,168
Primary insurance, net	1,634	552
Reinsurance, net	—	2,616
Telecommunications	1,634	3,701
Business, professional, and technical services	3,334	1,425
Accounting, auditing, and bookkeeping	—	37
Advertising	—	140
Computer and data processing	—	61
Database and other information services	—	28
Engineering, architectural, construction, and mining, net[b]	—	368
Installation, maintenance, and repair of equipment	—	506
Legal services	—	56
Management, consulting, and public relations	—	50
Medical services	—	—
Research and development, commercial testing, and laboratory services	—	127
Other	—	52
Other	995	1,122
Wages of temporary workers	740	888
Film rentals	73	48
Expenditures of foreign governments and international organizations	182	—
Other	—	186
Amount of change (current less previous)	—	3,600
New information	—	2,442
Transferred from other accounts	—	415
Revisions	—	743

NOTES: The original figures are those reported based on earlier surveys; the revised figures are based on later BEA surveys. A dash indicates the data are not available.

[a]Insurance receipts are published net of losses paid, and payments are published net of losses recovered.

[b]Engineering, architectural, construction, and mining receipts are published net of merchandise exports, which are included in the merchandise trade account, and net of outlays abroad for wages, services, materials, and other expenses.

SOURCE: *Survey of Current Business* (1989:57).

TABLE 5-4a Receipts, Other Private Services, Unaffiliated, 1988 (in millions of dollars)

Service	Original	Revised
Total	11,224	21,471
Education	—	4,111
Financial services	1,966	3,835
Insurance[a]	833	1,564
Primary insurance, net	—	1,311
Reinsurance, net	833	253
Telecommunications	1,970	2,357
Business, professional, and technical services	1,704	4,787
Accounting, auditing, and bookkeeping	—	—
Advertising	—	—
Computer and data processing	—	—
Database and other information services	—	—
Engineering, architectural, construction, and mining, net[b]	1,163	—
Installation, maintenance, and repair of equipment	—	—
Legal services	—	—
Management, consulting, and public relations	—	—
Medical services	541	541
Research and development, commercial testing, and laboratory services	—	—
Other	—	—
Other	4,751	4,817
Wages of temporary workers	129	129
Film rentals	724	776
Expenditures of foreign governments and international organizations	3,487	3,504
Other	411	408
Amount of change (current less previous)	—	10,247
New information	—	8,244
Transferred from other accounts	—	2,855
Revisions	—	–852

NOTES: The original figures are those reported based on earlier surveys; the revised figures are based on later BEA surveys. A dash indicates the data are not available.

[a]Insurance receipts are published net of losses paid, and payments are published net of losses recovered.

[b]Engineering, architectural, construction, and mining receipts are published net of merchandise exports, which are included in the merchandise trade account, and net of outlays abroad for wages, services, materials, and other expenses.

SOURCE: *Survey of Current Business* (1989:57).

TABLE 5-4b Payments, Other Private Services, Unaffiliated, 1988 (in millions of dollars)

Service	Original	Revised
Total	8,716	12,094
Education	—	555
Financial services	2,057	1,656
Insurance[a]	1,922	2,781
Primary insurance, net	—	603
Reinsurance, net	1,922	2,179
Telecommunications	3,681	4,264
Business, professional, and technical services	—	1,646
Accounting, auditing, and bookkeeping	—	—
Advertising	—	—
Computer and data processing	—	—
Database and other information services	—	—
Engineering, architectural, construction, and mining, net[b]	—	—
Installation, maintenance, and repair of equipment	—	—
Legal services	—	—
Management, consulting, and public relations	—	—
Medical services	—	—
Research and development, commercial testing, and laboratory services	—	—
Other	—	—
Other	1,056	1,192
Wages of temporary workers	793	950
Film rentals	70	50
Expenditures of foreign governments and international organizations	—	—
Other	193	192
Amount of change (current less previous)	—	3,378
New information	—	2,873
Transferred from other accounts	—	514
Revisions	—	–9

NOTES: The original figures are those reported based on earlier surveys; the revised figures are based on later BEA surveys. A dash indicates the data are not available.

[a]Insurance receipts are published net of losses paid, and payments are published net of losses recovered.

[b]Engineering, architectural, construction, and mining receipts are published net of merchandise exports, which are included in the merchandise trade account, and net of outlays abroad for wages, services, materials, and other expenses.

SOURCE: *Survey of Current Business* (1989:57).

work, BEA sets exemption levels for filing detailed data. Reports are mandatory for individual transactions of $250,000 or more (though this has been interpreted to mean annual transactions with a single customer); reports for smaller transactions are voluntary, with some indication to be provided of the overall magnitude of the transactions, but not by type or country.

In the initial distribution of these forms, over 20,000 were mailed directly to lists of firms considered to be likely respondents. Of that original universe, almost 1,000 returns were filed that contained statistics that could be used. Although this number appeared to be quite limited, the result was a notable increase in the amounts reported for these types of services, and amounts were reported for services not covered at all up to that time (see Tables 5-2, 5-3, and 5-4).

It is clear that the new BE-22 survey added considerably to the receipts of services shown in the balance-of-payments accounts, although some of the amounts shown as new information may reflect improved compliance with the reporting requirements rather than new transactions. According to BEA, the new survey was more successful in filling gaps on the receipt side than in identifying payments abroad for services by U.S. residents, but this is always to be expected when coverage on one side or the other requires canvassing a much more widely dispersed universe. The extent of the bias is not known, and there is no obvious practical solution to this imbalance, although persistent checking of source materials may help to broaden the coverage. Although the number of potential purchasers of foreign services is small, the introduction of the new survey did succeed in improving the coverage of payments. For telecommunications, data on payments were increased considerably more than those on receipts; this difference appears to reflect the fact that more companies responded to the new mandatory survey.

In addition to the improved reporting through form BE-22, there are three specialized surveys that were brought under the new act in 1986 and were strengthened in 1987 by increases in both coverage and detail. Form BE-93, revised in 1987, covers receipts and payments of royalties, fees, and charges for the use of intangible property between U.S. firms and unaffiliated nonresidents, supplementing the coverage of the multinational direct investment surveys. The number of respondents is now over 400. BEA continues its efforts to broaden the reporting base for this survey, checking with the Patent Office, booking agents, and other possible sources of mailing lists. Given the wide dispersal of participants in this type of services and the relatively small magnitude of individual contract arrangements, it seems unlikely that there will be major changes in these data.

Another special form (BE-48) covers premiums earned and paid and losses paid and recovered on reinsurance and premiums earned (and associated claims) on primary insurance transactions of insurance companies with nonresidents. Reinsurance had been covered for many years, but the revised mandatory form introduced in 1987 also covered U.S. sales of primary insurance, and the number of insurance companies or groups responding increased from just under 250 to about 300. As shown in Tables 5-2, 5-3, and 5-4, there were some sizable revisions from earlier reports, raising reinsurance payments considerably in 1987 (from $1.6 to $2.6 billion) and reducing reinsurance receipts in 1988 (from $0.8 to almost $0.3 billion). It should be noted that the insurance entries are shown on a net basis, reflecting the difference between premiums received and paid, as well as losses paid and recovered. Thus, the 1988 revision reflects a larger figure for losses paid than was reported earlier.

Primary insurance sales to nonresidents by U.S. insurance companies was first measured in 1987 and showed a sizable surplus of premiums over losses paid. However, there is little reporting on primary insurance between the U.S. residents and foreign insurance companies; the exemption level is high ($250,000), but, a priori, this would not seem likely to be a significant service activity. There are certain difficulties in calculating the value of these transactions—apart from the difficulties in measuring the direct investment transactions of this industry. Premium receipts are generally recorded on a cash basis, reinsurance premiums paid are as reported, and the report filers estimate the corresponding loss experience. No account is taken of any accumulating asset or liability positions that are built into some forms of insurance, which might be useful as part of the overall effect of this industry's operations.

A new annual reporting form (BE-47) also came under the new mandatory reporting system and was expanded. It improved and refined the coverage of services related to construction and engineering operations as well as architectural and mining services. The data showed that U.S. international transactions in these services were conducted by a fairly small number of firms. Currently, the number of respondents is fewer than 100. BEA continues to expand coverage by reference to trade publications and other information on sizable foreign projects. There is more limited coverage of foreign contractors, engineering, or architectural firms operating in the United States. It should be noted that it is especially difficult to separate the strictly service aspects of this industry from activities defined as direct investments. In principle, in addition to other criteria set up by BEA, when a firm establishes a relatively permanent presence to carry out a contract, the activity is reported under the heading of direct investments. Although BEA (in its instructions to form BE-47) provides criteria used for determining whether a foreign activity or operation should be reported as direct investment or cross-border services transactions (including the nature of the operation and the types of records kept), the distinction probably baffles some of the reporting companies, which may not maintain their records on those criteria.

TRADITIONAL SERVICES: SHIPPING AND TOURISM

International Shipping

Collection of data on international freight and shipping activities is one of the oldest and most complex activities reported in the U.S. balance of payments. These transactions involve very large receipts and payments, as shown in Table 5-5. A breakdown of the elements entering these accounts is shown in Table 5-6 for 1970-1988. Estimating each transaction involves several steps.

For ocean shipping, on the payments side, the convention is to consider that all payments for freight on imports are paid by the importer. To compile the balance-of-payments accounts, it is necessary to determine how much of the total freight bill for imports is paid to foreign fleets and how much to the U.S. fleet; payments by U.S. importers to the U.S. fleet do not enter the balance of payments

TABLE 5-5   Selected Service Transactions, 1986-1988 (in millions of dollars)

Service	1986	1987	1988
Exports of selected services	70,886	79,405	92,058
Travel	20,454	23,505	29,202
Passenger fares	5,546	6,882	8,860
Other transportations	15,458	16,989	18,930
Freight	3,969	4,700	5,345
Port services	10,480	11,575	12,830
Other	1,009	714	755

TABLE 5-5 *Continued*

Service	1986	1987	1988
Exports of selected services—*continued*			
Royalties and license fees	7,254	9,070	10,735
Affiliated, net	5,412	6,900	8,319
U.S. parents' receipts	5,518	7,049	8,431
U.S. parents' payments	106	150	112
Unaffiliated	1,842	2,171	2,416
Other private services	22,174	22,959	24,331
Affiliated services, net	3,024	2,196	2,858
U.S. parents' receipts	5,375	5,106	6,168
U.S. parents' payments	2,351	2,910	3,310
Unaffiliated services	19,150	20,763	21,471
Education	3,480	3,804	4,111
Financial services	3,301	3,731	3,835
Insurance[a]	2,041	2,285	1,564
Telecommunications	1,827	2,105	2,357
Business, professional, and technical services	4,368	4,270	4,787
Other unaffiliated services[b]	4,133	4,568	4,817
Imports of selected services	59,281	67,455	73,073
Travel	26,000	29,215	32,112
Passenger fares	6,774	7,423	7,872
Other transportations	16,715	18,062	19,641
Freight	10,687	10,999	11,841
Port services	5,201	6,360	7,059
Other	827	703	741
Royalties and license fees	1,062	1,365	2,048
Affiliated, net	602	843	968
U.S. affiliates' receipts	171	240	238
U.S. affiliates' payments	773	1,083	1,205
Unaffiliated	461	522	1,080
Other private services	8,730	11,390	11,400
Affiliated services, net	−1,284	−616	−694
U.S. affiliates' receipts	2,808	2,683	3,028
U.S. affiliates' payments	1,524	2,067	2,334
Unaffiliated services	10,014	12,006	12,094
Education	461	513	555
Financial services	1,769	2,077	1,656
Insurance[a]	2,201	3,168	2,781
Telecommunications	3,252	3,701	4,264
Business, professional, and technical services	1,252	1,425	1,646
Other unaffiliated services[b]	1,079	1,122	1,192

[a]Insurance receipts (exports) are published net of losses paid, and payments (imports) are published net of losses recovered.

[b]Other unaffiliated services receipts (exports) include mainly expenditures of foreign governments and international organizations in the United States. Payments (imports) include mainly wages of foreign residents temporarily employed in the United States and Canadian and Mexican commuters in U.S. border areas.

SOURCE: *Survey of Current Business* (1989:76).

TABLE 5-6 U.S. Receipts and Payments for International Transportation: 1970-1988 (in millions of dollars)

Item	1970	1980	1981	1982	1983	1984	1985	1986	1987	1988
Total receipts	3,669	14,208	15,671	15,491	16,200	17,824	19,062	21,004	23,870	27,790
Ocean transportation	2,256	7,757	8,028	7,685	8,133	8,849	8,846	9,169	10,060	11,116
Export freight earnings	604	2,641	2,803	2,549	2,881	2,702	2,866	2,610	2,806	2,959
Freight earnings on shipments between foreign countries	209	588	561	555	575	563	574	576	595	689
Port expenditures	1,406	4,435	4,552	4,468	4,562	5,457	5,274	5,843	6,514	7,315
Charter hire	37	93	112	113	115	127	132	140	145	153
Air transportation	1,240	5,946	7,160	7,326	7,596	8,460	9,735	10,966	12,825	15,652
Export freight earnings	187	742	752	762	576	645	706	783	982	1,385
Passenger fares	541	2,591	3,111	3,174	3,610	4,015	4,388	5,546	6,882	8,860
Port expenditures	512	2,613	3,297	3,390	3,410	3,800	4,641	4,637	4,961	5,407
Other transportation	173	505	483	480	471	515	481	869	985	1,022
Total payments	4,058	15,397	16,961	16,482	18,225	20,753	22,314	23,489	25,484	27,513
Ocean transportation	2,380	8,447	8,900	8,307	8,624	10,560	11,018	11,619	11,649	12,641
Import freight payments	1,444	5,809	6,073	5,562	5,827	7,755	8,114	8,636	8,657	9,505
Passenger fares	245	268	287	290	305	305	320	320	328	328
Port expenditures	316	1,905	2,054	1,957	1,980	1,972	2,048	2,125	2,114	2,244
Charter hire	375	465	486	498	512	528	536	538	550	564
Air transportation	1,581	6,705	7,785	7,938	9,361	9,950	11,070	11,581	13,527	14,525
Import freight payments	115	562	671	725	1,066	1,633	1,666	2,051	2,242	2,226
Passenger fares	970	3,339	4,200	4,482	5,698	5,605	6,351	6,454	7,095	7,544
Port expenditures	496	2,804	2,914	2,731	2,597	2,712	3,053	3,076	4,190	4,755
Other transportation	97	245	276	237	240	243	226	289	308	347
Balance	-389	-1,189	-1,290	-991	-2,025	-2,929	-3,252	-2,485	-1,614	277

SOURCE: *Survey of Current Business*, June issues, and unpublished data from the Bureau of Economic Analysis.

NOTE: Data are international transportation transactions recorded for balance-of-payment purposes. Receipts include freight on exports carried by U.S.-operated carriers and foreign carrier expenditures in U.S. ports. Payments include freight on imports carried by foreign carriers and U.S. carrier port expenditures abroad. Freight on exports carried by foreign carriers is excluded since such payments are directly or indirectly for foreign account. Similarly, freight on U.S. imports carried by U.S. carriers is a domestic rather than an international transaction.

since they are resident-to-resident payments. Determining the total freight bill on U.S. imports is relatively simple, since the merchandise trade data are tabulated on both cost-insurance-freight (c.i.f.) and free-on-board (f.o.b.) basis—the difference being freight and insurance. BEA makes an arbitrary estimate that 1 percent of the import bill represents insurance payments, and the rest of the c.i.f.–f.o.b. difference represents freight payments.

The next step is to determine how much of those payments is to the foreign fleet. The Census Bureau tabulations on merchandise imports identify the carriers bringing in the goods by flag of registry, and there are vessel clearance reports filed with the U.S. Customs Service that indicate the operator of each vessel. From this information and information gathered over many years of studying shipping industry practices, BEA prepares estimates of how much of the total ocean import freight bill is paid to foreign operators; this estimate is shown as part of import freight payments ($9.5 billion in 1988).

One feature of ocean ship operations is that a very large part of gross freight revenues is spent in the ports of the importing countries to cover a wide variety of operating expenses; BEA collects this information on foreign-operated ships calling at U.S. ports (form BE-29). At present, the procedure is to send this form early in the year to U.S. agents of foreign shippers, asking them to complete the form for 10 port calls during the year. A report is required from an agent handling 40 or more port calls with aggregate expenditures of $250,000; however, it is difficult to determine, a priori, whether a given agent is required to report. The form separates vessels into three classes (liner, tramp, and tanker) and collects information on several types of expenditures in U.S. ports. The agent is requested to fill in both the amounts spent by the vessels and the shipping weight of the cargo handled. Since the total shipping weight of imports is known from Census Bureau merchandise trade data, this factor can be used to blow up this sample of returns to the universe to estimate foreign port expenditures in the United States ($7.3 billion in 1988).

However, this estimating procedure is not smooth sailing. Agents' responses may not be reliable, and the data for shipping weight are often missing. Also, data for one of the most important elements, bunker fuel, may be incomplete. Furthermore, it is necessary to obtain sufficient coverage for each type of vessel for overall estimates. The reporting requirement changed in 1989 (covering 1988 data) to a 10 port-call sample rather than a report covering all port calls, as an inducement for better compliance with the request for data, but compliance is still not entirely satisfactory. When reports on the BE-29 by agents do not provide full breakdowns by the type of vessel or type of expenditures, the reliability of the sample is greatly reduced; BEA is working on procedures to arrive at improved estimates for more of the cells in the forms. For example, there is an external source for the bunker fuel component from Census Bureau data on fuel loaded in vessels by flag, giving both quantity and value.

Port expenditure receipts must be viewed as an element in the balance-of-payments accounts that still depends on a less than robust reporting and estimating procedure. There may be some possibility for bias, tending to overstate port expenditure receipts, in the method used to estimate totals from the BE-29 returns. However, there is a certain amount of discipline in deriving these port expenditure figures because of the historical relationship of freight payments to foreign vessels. Over the 1980-1988 period, port expenditure receipts averaged 74 percent of the ocean freight payments, and there were no large year-to-year variations. It might be noted, however, that the global shipping data suggest that port expenditure receipts for the world as a whole may be understated.

On the other side of the ocean shipping account, it is necessary to measure the freight earnings of the U.S. fleet from both shipping U.S. exports and carriage of cargoes in foreign countries, as well as the port expenditures abroad incurred by the U.S. fleet in earning those revenues. The main source for this information is form BE-30, which covers revenues from exports and from charter hire and expenses in foreign countries. It also contains information on inbound cargoes that helps to sort out the import freight bill between U.S. and foreign operators.

The number of U.S. carriers, or operators, is relatively small, fewer than 50. These carriers operate mainly as fleet or line operators or as tanker operators. It is believed the coverage of U.S. carriers is comprehensive. It can be seen from Table 5-6 (above) that the freight earnings of the U.S. fleet have scarcely changed during the 1980s and that the associated port expenditures have averaged only about 60 percent of revenues (including freight on cross-trade: that is, carriage of freight among foreign countries abroad by U.S. fleet). The U.S. fleet is reported to carry less than 20 percent of U.S. exports, and it would require an intensive study of the basic data to determine whether the low ratio is in the nature of the activities of the U.S. fleet or results from the estimating procedures. International shipping and freight activities yielded net receipts of about $1.5 billion to the U.S. balance-of-payments accounts.

Transportation by air has clearly become a major factor in the U.S. balance of payments, as shown in Table 5-6. For foreign airlines coming to the United States, relevant data are collected on form BE-36, which is filed by 80-85 percent of relevant airlines. Import freight is derived from this form, but Census Bureau data may also be used. The quantity data shown in the form can be used for cross-checking against Census Bureau data, and an annual check is made to determine coverage based on weight information. The BE-36 form is the prime source for aircraft port expenditures in the United States ($5.4 billion in 1988). These port expenditures relate primarily to the transportation of U.S. and foreign travelers, and the information on passenger fares paid or received is collected as part of the information on travel (described below). The combined total of U.S. payments to foreign airlines for freight and passengers was $9.8 billion in 1988 (see Table 5-6), and this was partially offset by port expenditures receipts of $5.4 billion (which relate essentially to passenger fares).

International receipts and payments by U.S. airline operators are reported on form BE-37. The coverage of this report is believed to be comprehensive, since there are few international operators. U.S. air carriers derive comparatively little from freight earnings ($1.4 billion in 1988), but they have larger revenues from carrying foreign passengers ($8.9 billion in 1988). The latter figure is obtained from data collected in connection with the travel estimates. Offsetting these revenues, the U.S. airlines spent $4.8 billion in foreign ports in 1988. Also, aircraft leasing to foreign airlines earns a substantial amount for U.S. carriers. (The passenger fare figures are net of interline settlements between U.S. and foreign carriers.) Since the coverage of the airline operators is believed to be comprehensive, any shortcomings in the data entered in the U.S. accounts would result from faulty reporting rather than from the estimating procedures used by BEA. In particular, there seems to be no basis for a systematic bias on the side of either receipts or payments.

There are a number of other smaller elements in the shipping account that require special treatment. One is pipeline freight from Canada, as some Canadian pipelines run partly through U.S. territory. Another is traffic across the Great Lakes, which is part of the ocean transportation account. For surface traffic, information is obtained from railroad companies on freight carried across land borders, and estimates are made for freight car rentals on the basis of the number of cars being rented and the rates paid. A sizable problem exists for the measurement of the earnings of U.S. truckers from hauling freight within Canada or Mexico and the corresponding earnings of foreign truckers in the United States. No data have ever been obtained from U.S. truckers. There are differences between U.S. and Canada in the treatment of payments to truckers involved in cross-border hauling, with the U.S. side counting inland freight paid in Canada as part of the value of U.S. imports, and Canadians counting inland freight in the United States as part of transportation (freight) payments. The amounts involved are large: the Census Bureau began collecting c.i.f.–f.o.b. data on imports by truck in July 1989; Canada began to do the same in 1991.

With additional funding, BEA plans to develop an improved method of covering overland freight payments and receipts for Canada and Mexico. One possibility is to treat such transportation payments analogously to air freight—that is, as covering the cost of delivering goods from the shipping point to the destination in the bordering country. This would be counter to the present definition of export valuation, which, in principle, counts freight costs within the exporting country as part of the value of goods, rather than a service element. However, the suggested change seems to make sense if it can be reconciled with other relevant data and if the bordering countries agree to such a reformulation. It might then be possible to amend the shipping documents to give the necessary information on transportation costs.

Travel and Tourism

The travel accounts in the balance of payments comprise expenditures by U.S. residents as travelers in foreign countries and on foreign airlines or other means of transportation and receipts from nonresident travelers in the United States for their expenditures within the United States as well as their fares paid to U.S. transportation companies. As can be seen in Table 5-5 (above), these receipts and expenditures are much larger than those for any other service category, and they will probably grow rapidly in line with the generally buoyant condition of the travel industry as a whole. However, in many respects the quality of the data in this sector of the accounts is less than robust. There are three major subdivisions of the travel category that require individual statistical treatment: air travel overseas, travel with Canada, and travel with Mexico.

Air Travel Overseas   Overseas air travel is the largest component of international travel, accounting for about two-thirds of both receipts and payments.   Collecting data covering either U.S. residents traveling abroad or foreigners traveling to the United States has been one of the perennial problem areas in the balance-of-payments accounts.   The basic concept is fairly simple: information on the number of U.S. residents traveling abroad, by principal destination, is available from the Immigration and Naturalization Service (INS), and therefore it is only necessary to obtain information on their length of stay and average expenditures per day. Similarly, data are available from the INS on the number of non-residents arriving by air from abroad, and this information can be combined with data on length of stay and daily expenditure rate. The difficulty is finding a way to obtain information on length of stay and expenditures (together with other information) from travelers, since there is no mandatory requirement that travelers supply such information to the government.

For a long time, the Commerce Department, through BEA and its predecessor agencies, and with the help of the Customs Service, distributed a questionnaire card to a sample of arriving passengers.   The U.S. travelers were requested to complete the card and mail it in as soon as possible, giving information on their foreign travel expenditures, itinerary, etc.   Foreign travelers were requested to mail in the card when their trip to the U.S. was completed.   Response rates to this questionnaire survey were very low and declining, and the coverage of information was limited to the essential needs of the balance-of-payments accounts.   Beginning with the second quarter of 1984, the U.S. Travel and Tourism Administration (USTTA) of the Commerce Department took over the task of distributing a more extensive questionnaire and developing a procedure that would raise the response rate.

The questionnaire that is now distributed is the Survey of International Air Travelers Departing the United States.   It is intended to serve the interests of the tourist industry in general, as well as the statistical needs of BEA.   For balance-of-payments purposes, there are several key items: for foreign travelers to the United States, their country, length of U.S. stay, and expenditures in the United States by type; for U.S. residents traveling abroad, number of nights outside the United States, principal places visited and length of stay, and estimated amount to be spent outside the United States by type.   In both cases, data on fares paid are also collected and the questionnaire shows which airline and which flight is being surveyed.   The technique used by USTTA is to seek agreements from airlines to pass out these cards to all passengers on selected flights, to collect them from passengers who choose to complete them, and to return them to USTTA. At present all 7 U.S. airlines that operate overseas do hand out cards, and 35 of 60 foreign airlines do so, covering about 80 percent of passengers carried on foreign airlines.

A random sample of flights departing the United States in each time period is selected by USTTA, and cards are sent to the participating airline for distribution on those flights. It should be noted that an important problem in this system is that the U.S. travelers are requested to estimate their expenditures abroad *before* they have made any foreign expenditures. The actual compilation of the data is contracted to an organization in San Diego, California. For each quarterly period, BEA receives a computer tape with the information for the period and prepares all the estimates of expenditures and receipts for the air travel account from these sample data. BEA uses these estimates for the balance-of-payments accounts and makes them available to USTTA as well.

In 1988 about 200,000 cards were handed out on planes, and about 50 percent were turned in and sent for tabulation. Of the 100,000 cards returned, USTTA found about 70,000 were usable for its purposes. BEA found useful information for the balance-of-payments accounts on about 37,000 cards, of which 17,000 were returned by foreign visitors and 20,000 by U.S. residents. In 1988 the number of foreign visitors carried by the airlines was 12,493,000, and the number of U.S. overseas travelers was 14,529,000, so the usable cards represented about one-tenth of 1 percent of U.S. international airline travel. Although that coverage seems small, it is considerably larger than the sample obtained under the earlier BEA procedure. Moreover, it is possible to test the reliability of the sample results by comparing the reported daily expenditure rates and fares to those estimated independently by industry researchers on travel costs and airfares and those estimated by researchers in other countries. Some of these tests are applied by BEA before arriving at the published estimates, and BEA also attempts to detect and eliminate extreme data.

The shift from the BEA system of collecting data on air travel to the USTTA system resulted in a major shift in the levels of receipts and payments and a considerable shift in the net result; see Table 5-7. For the travel account, receipts and payments were each raised by over $7 billion in the 1984-1987 period, with the result of raising net payments by $800 million to $1.8 billion in 1984 through 1986, but with no net change in the account in

TABLE 5–7 Differences in Data on International Travel Account
From Old and New Surveys (in billions of dollars)

Survey	Year			
	1984	1985	1986	1987
BEA card survey				
Travel				
Receipts	10.9	11.2	12.5	14.8
Payments	15.0	16.0	17.3	20.5
Net	−4.1	−4.8	−4.8	−5.7
Passenger Fares				
Receipts	3.6	3.6	4.2	5.4
Payments	7.0	7.9	7.5	8.8
Net	−3.4	−4.3	−3.3	−3.4
USTTA card survey				
Travel				
Receipts	17.8	17.9	20.5	23.5
Payments	22.7	24.5	26.0	29.2
Net	−4.9	−6.6	−5.5	−5.7
Passenger Fares				
Receipts	4.0	4.4	5.5	6.9
Payments	5.9	6.7	6.8	7.4
Net	−1.9	−2.3	−1.3	−0.5
Travel difference, net	−0.8	−1.8	−0.7	0
Fare difference, net	1.5	2.0	2.0	2.9
Combined difference, net	0.7	0.2	1.3	2.9

SOURCE: Data from *Survey of Current Business*, June 1988 and June 1989.

1987. However, the figures for passenger fares were raised on the
receipt side and lowered on the payments side, leading to an addition to net receipts of nearly $3 billion in 1987. These changes
imply large increases in estimated daily expenditures on both sides
of the account, together with a significant shift in average fares
paid by foreigners traveling on U.S. airlines (an increase in fares
received) and U.S. residents traveling on foreign airlines (a decrease in fares paid). No analysis has yet explored the reasons for
the changes in the results yielded by the two data collection methods.

Clearly, there are many possibilities of gaps and biases in the
new procedure, but there is also some degree of safeguard against
extreme errors. One safeguard is the continuity of the actual
count of travelers to and from the United States by air. That
particular data source has been consistent over many years. An-

other safeguard is the expectation of consistency over time in the average daily expenditures being reported, allowing for differences in different destinations or residences of travelers and for changes in price levels and exchange rates. Nonetheless, there is some question of whether the sampling procedure does result in consistent and reliable expenditure data, since some large abnormalities, in fact, have shown up.

The BEA procedure for expanding a sample of returns by U.S. travelers to an estimated universe is fairly detailed. BEA receives information on the cards returned from particular flights and has data on the number of passengers on that flight. BEA proceeds to use the sample from these flights to generate total data for all flights to that destination. BEA has data for the total number of U.S. travelers to that destination in the period being covered and expands the average expenditure data from the sample to the total for that destination on the basis of total U.S. travel traffic to that destination. BEA also has information on the breakdown of travelers between U.S. residents and others so that the correct population allocation can be closely approximated. In practice, a number of considerable difficulties must be overcome. One problem is that in the random sampling of the flights chosen by USTTA to receive cards there are episodes of underrepresentation or overrepresentation of particular destinations. Another problem is that cards are often returned with only some data: the missing data items are treated implicitly as if the reply matched the average for completed cards, possibly causing an overstatement of the coverage of the sample, though not necessarily affecting the estimates. Still another problem arises when a U.S. traveler visits several destinations in addition to the first destination of record. In that case, BEA uses the data on nights spent (or expected to be spent) at each destination to prorate the total expenditures for each destination. Allowance is made for differences in likely costs in each destination (based on data from returns by travelers who only visited one destination), but the precision of the data for individual countries, except for the most popular destinations, is clearly questionable. The data on a regional basis (for example, Europe, Asia, and Latin America) are presumably not much affected, although the estimates made by U.S. travelers under this system may have some unknown bias.

BEA has reported wide quarterly variations in the daily expenditure rates for particular destinations for which there are no explanations. However, as noted, the switch from the BEA-administered survey to the USTTA system resulted in large increases in both receipts and payments. Given the weaknesses in the BEA procedure, probably some large changes could be expected, but a test for possible biases in the new system and a detailed review of the estimated daily expenditure rates would certainly help to shore up the credibility of the expenditure data. There are similar problems when dealing with expenditures in the United States by foreign air travelers, and here, too, a test of the consistency of daily expenditures data would seem to be in order. However, these travelers do report on the basis of their *actual* expenditures.

As noted above, the questionnaire cards are also used to derive data on average fares paid by U.S. and foreign travelers. These average fares are combined with data available to BEA on the nationalities of travelers and the ownership of airlines to derive estimates of total fares paid by U.S. travelers to foreign airlines and by foreign travelers to U.S. airlines. The average fare data derived from the cards have not been checked for consistency with generally available data on air fares. Such a check might be worth doing on a spot basis for a sample of flights for which BEA would have specific information. One major difficulty reported by BEA is that the necessary data on the number of travelers by nationality and airline, provided by Department of Transportation, are very late in arriving, so the published fare data for the most recent two to four quarters are extrapolations based on earlier data. Also, the fare data received from cards for U.S. airlines alone, or for foreign airlines alone, yield questionable results, given what is known about air fares in general, so that the two data sets are merged to smooth out the result. This result also suggests some difficulties in the sampling process.

Travel With Canada For data on overland travel to and from Canada, the standard procedure for some years has been that BEA, through the Customs Service, carries out a questionnaire card survey of U.S. residents returning from Canada, and Statistics Canada surveys Canadians returning from the United States. The agencies then exchange the data on expenditures and length of stay, to be combined with data on the number of border crossings. This system seemed to be efficient and adequate, but the Canadians decided that they wanted a wider range of information on the expenditures of U.S. travelers in Canada and that the number of travelers covered on the U.S. side was insufficient. Starting in 1990, Statistics Canada has also been covering U.S. travel in Canada by giving questionnaires to Americans entering Canada and asking that they be mailed back, in Canada, before the traveler returns to the United States. The results will be made available to BEA. It remains to be seen what the new system will reveal and whether any revisions of the older data will be needed.

Travel With Mexico To cover most U.S. overland travel in Mexico, BEA uses a card (handed out by the Customs Service according to a program designed by BEA) covering U.S. travelers returning across the border. It is assumed that nearly all such travel takes place within a 3-mile wide border area. The INS provides data on the number of border crossings. For this segment of travel, the statistical routine is similar to the sampling technique for Canada, described above. The data on border travel is supplemented by data collected by the Bank of Mexico from U.S. travelers who travel farther than 3 miles into Mexico. The resulting estimates are supplied to BEA. There is, however, no procedure for checking the validity of the information provided.

For data on travel by Mexicans in the United States, BEA depends entirely on estimates developed by the Bank of Mexico. These estimates are based on personal interviews with returning visitors conducted by representatives of the Bank of Mexico. There is no independent check on these travel expenditure estimates.

FINANCIAL SERVICES AND EDUCATIONAL AND MEDICAL TRANSACTIONS

Financial Services

The rapid growth of the international activities of banks and other financial institutions and the introduction of new financial instruments and new services performed for investors and borrowers should result in a considerable escalation of the fees and commissions earned by resident financial institutions from nonresidents and in payments for services performed by foreign institutions for U.S. residents. In practice, however, it has been proved very difficult to establish procedures for obtaining information on international receipts and payments for financial services. This is not only a U.S. problem—most countries are having similar problems. As shown in Table 5-2 (above), the coverage of U.S. receipts for financial services was improved in the mid-1980s, and the level of such receipts has risen slowly to nearly $4 billion. Nearly one-half of the amount now recorded as receipts for financial services had been entered earlier as part of portfolio income receipts. Much work remains to be done before the coverage of financial services can be considered to be comprehensive.

At present, the major element in financial fees is the commissions generated in connection with transactions in securities between U.S. and foreign residents. The principal data on the turnover in these transactions are provided by the monthly Treasury S forms, which show purchases and sales, for an extended list of countries, in U.S. bonds, U.S. equities, foreign bonds, and foreign equities. The amounts reported in the S forms include the value of the securities and fees and commissions. Until recently, no effort was made to adjust the capital flow data by subtracting an estimate of the implicit services component. At present, the S form data are adjusted for fees and commissions estimated by BEA before being entered in the capital accounts.

To estimate the services component of securities transactions, BEA takes into account many aspects of the trades taking place: the nature of the security and the market where traded, the residence of the transactors, the size and other characteristics of the reported trades (for example, separating new issues and redemptions from trading in the secondary market), and the changes in the fee structure that are occurring. Information on fee structures is kept up to date by the use of a variety of published sources and discussions with market participants. For foreigners purchasing U.S. securities, separate fee structures are developed for each type of security, and separate account is taken of trade in U.S. government issues for which the fee may take the form of a markup on purchases. Fees paid on sales of new U.S. issues in foreign markets are also calculated. In short, BEA attempts to develop the estimates carefully. For U.S. trading in foreign securities, it is assumed that most transactions are effected abroad, and an estimated fee paid to foreign financial institutions is deducted from the gross trading prices reflected in the S form data.

There are many peculiarities of the fee structures—such as intercompany trading to adjust inventories or wholesale trading of certain kinds—that must be taken into account in constructing the fee structure applicable to these trades. In addition, there remains the difficulty that the S form data system is not capturing many kinds of transactions under present market conditions, such as ready direct access by investors to foreign markets and increased activity in these markets of mutual funds or pension funds that may by-pass the usual financial intermediaries. To the extent that portfolio capital flow data are deficient, there is also a deficiency in estimating the fees connected with such trading.

Difficult though it is to develop estimates for fees and commissions connected with transactions in securities, there are much greater obstacles in doing so for the various kinds of financial services performed by commercial banks. Certain kinds of bank fees can be covered fairly easily (though not with great confidence) because data on the volume of business are available or can be estimated—including fees on acceptances and on commercial and standby letters of credit, commitment fees from potential borrowers, and charges for collections. In all these cases a fee structure can be established by consultations with a sample of large banks. The situation is much more difficult, however, for other important types of transactions—including foreign exchange trading, fees related to the rescheduling or renegotiation of loans, and syndication fees.

For foreign exchange trading, it is believed that nearly all trading in foreign exchange for U.S. customer accounts takes place in markets abroad, and any fees that are earned are booked to the foreign branches of the U.S. bank or broker. Most trading in the U.S. market is believed to be resident-to-resident, so no international fee payment is involved. Consequently, there is no balance-of-payments entry in the United States for earnings on foreign exchange trading. In principle, the accounts of the countries in which the trading occurs should be picking up a financial services receipt that, from the U.S. point of view, is part of the revenue of a direct investment establishment abroad. This is an illustration of the difficulty of comparing data on specific services transactions across countries.

For fees related to loan reschedulings or the conduct of financial deals (for example, takeover bids) that involve many kinds of services, the complexity of the internal organization of major financial institutions creates barriers to the extraction of the pieces of the transaction that can be accounted for as fees earned from nonresidents. Even when that can be done, the fees may be parceled out arbitrarily between the U.S. and foreign components of the organization, confusing the national residency basis for international data collection.

In addition to sorting out the relevant data from these complex operations, there are other kinds of transactions and transactors that are not now covered by any data collection—including the business of U.S.-resident foreign banks with nonresidents, certain major operations of investment bankers or merchant banks, income of banks' custody or trust departments, and fees charged for financial consulting.

There are serious definitional and theoretical problems connected with trading in financial assets that are under consideration in the context of the revision of the U.N. systems of national accounts and the revision of the IMF *Balance of Payments Manual* on balance-of-payments accounting. These considerations may lead to further modifications of the distinctions between capital gains, investment income, and returns for the provision of financial services. Some convention is likely to be adopted that will come to terms with the kinds of accounts maintained by financial institutions. Other difficulties that need to be overcome arise from the complexity of these operations and of the organization of financial institutions. BEA is currently studying the problems of collecting data on noninterest income of U.S. financial firms and has requested funding for fiscal 1992 to develop a survey to collect such information.

Medical Services Receipts

Estimates for U.S. receipts for medical services are based on a special informal inquiry conducted in 1985, in which hospital administrators at medical centers and university hospitals were asked to analyze their records to determine how many of their patients were nonresidents and to provide data on average hospital costs and on associated physicians' fees. The hospitals covered were estimated to account for about two-thirds of the medical treatment services for foreigners, and the reported totals were raised by 50 percent to reflect the missing one-third. It was also estimated that about 10 percent of the gross foreign payments for medical care was paid by U.S. charitable or other sources.

The estimates prepared for 1985 were carried back to 1981 and are being carried forward, based essentially on changes in relevant costs as measured in the Consumer Price Index. There has not been a repeated attempt to collect data from hospital administrators, primarily because the necessary records identifying the nationality of patients are very difficult to obtain and analyze, so that an effort of this magnitude cannot be undertaken frequently. Although the apparent magnitude of the receipts (about $550 million annually) would not seem to justify a more intensive effort, the 1985 effort is becoming increasingly dated as a basis for current estimates. In the future, BEA may want to consider investigating whether questions on sales of medical services to foreign patients can be added to existing surveys of health care providers. There are no similar data for medical expenditures abroad by U.S. residents. It is believed that the amount is not large, and it would be extremely difficult, in any case, to arrive at a satisfactory estimate.

Education Services

As shown in Tables 5-2, 5-3, 5-4 (above), the introduction of estimates for expenditures by foreign students in the United States resulted in a significant increase (over $4 billion in 1988) in services receipts. These estimates are developed by BEA from several sources (for a detailed description of the methodology used, see *Survey of Current Business* [June 1989:58]). Statistics on the population of foreign students at U.S. institutions of higher learning are developed by the Institute for International Education, including considerable detail about the characteristics of the population. Estimates of expenditures for tuition and room and board come through the U.S. Department of Education and are refined by BEA to match the profile of the foreign student population. Data on living expenses are derived from Bureau of Labor Statistics budget data. Some of this gross expenditure figure is offset elsewhere in the international accounts to allow for financing received by foreign students from U.S. private and public sources and for earnings by the students.

A similar process is used to estimate the much smaller amount of expenditures abroad by U.S. students. Again, a student population figure is obtained through the Institute for International Education. Estimates of expenditures per student come from U.S. institutions that are the sponsors of most of the foreign study programs. Estimates of living expenses abroad are based on data on living costs abroad. The coverage of U.S. students abroad is smaller than the coverage for foreign students in the United States, and BEA makes estimates for nonresponse cases. The coverage of U.S. study abroad is narrowly confined to those students who receive academic credit from a U.S. institution. There is no coverage of the large population of students following independent casual courses; some of their expenditures are included in the tourist expenditure and fare estimates.

LIMITATIONS OF THE DATA

Although the coverage and accuracy of the data on U.S. international services transactions have been improved in recent years, the considerable range in the quality of the data now available warrants significant additional attention.

A major concern about international services data is the difficulty of developing a complete sampling frame. BEA can use the press or other publicity avenues to call to the attention of the public the existence of the reporting requirements and especially to bring to the attention of businesses that may be participants in the services transactions the importance of accurate and comprehensive U.S. international services data. To enhance the usefulness and reliability of the data, BEA needs to work closely with industry representatives and trade associations in developing new inquiries, conferring with them on kinds of records that are available in firms and the kinds of information that can and cannot be reported. This should be done because complete and consistent reporting of transactions depends on the manner in which records are kept by respondents as well as clear and uniform understanding of the types of transactions to be included. BEA should also conduct periodic reviews of the quality of the incoming data to assure their quality. Cooperation from the services industries in providing accurate and timely information is critical to enhancing the usefulness of data on U.S. international services transactions.

Another concern relates to the fact that the size and complexity of services transactions are growing, requiring constant effort just to keep up with more or less routine development. This leaves little opportunity for new initiatives. Additional efforts are needed to improve concepts and methodologies, especially to determine, by sector, how trade in services should be measured, develop appropriate sampling frames and sample sizes, and refine survey questionnaires. There is also need to broaden coverage to reach new respondents and new services and to produce estimates providing greater detail by industry. Exemption levels also need to be reviewed because the present exemption level is adversely affecting the validity of some of the data being sought. Other limitations pertaining to specific services data are discussed below.

TRANSACTIONS BETWEEN AFFILIATED PARTIES OF MULTINATIONAL CORPORATIONS

The most reliable U.S. international services data appear to be those derived from long-standing mandatory surveys of multilateral corporations, covering intracorporate service receipts and payments. As indicated in Table 5-1 (above), revisions in intracorporate data for royalties, fees, and other services have been relatively small. Nonetheless, given the present interest in data on international services, there are inadequate detailed breakdowns of the types of services between affiliated parties, and more precision is required in defining royalties, fees, and charges for the use of intangible property.

Also, although the reporting systems for these transactions are well developed, there are some reasons for concern. Most important is the less than satisfactory compliance by filers with the reporting requirements, especially by certain U.S. affiliates of foreign firms in the United States. When there are increasing delays in filing reports, the blow-up procedures used by BEA involve more potential error and larger revisions between preliminary and final estimates. Part of the problem of tardy returns may reflect the rather demanding questionnaires, which represents a formidable reporting burden. To a large extent, the details of the questionnaires, in turn, reflect the rising interests in aspects of the operations of the multinational corporations that are not covered by the balance-of-payments accounts.

OTHER PRIVATE SERVICES, UNAFFILIATED

Great strides have been made by BEA in recent years in improving coverage of other services and in covering services that were previously not covered. The new mandatory reporting requirements have helped. Nonetheless, the present exemption levels for some services are so high that some types of transactions (for example, legal services) are substantially underreported or simply not represented.

In addition, in the specialized survey on royalties and fees with nonaffiliated foreign persons, which covers services for which there are many widely dispersed potential filers and for which individual transactions are typically small, omissions are possible. The estimates now being published seem low on both the receipts and payments sides. The less than satisfactory response rate to this mandatory questionnaire also poses a problem. The other two specialized surveys—on reinsurance and primary insurance and on construction, engineering, architectural, and mining services—cover relatively specific and well-identified industries, and coverage is believed to be reasonably complete. There are technical problems with both surveys, however. In particular, the insurance sector does not have adequate data on insurance claims paid. It is also difficult to separately identify investment activities and services transactions undertaken by insurance companies. Likewise, for the engineering industry, the main problem is the possible duplication of trade data and direct investment data. Some of these definitional problems are currently being reviewed under the U.N.'s efforts on the system of national accounts.

TRADITIONAL SERVICES: SHIPPING AND TOURISM

There are classic problems with the data on shipping and tourism. In the case of the shipping account, the identification of the "U.S. fleet" by residence of operator is difficult, although the number of potential filers is small. It is also extremely difficult to check the data being reported as port expenditures abroad. Similar obstacles exist for ascertaining the accuracy of freight earnings, especially in cross-trades. For freight payments to foreign carriers, however, the existence of both c.i.f. and f.o.b. valuations of imports helps to confine any error within reasonable limits.

There is the possibility of major errors or biases in the travel account, in which major revisions of expenditures and fares have been made in recent years. The samples used to establish levels for land expenditures and fares are small; there is no assurance of consistency of the data collected from the respondent; and there is also no standard procedure to monitor for biases. In addition, steps are needed to revise the present questionnaire so as to present the balance-of-payments data up front, rather than buried in a rather lengthy inquiry. A better procedure would be to separate the balance-of-payments questions on a separate card, or a detachable part of the card, and urge flight attendants to give more emphasis to having these cards turned in. Since there are serious misgivings about the quality of the tourist and fare data now entering the travel account, benchmarks for daily expenditure levels and average fares can be used to check the validity of the sample responses and guard against major biases or arbitrary quarter-to-quarter or year-to-year variations.

FINANCIAL SERVICES AND EDUCATIONAL AND MEDICAL TRANSACTIONS

For financial services, the main data problem is that there are substantial sectors in the financial industry, and certain kinds of transactions, for which little or no data or estimates are available. To some degree this results from the inherent complexity of the industry and the arbitrariness of the allocations of earnings from the provision of financial services. However, it is clear that BEA does not have adequate resources to conduct the exploratory work needed to form a basis for designing a reporting or estimating system—or even for testing the feasibility of establishing such a system. In view of the growing importance of international sales of financial services by U.S. firms and substantial funds involved, accurate reporting of these transactions will substantially enhance the quality of U.S. international services data. In addition to BEA, the agencies responsible for oversight of the financial system, notably the Treasury Department and the Federal Reserve, should have a role in closely studying this feature of the activities of banks and other financial institutions.

For medical services in the United States purchased by foreigners, the present estimates depend on a single survey in 1985. The quality of current estimates is inevitably affected by the dated information. There is no information on medical expenditures abroad by U.S. residents.

The estimates of expenditures in the United States by foreign students are probably as well done as can be expected, given the inherent difficulty in covering such a diffuse population. There is a possible understatement of expenditures abroad by the floating population of U.S. "students."

RECOMMENDATIONS

Our recommendations for improving data on U.S. international services data are listed in the order of their relative importance, with the most important one listed first.

Recommendation 5-1 Among the international services categories, improvements in data on international financial services should be accorded a high priority. The Bureau of Economic Analysis, the Treasury Department, and the Federal Reserve should work together to develop a clear conceptual framework, as well as effective statistical methods and procedures for collecting the information.

Recommendation 5-2 The Bureau of Economic Analysis should place greater emphasis on increasing the response rates of the mandatory surveys.

Recommendation 5-3 For the travel accounts, a study should be made of the feasibility of introducing methods other than the current questionnaire card surveys or of obtaining improved responses from the present method.

Recommendation 5-4 For information on international sales and purchases of services by affiliates, beyond that required for the balance-of-payments tabulations, the Bureau of Eco-

nomic Analysis should develop separate and expressly designed surveys, in coordination with the service sectors concerned, to obtain the additional data. Burdening the existing system with additional details would increase time lags in reporting, reduce the quality of responses, and weaken the basic data requirements of the balance-of-payments accounts.

Recommendation 5-5   To maintain and enhance the quality of services data, the Bureau of Economic Analysis should allocate additional resources to improving the analytical usefulness of the data. BEA should also enhance its capacity to analyze the statistics compiled and to present the analyses in ways that contribute to public understanding of this growing component of U.S. international transactions. At the same time, public access to detailed information should be as free as possible. Efforts to establish comparability with Census Bureau industry data should be encouraged.

Recommendation 5-6   The Bureau of Economic Analysis should be given the authority to establish appropriate exemption levels for reporting requirements for various services categories consistent with the nature of the data to be collected.

Recommendation 5-7   The Bureau of Economic Analysis should take further steps to obtain better information on payments to foreigners for services performed for U.S. residents abroad.

6

International Capital Flows

O_f all the data on U.S. international economic transactions, capital flow statistics are the most subject to errors and gaps. Although the United States collects as much detailed data on its capital flows as any country in the world, the explosion in direct and portfolio investments across U.S. national boundaries in the 1980s outpaced improvements in the statistical system that monitors them. Specifically, the existing system is designed to collect most of the information on international capital flows from a group of large financial intermediaries and corporations. Yet the integration of world financial markets and innovations in electronic and communications technology have greatly increased the number of financial transactors and facilitated new modes of transactions, bypassing traditional financial intermediaries and channels. This change has made it increasingly difficult and costly to capture comprehensive and accurate capital flows under the current reporting systems. In addition, growing numbers of new financial instruments have outstripped the coverage of existing data, further rendering them incomplete and inaccurate.

Efforts to collect accurate and comprehensive information on the rapidly growing capital flows should yield high payoffs in improving the usefulness of existing data on U.S. international transactions because capital flows are of substantial magnitude and are inadequately measured. In fact, over the past decade, values of capital flows surpassed those of trade flows. Information on capital flows is especially needed to examine the extent of internationalization of the U.S. economy; the changing operations of U.S. financial markets; the impact of foreign direct investment on the domestic economy; the incomes on U.S. international investments and net servicing burden on U.S. external indebtedness; and the relationship of flows of foreign capital and U.S. interest and foreign exchange rates. In addition, since net capital flows should match the balance of international transactions in goods and services and transfers (the current account), improved information on capital flows would help illuminate the accuracy of data on the U.S. current account. Improved capital flow data would also contribute to more accurate estimates by the Bureau of Economic Analysis (BEA) of the U.S. international investment position (which measures the value of accumulated stocks of U.S. assets abroad and of foreign assets in the United States).

More important, improvements in data on international capital transactions can improve the preparation of the flow-of-funds accounts and the balance sheets of the U.S. economy (both published by the Federal Reserve). The flow-of-funds accounts detail the sources and uses of savings in the U.S. economy by sector and by type of transaction. Sectors include households; nonfinancial businesses (corporate and noncorporate); state and local governments; the federal government; foreigners; and financial institutions, including banks, savings and loan associations, life insurance companies, and pension funds. The account for each sector shows changes in financial assets and liability items, such as deposits, mortgages, loans, open-market papers, federal government securities, and bonds. Along with the national income and product accounts published by BEA, the flow-of-funds accounts provide an integrated set of financial accounts that are used to analyze economic developments in the United States. U.S. balance-of-payments data are major inputs to the flow-of-funds accounts; that information is modified and supplemented with other data on international transactions from bank regulatory reports and the Treasury International Capital (TIC) reporting system to make it compatible with the sector and instrument classifications used in the flow-of-funds accounts. The foreign data are also used for estimating aggregate levels of outstanding debt by sector and measures of national net worth. At the Federal Reserve, the flow-of-funds accounts have been useful in assessing the impact of monetary policy and the general financial conditions of the various sectors. The domestic nonfinancial debt aggregate measure that is monitored by the Federal Reserve's Federal Open Market Committee is derived from the flow-of-funds accounts. The accounts are also widely used for a variety of purposes in the academic and business communities and elsewhere in the government. Flow-of-funds publications include the quarterly *Flow of Funds Accounts*, the semiannual *Balance Sheets for the U.S. Economy*, and the annual *Financial Assets and Liabilities*.[1]

DATA ON CAPITAL FLOWS: KEY FEATURES

Capital flows refer to transactions in financial assets between U.S. residents and residents of foreign countries. Financial assets include loans, bank deposits, drafts, acceptances, notes, government and private debt and equity securities, and intracompany accounts for the financing of direct investments.

There are two major types of capital flow transactions: official and private. U.S. official capital flows include changes in the reserves of U.S. monetary authorities in monetary gold, foreign exchange, special drawing rights at the International Monetary Fund, and loans and credits to foreigners by U.S. government agencies. Official capital flows are estimated quarterly by BEA on the basis of data provided to it by Treasury, the Federal Reserve System, and the International Monetary Fund (IMF). Changes in foreign official assets in the United States can take place through transactions in U.S. Treasury securities, other U.S. government obligations, and bank deposits, as well as U.S. corporate bonds and stocks. BEA estimates these transactions quarterly on the basis of data provided by Treasury and a number of other U.S. government agencies that possess relevant information (Bureau of Economic Analysis, 1990c).

Private capital flows encompass direct investment and portfolio investment undertaken by both U.S. residents abroad and foreigners in the United States. As stated in the International Investment and Trade in Services Survey Act, direct investment is defined as "the ownership or control, directly or indirectly, by one person of 10 per centum or more of the voting securities of an incorporated business enterprise or an equivalent interest in an unincorporated business enterprise," and portfolio investment is defined to include "any international investment which is not direct investment." These definitions conform to the general guidelines provided in the IMF's *Balance-of-Payments Manual*. Direct

---

[1]We appreciate the information on the flow-of-funds accounts provided by Albert M. Teplin of the staff of the Federal Reserve Board.

investment reflects an investor's interest in and influence over the management of an enterprise (Bureau of Economic Analysis, 1990c:84). All investment transactions between parent organizations and their foreign affiliates are direct investment flows. Portfolio investment primarily refers to ownership of financial securities, broadly defined to include sales and purchases of securities and amounts of outstanding claims and liabilities reported by banks and nonbanking concerns.

In the balance-of-payments accounts, incomes on direct and portfolio investment are reported in the current account; exchanges in financial assets between U.S. and foreign residents are measured in the capital account. The value of accumulated stocks of U.S. assets abroad and of foreign assets in the United States— resulting from capital flows in and out of this country over time— is annually compiled and published by BEA in the statement of U.S. international investment position.

The responsibility of gathering data on private capital flows is divided between BEA and Treasury.[2] BEA collects information on direct investment and Treasury, using Federal Reserve banks as agents, compiles data on portfolio investment. The two data systems have evolved together over the years and reflect a high degree of collaboration between the two agencies. Various exemption levels are applied to different types of transactions. Since the 1980s—with the influx of foreign direct investment in U.S. industries covering manufacturing, wholesaling, retailing, as well as banking, securities, finance, and other services, together with the surge in foreign portfolio investment in U.S. securities during the same period—the pressure on both BEA and Treasury to collect adequate information on these burgeoning transactions has increased.

DATA SYSTEMS FOR PRIVATE CAPITAL FLOWS

DIRECT INVESTMENT

BEA (and its predecessor, the Office of Business Economics) has been collecting data on U.S. direct investment abroad and foreign direct investment in the United States since the 1920s. It has gradually increased coverage and moved from voluntary reporting by enter-

---

[2]Foreign income statistics compiled from tax returns can be found in the *Statistics of Income* data series published by the Internal Revenue Service of the Department of the Treasury.

prises to more comprehensive mandatory reporting. Current legal authority for the collection of direct investment data is provided by the International Investment and Trade in Services Survey Act.

BEA uses a hierarchy of surveys to cover both U.S. direct investment abroad and foreign investment in the United States. These include benchmark surveys (censuses) at 5-year intervals, as well as annual and quarterly surveys. Benchmark surveys are designed to collect a wide range of information on affiliates' transactions, as well as to update the universe of the database from which annual and quarterly surveys of smaller samples are drawn.

BEA defines a direct investor as a person who has a 10 percent or more ownership in a business enterprise located in a foreign country. This definition applies to both outward investment by U.S. residents and foreigners' inward investment in the United States. Separate surveys are conducted for U.S. direct investment abroad and foreign direct investment in the United States. Information collected from direct investment surveys includes not only data required by the U.S. balance-of-payments accounts, but also those on affiliates' operations such as their production, sales, trade, employment, financial statements, technology, and external financing (Bureau of Economic Analysis, 1990c).

Benchmark surveys are comprehensive and cover the universe of filers; exemption levels are minimal. These mandatory surveys cover information on a direct investor's share of income, distributed earnings, and capital gains and losses of its foreign affiliates; interest, royalties, fees, allocated expenses, and other charges; and the changes in a direct investor's equity and debt positions in its foreign affiliates. In addition to these balance-of-payments data, benchmark surveys cover financial structures and operations of parent companies and affiliates, including information on balance sheets and income statements, composition of external financing, production, employment, and intracompany trade, as well as technology, property, plant, and equipment. At the time this report was in print, BEA was tabulating its latest benchmark survey for U.S. direct investment abroad, covering 1989. The most recent available benchmark survey on U.S. direct investment abroad covered the year 1982. For that year, 2,245 U.S. parent corporations filed complete financial and operating data on their own operations, and 18,339 reports on their investment positions and transactions with their foreign affiliates. The most recent benchmark survey of foreign direct investment in the United States was undertaken for 1987. For that year, 8,577 reports were filed by U.S. affiliates of foreign direct investors.

On an annual basis, BEA collects key information on the operations of a sample of parent companies and their affiliates (excluding banks). The annual surveys cover the operational aspects of the affiliates (for example, sales and employment) to supplement the data that enter the balance-of-payments accounts. The results of these surveys are published annually by BEA in detail. For 1988 the survey on U.S. direct investment abroad covered the operations of 9,500 U.S. companies and their affiliates; the one on foreign direct investment in the United States surveyed the operations of 5,500 U.S. affiliates of foreign corporations. Mandatory quarterly surveys cover information required for balance-of-payments purposes. In 1988, 1,300 U.S. parent companies filed 9,100 quarterly reports covering their foreign affiliates, and 3,400 U.S. affiliates of foreign companies filed quarterly reports.

The universe of direct investors is heavily skewed toward large companies and is also heavily skewed toward investors with ownership percentages of 50 percent or more. For instance, the 10 largest U.S. parent companies, in terms of the assets of foreign affiliates, owned 32 percent of such assets; the 100 largest owned 72.4 percent. Smaller foreign affiliates ($15 million of assets or less) account for 47 percent of the number of affiliates, but only 5 percent of assets. Similarly, in the United States in 1989, majority-owned U.S. affiliates of foreign companies accounted for 72 percent of the total assets of U.S. affiliates of foreign firms (Bezirganian, 1991:80).

All this survey information is confidential. Data are published only in aggregate form. When one or two filers account for the dominant share of the information in a data cell, the cell is suppressed. "Secondary suppressions" also are imposed to prevent derivation of such cells by subtraction. To augment the content of the information on foreign direct investment in the United States, the Foreign Direct Investment and International Financial Data Improvements Act of 1990 provides that the Census Bureau exchange information with BEA on data collected on business enterprises operating in the United States. This legislative action is necessary because BEA collects information on foreign direct investment in the United States at the enterprise or consolidated level: that is, if a manufacturing company also owns a retail operation, the manufacturing company would file information with BEA, consolidating the retail operations. The Census Bureau, in contrast, collects information (pursuant to its authority under Title 13, U.S. Code) at the establishment level: that is, information on individual plants. BEA, through its access to information in the

Census Bureau's Standard Statistical Establishment List (SSEL), will be able to produce more disaggregated data on foreign direct investment in the United States, facilitating the analysis of the relative share of such investment in the domestic economy at more detailed industry-by-industry establishment levels.

In June 1991, using two new measures, market-value and current-cost estimates, BEA revaluated U.S. foreign direct investment abroad and foreign direct investment in the United States for 1982 through 1989. These new estimates of inward and outward direct investment represent BEA's attempt to put U.S. assets abroad and foreign assets in the United States on a comparable basis. The comparability problem arises because U.S. direct investment abroad is, on average, older than foreign direct investment in the United States. Together with the revaluation of U.S. gold reserves using the market price of gold as a basis, these new estimates resulted in a change in the value of the 1989 U.S. net international investment position from the previously reported –$663.7 billion to –$281.0 billion under the market-value basis, and to –$464.0 billion under the current-cost basis (Bureau of Economic Analysis, 1991a).

BEA publishes and discusses data on direct investment periodically in its monthly *Survey of Current Business* and issues more extensive annual and periodic specialized census data in separate publications.

PORTFOLIO INVESTMENT DATA

The Treasury International Capital (TIC) reporting system, with Federal Reserve banks serving as agents for the Treasury Department, provides monthly and quarterly data on holdings of, and on transactions in, portfolio investment: investment in the forms of debt instruments between unaffiliated parties, equity positions of less than 10 percent, and other claims and liabilities (Bureau of Economic Analysis, 1990c:14). Treasury uses a number of TIC forms to capture sales and purchases of securities and amounts of outstanding claims and liabilities reported by banks and nonbanking concerns: the TIC S forms cover securities transactions; TIC B forms, banks' own claims and liabilities and custodial transactions; and TIC C forms, nonbanks' assets and liabilities in relation to unaffiliated foreigners, such as foreign trade credit by corporations.

Filing of TIC S forms is required on sales and purchases of long-term U.S. and foreign securities (original maturities longer than 1 year). Filers include banks, banking institutions, brokers, dealers, and other persons in the United States who engage in these transactions, as well as corporations that issue Eurobonds directly from their U.S. offices. Monthly reports of sales and purchases are required. Reports must be filed if the total of purchases or sales amounts to $500,000 or more during a given month.

TIC B form filings by U.S. banks, depository institutions, international banking facilities, bank holding companies, brokers, and dealers in the United States report information on loans, advances, and overdrafts; placements of funds; acceptance financing and depositing; and borrowing through repurchase and resale agreements. Also included on the form are operating transactions between U.S. banks and their foreign branches, agencies, and subsidiaries, as well as those between U.S. branches, agencies, and subsidiaries of foreign banks and their parent corporations (excluding their permanent direct investment positions). Depending on the particular institution and form involved, monthly or quarterly reports are required. Banking data are monthly positions as of ends of the month. Reported transactions include both those undertaken for the banks' own accounts and those undertaken for the accounts of their domestic and foreign customers (custodial positions). Reports are required if total claims on, or liabilities to, foreigners are $15 million or more for any month-end closing balance.

Nonbanking businesses are required to file TIC C forms on a quarterly basis. Such businesses include exporters, importers, industrial and commercial firms, some nonbanking financial institutions, and U.S. affiliates of foreign business enterprises. Transactions include financial claims or liabilities (such as deposits in foreign banks or direct borrowings from foreign investors) and commercial claims or liabilities related to the sale of goods and services in normal business operations (for example, trade credits). Direct investment flows are excluded. Reports are required for financial or commercial claims on, or liabilities to, unaffiliated foreigners totalling $10 million or more at the end of the quarter.

According to the Treasury Department, in 1990 approximately 350 institutions filed regular monthly S forms; about 975 filed regular monthly and quarterly B forms; and 475 filed quarterly C forms. TIC forms are filed with district Federal Reserve banks by banks and banking institutions and with the Federal Reserve Bank of New York by all brokers, dealers, and corporations. The costs to the Federal Reserve banks of collecting the TIC data are borne by their own budgets. The Federal Reserve Bank of New York consolidates the data and makes them available to Treasury for publication in the quarterly *Treasury Bulletin*. The data remain on the Federal Reserve Bank of New York's computer, loaded to databases to which Treasury has access. Treasury, in turn, transmits aggregate TIC data to BEA, which uses the TIC data to estimate portfolio investment income and compile capital flow statistics for the balance-of-payments accounts.

LIMITATIONS OF THE DATA

Under the current reporting systems, data on direct investment appear to provide a reasonably accurate picture of these transactions, although problems remain. Data on portfolio investment, however, are questionable. The latter are particularly affected by the growing numbers of financial transactors and products, as well as intermediaries. In compiling capital flow data, both BEA and Treasury have also encountered growing technical and operational problems. The increasingly complex nature of the transactions and the less than satisfactory compliance by filers have affected the accuracy and timeliness of the data. Despite BEA and Treasury efforts to broaden the data coverage and update filer lists, major data gaps remain.

U.S. DIRECT INVESTMENT ABROAD

Although it is generally acknowledged that data on U.S. direct investment abroad are of high quality, especially in view of the size of the universe to be covered and the complexity of the financial structures of U.S. multinational companies, sizable revisions of quarterly data do occur at times when tardy reports are received and errors detected. According to BEA, it generally does not attempt to expand, or blow up, reported capital flow data to account for late responses because capital flow data tend to be volatile and are subject to sign reversals. However, BEA plans to study the feasibility of including in direct investment capital flows an allowance for late reports, particularly when systematic patterns of late-reported data can be discovered.

Another shortcoming relates to the fact that the wide range of economic and financial data gathered on operations between parent corporations and their affiliates, beyond the balance-of-payments requirements, are not well synthesized and summarized, making them difficult to use and to interpret. In addition, BEA undertakes few in-depth analyses of these data. As a result, the wealth of information collected is not well understood and utilized by the users who could benefit from greater information on changes in U.S. direct investment abroad. In effect, the information BEA collects and publishes on direct investment is not sufficiently well known to either the public or specialists.

Foreign Direct Investment in the United States

Except for transactions undertaken by small investors who may not be familiar with the reporting requirements (especially in real estate transactions), data on foreign direct investment in the United States probably accurately represent the overall trend, since most large acquisitions or new investments in the United States by foreigners are well publicized and are monitored by BEA. In addition, BEA uses information collected by industry groups to identify incoming direct investment and to broaden mailing lists of filers. On a limited basis, BEA is currently adjusting its data to account for capital flows related to establishment or acquisition of new affiliates by foreign direct investors. Nonetheless, problems persist.

One problem is that compliance with reporting requirements is not as good as it could be. U.S. affiliates of foreign parent companies often fail to respond or to respond fully and often refer inquiries to their foreign parent companies. Late reporting is also a problem. Increased funding provided to BEA to track new inward investments and to pursue cases of noncompliance and inadequate reporting, together with heightened penalties for noncompliance and greater enforcement efforts, should ameliorate the situation. In the case of foreign investment in U.S. real estate, it is suspected that much of it is not captured in the U.S. balance of payments. This is because many of these transactions are in the form of limited partnerships, which are also not captured under the TIC system unless they are listed on the exchanges (Stekler, 1991b).

Another problem relates to the adequacy of data on income on (payments to) foreign direct investment in the United States. While such foreign direct investment rose by $342 billion between 1980 and 1990 (from $124 billion to $466 billion, valued at current costs), income payments related to it did not show an upward trend; they fluctuated between $3 billion and $11 billion during the period. And in 1990 such payments were reported to be less than $2 billion. The trend of these income payments contrasts with that of income receipts from U.S. direct investment abroad. During 1980-1990, U.S. direct investment abroad rose from $385 billion to $598 billion (valued at current costs), or an increase of only $213 billion. Yet income receipts from such investment rose from $37 billion to almost $55 billion during the same period (Bureau of Economic Analysis, 1991d). Although variations between incomes on foreign direct investment in the United States and those on U.S. direct investment abroad can result from differing cyclical conditions in the United States and abroad, as well as from variations in foreign exchange rates, the drastic differences in their magnitudes and trends raise concerns about the underlying causes for the relatively small income payments on foreign direct investment in the United States. Deliberate understatements of incomes by filers (often through transfer-pricing practices) can result in losses of tax revenues to the Treasury Department.

SECURITIES

There appear to be significant gaps in data on securities transactions. Such lacunae also exist in securities reporting in other countries. The main difficulty with both U.S. and foreign data is that the information collected comes primarily from resident financial institutions. In some countries, that process would be adequate, since residents would almost always effect their international portfolio purchases or sales through a resident bank, broker, or dealer, but it is no longer always the case for many countries. Modern communications facilities and the withering away of exchange controls or other official restrictions have made it not only possible, but often quicker and cheaper, for residents of one country to deal directly with markets in another country. In addition, money managers and large institutional investors (such as pension or mutual funds) increasingly maintain their own facilities for conducting business, without dealing with a financial institution that reports on the TIC S forms. In these cases, unless the Federal Reserve Bank of New York contacts the transactors, these transactions are not captured by the existing system. In principle, the S form reporting requirement extends to all U.S. residents whose transactions are above the exemption level in any month, but there is no system for identifying all such residents. Although reports filed by large financial institutions cover many transactions and transactors, given the changing international financial trading environment, the number of filers of monthly reports—about 350—casts doubt that the data fairly represent the cross-border business done by residents, including those removed from the traditional channels of resident financial institutions. According to the Federal Reserve Bank of New York, there is also no assurance that the reported transactions are complete and accurate.

A second difficulty relates to U.S. borrowers' use of Euromarkets. Eurobonds account for most U.S. corporate bonds sold to foreigners. When a U.S. corporation issues securities directly in Euromarkets (usually through underwriters in London), there may be no U.S. financial institutions directly involved (with the possible exception of an affiliated office in Europe), so that reporting of the inflow and subsequent redemption would occur only as a result of direct reporting by the borrower. Although the Federal Reserve Bank of New York or BEA can track these issues when they are well publicized, comprehensive coverage is difficult to obtain. Similarly, domestic borrowers in domestic markets may not know when the resident lender has resold a loan to a foreigner. Although there is a provision for recovering such resales of loans— on the BL-2 form through custodial reporting when the originating lender acts as the loan-servicing agent and a foreign bank is the purchaser—such transactions involving nonbank entities may not be adequately captured.

In addition to these examples of capital inflows that may not be captured, unreported capital outflows pose even greater problems, since it is more difficult to monitor financial activities undertaken abroad by residents. Global studies on capital flows conclude that most countries, including the United States, are better positioned to capture inflows of capital in their statistical frameworks than outflows by residents. (In some countries, not especially the United States, there is also an incentive to hide outflows of funds illegally or to avoid taxes or other restrictions.) The last Treasury Department benchmark survey of U.S. portfolio investment abroad was undertaken during World War II. This raises the concerns about the adequacy of the coverage of U.S. holdings of foreign securities.

A third difficulty with securities data is the proliferation of short-term marketable instruments and derivative instruments such as warrants, options, puts, and calls. These are not ordinarily covered by the TIC S forms, which deal primarily with long-term securities. The S forms cover warrants and options only when the underlying security is a stock or long-term bond. But since data on purchases and sales of these instruments are not disaggregated with purchases and sales of U.S. or foreign bonds, an evaluation of the adequacy of coverage of these transactions is currently not possible. And all other options or warrants are not covered. Although BEA includes margin accounts and profits and losses on

futures trading by foreigners on U.S. futures exchanges in its estimates of U.S. nonbank liabilities to unaffiliated foreigners, U.S.
residents' trading in foreign futures exchanges are not captured by
the TIC system (Stekler, 1991b). In addition, as noted above,
limited partnerships are not adequately covered.

A fourth difficulty—which generally applies to data on U.S.
international transactions and which particularly complicates any
attempt to identify gaps in the reporting of securities—is the con-
fusion of geographical allocations, especially when trading takes
place through offshore centers or foreign financial centers. The
latter often act as intermediaries on behalf of residents of many
countries. In the U.S. data, the geographical identity of the foreign
transactor is simply the address from which, or to which, orders are
placed or transmitted. As a result, when such transactions are
reported, they are often reported as transactions between the United
States and countries with well-developed financial markets, such
as the United Kingdom and Switzerland, instead of the country
that is the ultimate source of foreign funds or the ultimate destination of U.S. funds (Bureau of Economic Analysis, 1990c). Consequently, the U.S. data show the bulk of recorded transactions
for major foreign financial centers, regardless of whether the ultimate buyer or seller actually resides in those locations. In those
foreign financial centers, the statistical offices tend to net out
their foreign-to-foreign transactions on the ground they have no
relation to the economies of those centers, so that it is not possible, in most cases, to rely on data collected by partner countries
as a check on the data available to the home country.

International comparisons are further made difficult by the varying
data definitions used by different countries. For example, there
are sizable discrepancies between U.S. and Japanese data on purchases of U.S. Treasury securities, because the Japanese data include all Japanese purchases of U.S. Treasury securities worldwide while the U.S. data include only U.S. Treasury securities
sold directly to Japan (Stekler, 1991b).

A fifth difficulty with securities data concerns changes taking
place in the institutional and functional arrangements of financial
organizations. One change is the increased complexity of individual organizations: as they develop new techniques and instruments and spread around the world, the responsibility for reporting on U.S. statistical forms becomes decentralized, the actual
locus of a transaction becomes arbitrary, and participation with
institutions headquartered in other countries further obscures the
responsibility for statistical reporting.

BANKING

There are numerous difficulties related to the use of the TIC B forms for banking that can distort the data. A basic problem is that the B form data are end-month positions, which must be converted into flows for use in the balance-of-payments accounts. This means that write-offs or renegotiated balances must be detected and adjusted from the flows, and balances in foreign currencies must be adjusted to reflect changes in the foreign exchange value of the dollar. In practice, however, this is not done in the U.S. accounts because the currency composition is not known. In addition, apparent flows may occur because an address changes from domestic to foreign, or vice versa. All these adjustments can result in large swings in the statistical discrepancies in the balance-of-payments accounts.

Furthermore, although it appears that U.S. banks generally do a conscientious job of reporting under the TIC system, problems arise in dealing with some U.S. affiliates of foreign banks. The problems concern whether the instructions for the forms are always fully understood and acted on properly and whether accounts owned by foreigners in the United States can always be identified as such by reporting banks. It is comparatively simple for a nonresident to acquire a U.S. bank account in the name of a resident or to establish a temporary residence in the United States.

Interbanking business between U.S. and foreign banks seems to be accurately reported, and transactions can be verified with the banking data collected by the Bank for International Settlements from partner banks. However, cross-border banking is increasingly done without the intervention of international banking facilities. This is a gap in the statistics for which banks are not responsible, but it means that reliance on reporting by banks no longer gives the assurance of nearly complete coverage that was assumed in earlier years.

Another change of considerable importance is the growth of direct transactions between nonfinancial lenders and borrowers, with financial intermediaries increasingly acting as agents or arrangers of deals for a fee or commission. This process is partly driven by the tightening of minimum capital standards for internationally active banks by the Basle Committee on Banking Supervision, which indirectly encourages banks to do business in ways that do not appear directly on their balance sheets. Under these circumstances, it is unlikely these transactions are included in the TIC reporting system.

NONBANKING BUSINESSES

Many attempts have been made to broaden the coverage of the TIC C forms and to review the accuracy of reporting for transactions by nonbanking businesses, but the results of efforts to include more respondents or detect significant errors in reporting have been only marginally successful. Current filers are believed to include only a fraction of those that should report. One reason to doubt the effectiveness of the C forms comes from comparing U.S. data on cross-border positions of nonbanks with the data reported by partner-country banks in the Bank for International Settlements (BIS) and IMF accounting frameworks. In September 1990, for example, TIC data on U.S. nonbank financial assets abroad (including bank custodial accounts for nonbanks) amounted to about $65 billion; the data derived from foreign banks as reported by the BIS and IMF show liabilities to U.S. nonbanks of about $250 billion. On the other side of the accounts, the TIC reports that the liabilities of U.S. nonbanks to foreign banks were about $80 billion; the BIS and IMF report that foreign banks' claims on U.S. nonbanks amounted to $235 billion. Although there are differences between the TIC and the BIS and IMF reporting systems in definition and, in particular, in coverage, such sizable discrepancies suggest the need for an examination of the possibility of underreporting in the U.S. data.

CURRENCY FLOWS

Currently, increases in foreign holdings of U.S. currency are not included in the U.S. balance of payments. Yet these holdings represent noninterest bearing obligations of the U.S. government to foreigners. Unreported currency shipments can be related to drug trade, to money brought in and out of the country by tourists, and to money mailed by U.S. residents to relatives abroad. Although Treasury requires persons taking more than $10,000 in currency into or out of the United States to file a Currency and Monetary Investment Report (CMIR) with the Customs Service, compliance and enforcement are far from satisfactory.

On the basis of various surveys of household and business currency holdings, IRS estimates of the magnitude of drug trade, estimates of currency lost or destroyed, and other sources, it has been estimated that as much as one- to two-thirds of U.S. currency outstanding may be held by foreigners, or $85-170 billion. Increases in foreign holdings of U.S. currency were estimated at more than $15 billion in 1990 (Stekler, 1991b). An accurate account of foreign assets in the United States would require that data gaps on the Treasury CMIR, as well as currency flows related to drug trade, tourists, and other transfers, be closed.

INCOMES ON PORTFOLIO INVESTMENT

Unlike data on incomes on direct investment, which are reported by filers, data on incomes on portfolio investment are largely estimated by BEA, on the basis of accumulating stocks derived from Treasury's TIC reports and rates of return on these investments assumed by BEA. Both inadequate data on portfolio investment as filed in the TIC reports and inappropriate rates of return applied by BEA can result in misleading estimates on portfolio investment incomes.

A 1986 study on statistical discrepancies in the world's current account identified portfolio investment incomes as one of the most serious problem areas (International Monetary Fund, 1986a). Reported portfolio investment payments worldwide far exceeded reported portfolio investment receipts. The U.S. transactions account for a large proportion of the world current account transactions. More recently, Federal Reserve and IMF data indicate that the TIC reports underestimated U.S. residents' bank deposits abroad by $80-180 billion at the end of 1988. Using the 3-month Eurodollar interest rates, this implies that U.S. interest earnings were underestimated by $6-14 billion in that year (Stekler, 1990). Furthermore, in estimating income on equities, BEA assumes that income in the current period is the same as in the previous period plus dividends on additions to securities holdings. This methodology cannot yield reliable estimates because it assumes a stock acquired in 1960 is earning the same dividend today as it did three decades ago. Also, the value of holdings on which dividends are calculated is not current because the last benchmark survey of U.S. portfolio investment abroad was undertaken during World War II (Stekler, 1990).

According to the Treasury Department, it is considering conducting a new benchmark survey on U.S. holdings of foreign securities and undertaking a number of research projects to estimate more closely the magnitude and nature of other reporting defects. These projects include an examination of pension funds' offshore purchases of securities, the size of the reporting panel for the TIC C forms and the quality of the nonbanking reports, the volume and nature of currency flows, and effects of synchronization of payments and delivery. These efforts should yield insights into ways of enhancing the accuracy of existing U.S. portfolio investment data and lead to more accurate estimates of incomes from such investments.

RECOMMENDATIONS

Our recommendations for improving U.S. international capital flow data are listed in order of their relative importance, with the most important one listed first.

Recommendation 6-1 Because the existing system for collecting data on international portfolio transactions was developed before the advent of modern electronic and telecommunications technology currently used by growing numbers of transactors, research is needed to explore alternative methods of data collection. Over the long term, the clearing systems for securities, the payments systems for banking transactions, and other clearing channels for nonbanking transactions should be explored as alternative sources of information. Increased automation in trading and clearing systems would facilitate the compilation of data from such sources.

Recommendation 6-2 Research should be performed to develop ways to broaden coverage and to enforce compliance of reporting by filers. For securities transactions, improvements in coverage of U.S. outward investment in foreign securities and transactions by nonfinancial entities are of particular importance. For reporting by banks, the principal research effort should focus on enhancing the timely and accurate reporting of U.S. affiliates of foreign banks. For transactions on nonbanking concerns, improvements in the coverage of activities of the U.S. nonfinancial population, both corporate and personal, are needed. A broadening of the filing of TIC C forms, perhaps through lowering exemption levels for reporting, should also be considered.

Recommendation 6-3 The adequacy of data on official U.S. government international capital transactions should be examined. Official U.S. government international capital transactions are of growing importance, but the myriad forms of transactions in U.S. official reserve assets and other government assets and the involvement of numerous government agencies make them susceptible to inadequate reporting. There have also been few evaluations of government agencies' compliance with reporting requirements.

Recommendation 6-4 The methodology of estimating portfolio investment incomes should be improved, including new methods to measure current values of U.S. securities holdings abroad, as well as other forms of U.S. international financial assets and liabilities. Appropriate rates of return can be developed through close consultations with financial institutions at home and abroad.

Recommendation 6-5 In view of the difficulties of obtaining data on residents' direct purchases or sales of foreign securities, research should be undertaken to explore the feasibility of exchanging data with partner countries. This would require, among other things, the development of universal codes for identifying securities and uniform standards for reporting, as well as common definitions of the residence of the immediate transactor and of the ultimate owner.

Recommendation 6-6 To gauge the effectiveness of the existing reporting systems, "experiments" should be conducted in which capital transactions of various types are earmarked and purposefully injected into the economy and then methodically followed. Follow-up actions could then be taken to determine which transactions are captured by the existing systems.

Recommendation 6-7 The Bureau of Economic Analysis, in cooperation with the Internal Revenue Service of the Treasury Department, should examine the causes of the relatively low income payments on foreign direct investment in the United States.

Recommendation 6-8 Additional efforts are needed to exploit more fully the analytic potential of existing data on U.S. inward and outward direct investment and to disseminate them more effectively to users. Existing data should be reviewed to determine if additions, deletions, or modifications are necessary. Research should also be conducted to examine how data can be better synthesized and tabulated in more usable formats to enhance their analytic usefulness.

APPENDICES

APPENDICES

A

Sales and Purchases of Goods and Services Between Americans and Foreigners

$$T$$he first part of this appendix describes the exchange relationships that exist between various groups of Americans and foreigners and discusses how they can be estimated; the second presents a more detailed set of estimates of net sales of goods and services by Americans to foreigners than that in Chapter 1 and discusses the various aspects of these estimates.

EXCHANGE RELATIONSHIPS

Figure A-1 is a diagram of major exchange relationships between Americans and foreigners. As shown in the diagram, Americans and foreigners can be grouped by their locations. In the United States, these include: (1) U.S. affiliates of foreign firms located in the United States, (2) U.S.-owned firms in the United States, (3) households of U.S. citizens and U.S. government units in the United States, and (4) households of foreign citizens living in the United States. In foreign countries, these include: (5) foreign affiliates of U.S. firms located abroad, (6) foreign-owned firms located abroad, (7) households of foreign citizens abroad and foreign government units abroad, and (8) households of U.S. citizens living abroad. In

---

This appendix was prepared by panel chair Robert E. Baldwin. He appreciates the assistance of study director Anne Y. Kester and Fukunari Kimura, assistant professor, State University of New York at Stonybrook.

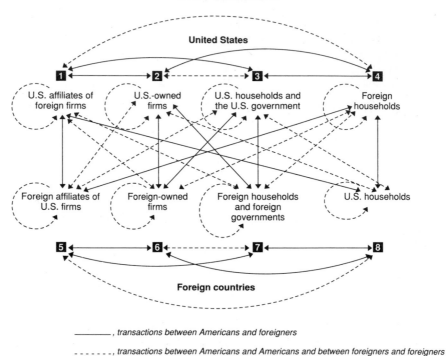

_____ , transactions between Americans and foreigners

- - - - - - , transactions between Americans and Americans and between foreigners and foreigners

FIGURE A-1   International and national exchange relationships.

the diagram the point of the arrowhead > indicates the direction of trade between trading units and the solid and dashed lines represent trade flows between trading units of different national ownership and the same national ownership, respectively.

We first consider the sales of goods and services to foreign-owned firms, private foreign citizens within and outside of the United States, and foreign governments by U.S.-owned firms, U.S. government units, and private U.S. citizens in the United States and abroad. These are the sum of the trade flows between the following trading units: 2>1, 2>4, 3>1, 3>4, 2>6, 2>7, 3>6, 3>7, 5>6, 5>7, 8>6, 8>7, 5>1, 5>4, 8>1, and 8>4.

These exchange flows are the sum of three components:

(A) the cross-border sales of goods and services by U.S.-owned firms, the U.S. government, and private U.S. citizens located in the United States to foreign-owned firms, foreign governments, and foreign citizens located abroad, namely, 2>6, 2>7, 3>6, and 3>7;

(B) sales of goods and services by U.S.-owned firms, U.S. government units, and private U.S. citizens located in the United States to foreign-owned firms and foreign citizens located within the United States, namely, 2>1, 2>4, 3>1, and 3>4; and

(C) sales of goods and services by foreign affiliates of U.S. firms and private U.S. citizens located abroad to U.S. affiliates of foreign firms and foreign citizens in the United States and to foreign-owned firms, foreign governments, and foreign private citizens located abroad, namely, 5>1, 5>4, 5>6, 5>7, 8>1, 8>4, 8>6, and 8>7.

The first of these components, (A), can be estimated by taking U.S. exports, the sum of 1>5, 1>6, 1>7, 1>8, 2>5, 2>6, 2>7, 2>8, 3>5, 3>6, 3>7, 3>8, 4>5, 4>6, 4>7, and 4>8, and subtracting both U.S. exports to foreign affiliates of U.S. companies, the sum 1>5, 2>5, 3>5 and, 4>5, and U.S. exports shipped by U.S. affiliates of foreign companies, the sum 1>5, 1>6, 1>7, and 1>8. This net figure is the sum of 2>6, 2>7, 2>8, 3>6, 3>7, 3>8, 4>6, 4>7, and 4>8 minus 1>5. Thus, the approximation exceeds the desired figure by 2>8, 3>8, 4>6, 4>7, and 4>8, minus 1>5. These latter figures are likely to be fairly small in comparison with the total trade of this component.

No direct information is available on the second component, (B). However, the Bureau of Economic Analysis (BEA) has estimated local purchases of goods and services by U.S. affiliates of foreign firms by subtracting estimates of factor incomes earned in U.S. affiliates of foreign firms and inputs of goods and services of these U.S. affiliates from their sales and their change in inventory (see Lowe, 1990). It is not possible to subtract purchases from other related or unrelated U.S. affiliates of foreign firms from these local purchases to obtain local purchases just from U.S.-owned firms, since BEA does not collect purchases by U.S. affiliates from related U.S. affiliates (presumably because they are not large) nor from unrelated U.S. affiliates. There is some interest in knowing purchases from related U.S. affiliates, but attempts to gather data on purchases from unrelated U.S. affiliates does not seem worth the effort that would be required.

The third component, (C), can be estimated by taking the total sales of foreign affiliates of U.S. companies, the sum of 5>5, 5>6, 5>7, 5>8, 5>1, 5>2, 5>3, and 5>4, and subtracting sales to the United States by foreign affiliates of U.S. companies, the sum of 5>1, 5>2, 5>3, and 5>4, and sales to other foreign affiliates of U.S. companies abroad, 5>5. This calculation yields the sum of 5>6,

5>7, and 5>8, which is greater than the desired figure by 5>8 but less than it by the sum of 5>1, 5>4, 8>1, 8>4, 8>6, and 8>7. The differences between the desired and actual figures are not likely to be large.

We next consider purchases of goods and services from foreign-owned firms abroad and in the United States, foreign governments, and households of foreign citizens within and outside of the United States by U.S.-owned firms in the United States and abroad, the U.S. government, and households of U.S. citizens in the United States and abroad. In terms of the diagram, these purchases are the sum of trade between the following trading units: 1>2, 1>3, 4>2, 4>3, 6>2, 6>3, 7>2, 7>3, 6>5, 7>5, 6>8, 7>8, 4>5, 1>5, 1>8, and 4>8.

These purchases can be represented as the sum of three components:

(D) cross-border purchases of goods and services by U.S.-owned firms, the U.S. government, and private U.S. citizens in the United States from foreign firms, foreign governments, and foreign citizens outside of the United States, namely 6>2, 7>2, 6>3, and 7>3;

(E) purchases of goods and services by U.S.-owned firms, the U.S. government, and U.S. citizens in the United States from U.S. affiliates of foreign companies and foreign citizens located in the United States, namely 1>2, 1>3, 4>2, and 4>3; and

(F) purchases of foreign affiliates of U.S. firms and U.S. citizens abroad from foreign firms, foreign governments, and foreign citizens abroad and purchases from U.S. affiliates of foreign firms and foreign citizens in the United States, namely 6>5, 7>5, 1>5, 4>5, 7>8, 6>8, 1>8, and 4>8.

The first of these components, (D), can be estimated by taking U.S. imports, the sum of 5>1, 5>2, 5>3, 5>4, 6>1, 6>2, 6>3, 6>4, 7>1, 7>2, 7>3, 7>4, 8>1, 8>2, 8>3, and 8>4, and subtracting both U.S. imports from foreign affiliates of U.S. companies, the sum of 5>1, 5>2, 5>3, and 5>4, and U.S. imports shipped to U.S. affiliates of foreign companies, the sum of 5>1, 6>1, 7>1, and 8>1. This calculation yields the sum of 6>2, 6>3, 6>4, 7>2, 7>3, 7>4, 8>2, 8>3, 8>4, minus 5>1, which exceeds the desired figure by 6>4, 7>4, 8>2, 8>3, and 8>4, minus 5>1. It does not seem that these differences will be large.

The second component, (E), can be estimated by taking the total sales of U.S. affiliates of foreign companies, the sum of 1>1, 1>2, 1>3, 1>4, 1>5, 1>6, 1>7, and 1>8, and subtracting U.S. exports shipped by U.S. affiliates of foreign companies, the sum of 1>5,

1>6, 1>7, and 1>8, and purchases from other U.S. affiliates of foreign firms, 1>1. This calculation yields the sum of 1>2, 1>3, and 1>4. The proper number should not include 1>4, but should include 4>2 and 4>3.

No direct published information is available for (F). BEA apparently has the information necessary to estimate the local purchases of foreign affiliates of U.S. firms abroad in the same manner it estimates the local purchases of U.S. affiliates of foreign firms in the United States, but there has been less interest in obtaining data on local purchases of foreign affiliates of U.S. firms. Using data from the benchmark survey of U.S. direct investment abroad, a related method of estimating (F) is to subtract from the cost of goods and services sold by foreign affiliates of U.S. firms the sum of U.S. exports shipped to foreign affiliates of U.S. firms, purchases from related foreign affiliates of U.S. firms, and employee compensation and other direct factor payments by these firms. However, the resulting figure incorrectly excludes U.S. exports shipped to foreign affiliates of U.S. firms by U.S. affiliates of foreign firms in the United States and incorrectly includes purchases from unrelated foreign affiliates of U.S. firms abroad.

AN ESTIMATE OF NET SALES OF GOODS AND SERVICES BY AMERICANS TO FOREIGNERS IN 1987

Table A-1 provides estimates of sales and purchases of goods and services by Americans from foreigners for 1987. Because of the difficulty of obtaining sales and purchases data on households of U.S. citizens living abroad and households of foreign citizens living in the United States, households are classified on a country-of-residency basis, as in the balance-of-payments accounts. That is, households of private foreign citizens in the United States (not employed by foreign governments) are combined with households of U.S. citizens living in the United States and the U.S. government and regarded as an American unit. (However, as in the balance-of-payments accounts, households of foreign residents living in the United States who are employed by foreign governments are regarded as residents of the country of that government.) Similarly, households of private U.S. citizens living abroad (not employed by the U.S. government) are combined with households of foreign citizens living abroad and foreign governments and regarded as a foreign unit. (Households of U.S. citizens abroad who work for the U.S. government are, however, as in the balance-of-payments accounts, regarded as U.S. residents.)

TABLE A–1 Net Sales of Goods and Services by Americans to Foreigners, 1987 (in millions of dollars)

Transaction	Amount
I. Cross-Border Sales to and Purchases from Foreigners by Americans[a]	
Exports to foreigners	
+ U.S. exports of merchandise and services	335,765
− U.S. exports to foreign affiliates of U.S. firms abroad	87,286
− U.S. exports shipped by U.S. affiliates of foreign firms	51,843
Total	196,636
Imports from foreigners	
+ U.S. imports of merchandise and services	483,933
− U.S. imports from foreign affiliates of U.S. firms	75,986
− U.S. imports shipped to U.S. affiliates of foreign firms	143,767
Total	264,180
Net cross-border sales to foreigners	−67,544
II. Sales and Purchases by Foreign Affiliates of U.S. Firms[b]	
Sales by foreign affiliates of U.S. firms	
+ Sales by foreign affiliates of U.S. firms abroad	815,541
− Sales among foreign affiliates of U.S. firms abroad	125,107
− Sales to the United States by foreign affiliates of	
U.S. firms	88,923
Total	601,511
Local purchases abroad by foreign affiliates of U.S. firms[c]	359,076
Net sales to foreigners by foreign affiliates of U.S. firms	242,435
III. Value-Added Abroad by Foreign Affiliates of U.S. Firms	
+ Sales by foreign affiliates of U.S. firms	815,541
− Local purchases abroad by foreign affiliates	359,076
− Imported goods and services	87,286
− Purchases from other foreign affiliates of U.S. firms	125,107
Total	244,072
Foreign content of foreign affiliate sales	
(244,072 + 359,076 + 125,107)	728,255
IV. U.S. Sales to and Purchases from U.S. Affiliates of Foreign Firms[d]	
U.S. sales to U.S. affiliates of foreign firms[e]	440,391
U.S. purchases from U.S. affiliates of foreign firms	
+ Sales by U.S. affiliates of foreign firms	731,392
− Sales among U.S. affiliates of foreign firms in the U.S.	n.a.
− U.S. exports shipped by U.S. affiliates of foreign firms	51,843
Total	679,549
Net U.S. sales to U.S. affiliates of foreign firms	−239,158
V. Value-Added in the U.S. by U.S. Affiliates of Foreign Firms[f]	
+ Sales of U.S. Affiliates of Foreign Firms	731,392
− Purchases within the United States by foreign affiliates	440,391
− Imported goods and services	143,767
− Purchases from other U.S. affiliates of foreign firms	n.a.
+ Inventory changes	4,671
Total	151,905
Local content of U.S. affiliate sales	
(151,905 + 440,391)	592,296
VI. Net Sales by Americans to Foreigners	−64,267

TABLE A–1 *Continued*

[a]Data of U.S. merchandise exports and imports are on the calendar basis; data on direct investment are reported on the financial year basis.

[b]Data on foreign affiliates of U.S. firms for goods cover only those firms for which the combined U.S. ownership of U.S. firms is 50 percent or more, that is, only majority-owned affiliates are covered.

[c]This rough estimate of local purchases from foreigners by foreign affiliates of U.S. firms was made as follows: employee compensation (105,452); depreciation, depletion, and production royalty payments (28,231); purchases from other foreign affiliates of U.S. firms (110,606); and U.S. exports shipped to foreign affiliates of U.S. firms (74,907). These figures were subtracted from the cost of goods sold by foreign affiliates of U.S. firms (629,137) to give a figure for local purchases of goods from foreigners of (309,941). These data are from Bureau of Economic Analysis (1990a,b).

Local purchases of services from foreigners was obtained by applying the ratio of total purchases of U.S. affiliates of foreign firms by the finance, insurance, and services sectors to the total sales of these sectors, namely, 0.78 (as calculated from Lowe (1990), to the total sales of services by foreign affiliates of U.S. firms (97,455) (as reported in DiLullo and Whichard, 1990) to give a total purchases estimate of 76,015. Imports of services from the United States (12,379) (see DiLullo and Whichard, 1990:Table 2) and purchases from other foreign affiliates of U.S. firms (14,501) (see DiLullo and Whichard, 1990:Table 11) are then subtracted from the total purchases figure to give 49,135 for local purchases of services from foreigners. Adding this to the goods figure yields a total for goods and services of about 359,076.

[d]Data on goods from U.S. affiliates of foreign firms, unlike those on foreign affiliates of U.S. firms, cover firms for which ownership by a single person or firm is 10 percent or more.

[e]This figure is somewhat lower than the figure estimated by Lowe (1990) since, as the author states, his estimate is overstated by the inclusion of purchases of services from foreigners. The later paper by DiLullo and Whichard (1990) includes an estimate for such imports and this estimate is used to revise the Lowe estimate.

[f]These data are from the Lowe article. However, the local purchases and import figures have been modified to take into account the figure on imports of services available from DiLullo and Whichard (1990).

SOURCES: Data on merchandise exports and imports are from the *Economic Report of the President*. Data on cross-border trade in services is from DiLullo and Whichard (1990). Data on sales and purchases of foreign affiliates of U.S. firms are from the 1987 benchmark survey (Bureau of Economic Analysis [1990a,b]) and DiLullo and Whichard (1990). Data on sales and purchases of U.S. affiliates of foreign firms are from Lowe (1990), DiLullo and Whichard (1990), and Bureau of Economic Analysis (1990a,b).

The focus is on identifying the cross-border selling and purchasing activities of foreign affiliates of U.S. firms abroad and U.S. affiliates of foreign firms in the United States. Thus, the term "Americans," as used here, consists of U.S.-owned firms in the United States and abroad, households of U.S. and private foreign citizens residing in the United States (U.S.-resident households), and U.S. government units. The term "foreigners," as used here, consists of foreign-owned firms in the United States and abroad, households of foreign and U.S. citizens residing abroad (foreign-resident households), and foreign governments.

Table A-1 reveals the high degree of internationalization of the American economy. Although the cross-border sales of goods and services by U.S. residents to foreign residents (Part I of the table) in 1987 fell short of the cross-border purchases from foreign residents by $148 billion ($336 billion – $484 billion) in 1987, the difference declines to –$67 billion ($197 billion – $264 billion) when the cross-border trade of U.S. affiliates of foreign firms in the United States and the cross-border trade of foreign affiliates of U.S. firms abroad are excluded.[1]

As Part II of the table indicates, net sales of goods and services by foreign affiliates of U.S. firms located abroad exceeded local purchases by these firms abroad by $242 billion in 1987. At the same time, net purchases by Americans of goods and services from U.S.-based affiliates of foreign firms exceeded sales of goods and services to these firms (Part IV of the table) by $239 billion. Consequently, the balance of these three accounts—net sales by Americans to foreigners—shows a balance (an excess of purchases) of –$64 billion. This is less than one-half of the trade deficit in that year.

---

[1]This figure is only an approximation. As pointed out above, in calculating cross-border sales of Americans to foreigners, exports of U.S. affiliates of foreign firms to foreign affiliates of U.S. firms are included in both figures and subtracted from total exports and thus are incorrectly subtracted twice instead of only once. Similarly, in calculating cross-border sales of foreigners to unaffiliated Americans, U.S. imports from foreign affiliates of U.S. firms going to U.S. affiliates of foreign firms are incorrectly subtracted twice.

More important, all data on goods of foreign affiliates of U.S. firms refer to majority-owned foreign affiliates (firms in which the sum of ownership interest of individual firms or persons, each of which has at least 10 percent of ownership interest, exceeds 50 percent), but data on U.S. affiliates of foreign firms refer to any firm in which there is at least a 10 percent or more foreign ownership interest by a single firm or persons. Data for majority-owned U.S. affiliates of foreign firms are not published.

The activities of foreign affiliates of U.S. firms and U.S. affiliates of foreign firms can be better understood by considering various components of the three accounts. Sales of goods and services by affiliates of U.S. firms located abroad (the first item in Part II) exceeded sales by U.S. affiliates of foreign firms (the second item in Part IV) in 1987 by $85 billion ($816 billion – $731 billion). However, as the other components of these two accounts indicate, sales among foreign affiliates of U.S. firms located abroad ($125 billion) plus sales of these foreign affiliates to the United States ($89 billion) are considerably larger than sales among U.S. affiliates of foreign firms in the United States (data not available) plus export sales of these U.S. affiliates to foreign countries ($52 billion). Consequently, net sales to Americans in the United States (purchases in the United States) by U.S. affiliates of foreign firms ($680 billion) (see Part IV) exceeded net sales to foreigners abroad by foreign affiliates of U.S. firms ($602 billion) (see Part II) by $78 billion.[2]

However, Americans sell more goods and services to U.S.-based affiliates of foreign firms than foreigners sell to foreign-based affiliates of U.S. firms: $440 billion and $359 billion, respectively (a rough estimate). This $81 billion excess of sales of goods and services by Americans to U.S.-based affiliates of foreign firms over sales of goods and services by foreigners to foreign-based affiliates of U.S. firms more than offsets the $78 billion shortfall of net sales by foreign affiliates of U.S. firms, compared with net sales in the United States of U.S. affiliates of foreign firms. Consequently, the difference of $3 billion is subtracted from the $67 billion shortfall of cross-border trade to give the $64 billion negative balance of net sales of Americans to foreigners.

As noted in the body of the report, the value added by U.S. affiliates of foreign firms in the United States to the U.S. gross

---

[2]The $602 billion figure incorrectly excludes sales of foreign affiliates of U.S. firms abroad to U.S. affiliates of foreign firms in the United States, and the $680 billion figure incorrectly includes the sales of U.S. affiliates of foreign firms to other affiliated and unaffiliated foreign-owned companies in the United States. BEA collects data on sales of foreign affiliates of U.S. firms abroad to other affiliates of these firms, but it does not collect data on the sales of U.S. affiliates of foreign firms in the United States to other affiliates of these firms; presumably, the number is small. It is probably not worthwhile to try to collect data on sales of U.S. affiliates of foreign firms in the United States to unaffiliated foreign-owned firms in the United States. Thus, data on sales of U.S. affiliates of foreign firms in the United States will, at best, include sales to unaffiliated foreign-owned firms in the United States, as well as to U.S.-owned firms in the United States.

domestic product and the local content of sales of U.S. affiliates of foreign firms can be calculated from the various components of the sales and purchases figures: they are shown in Part V of the table. Part III contains estimates of the value added to the gross domestic product of foreign countries by foreign affiliates of U.S. firms abroad and the foreign content of the sales of these firms.

B

Canvass of Data Users

Although many of its members are experienced users of foreign trade data, the panel considered it essential to consult with a broad spectrum of data users. It wanted to learn from them what kinds of foreign trade data they use; how they use the data; their evaluation of the quality, cost, and accessibility of the data; their unmet needs; their anticipated future needs; and their suggestions for improving foreign trade statistics. Thus, the panel undertook a canvass of the users of foreign trade statistics.

CANVASS METHOD

The best way to find out how well a program is serving its clients—if the client population is well defined, accessible, and large—is to conduct a formal survey of clients, using probability sampling. There have been numerous attempts, some more successful than others, to survey users of the statistics produced by federal agencies (see, for example, a recent Bureau of Labor Statistics survey of users of Consumer Price Index data [Kamalich and Kwiecinski, 1989]).

The panel examined carefully and then rejected the idea of conducting a formal survey of users of foreign trade data for three main reasons. First, there are so many different sources of foreign trade data that it would be virtually impossible to develop a comprehensive, unduplicated list of users. Second, the development of a structured questionnaire that would adequately cover all kinds of users and uses of foreign trade data proved to be extremely difficult. Panel members concluded that a highly structured questionnaire with predetermined response categories would not elicit the detailed and explicit information about user views needed. Third, the panel did not have the resources to conduct a formal user survey whose design and execution would meet generally accepted standards for high-quality survey research.

Fortunately, there were other options available. The panel used three methods of collecting information from users of foreign trade statistics: presentations by users at its meetings, on-site interviews of users by panel members, and solicitation of written statements. (See the invitation letter and the protocol for the interviews at the end of the appendix.)

For descriptive purposes, the users and types of responses have been divided into four groups. Group 1 is recognized key users of foreign trade data, most of them from U.S. federal agencies and international organizations; they were invited to make oral presentations at panel meetings or to submit written statements. Many of the presenters also submitted written statements; for those who did not, the minutes of the meetings served as documentation of their views. (This group does not include any of the agency representatives who made presentations solely as primary producers of foreign trade statistics, who were not considered to be part of the user population.)

Group 2 is data users from several types of organizations who were interviewed on-site, singly or in groups, by members on the panel. Some of the interviews followed a protocol designed to ensure coverage of all relevant aspects of the subject (see end of the appendix). The documentation for these interviews consisted of notes prepared by the interviewers and, in a few instances, written postinterview statements submitted by the person interviewed.

Group 3 is subscribers to the Census Bureau's foreign trade data products. The invitation for written comments was mailed to 589 organizations and individuals on subscription lists provided by the Census Bureau, with a follow-up mailing two months later. The response rate was slightly under 10 percent: after combining multiple responses from the same organization, there were usable responses from 48 organizations.

Group 4 is people who had participated in a November 1989 Conference, "International Financial Transactions: Issues in Measurement and Empirical Research," sponsored by the National Bureau of Economic Research (NBER). The invitation for written comments was mailed to 186 conference participants. A total of 17 responses were received, again slightly less than 10 percent of those invited to comment.

In sum, we received 111 responses. To provide an overall view of the kinds of users whose views we obtained, Table B-1 shows the distribution of the four groups by type of organization, using a slightly modified version of the U.S. Standard Industrial Classification.

About two-thirds of the responses came from the private sector and one-third from users at various government levels. The invited presentations and the responses from Census Bureau subscribers covered a broad spectrum of users from both sectors. We do not know for certain why manufacturers of chemical products were so heavily represented in the latter group; possibly a particularly interested and active industry association encouraged responses by its members. On-site interviews were limited to private-sector users because at that stage of the study the panel had already

TABLE B-1   User Responses By Type of Group

Type of organization	Group[a]				
	1	2	3	4	Total
Chemical manufacturers	–	–	16	–	16
Other manufacturers	1	4	11	–	16
Universities	2	1	–	7	10
Membership organizations	1	2	4	–	7
Consulting and research firms	2	3	6	1	12
Other private-sector organizations	3	–	4	–	7
U.S. federal agencies	10	–	–	8	18
Congress, state and local government	12	–	1	–	13
Other countries	1	–	6	–	7
International organizations	4	–	–	1	5
Total	36	10	48	17	111

[a]Groups: 1, invited presentations; 2, on-site interviews; 3, Census Bureau data subscribers; 4, participants, conference of the National Bureau of Economic Research. See text for more detailed description.

received presentations from all of the key government organizations. The participants in the NBER conference were mostly university-based researchers who use foreign trade data and representatives of U.S. executive branch agencies.

The user database contains a large number of responses, covering all of the major categories of users of foreign trade data. Many of the responses were detailed, thoughtful, and informative. Virtually all of those who were invited to make presentations to the panel or to participate in on-site interviews agreed to do so, although a small proportion of the Census Bureau subscribers and NBER conference participants responded to our invitation for written comments. Like the subgroups of the general population who write letters to newspapers or to their representatives in Congress, foreign trade data users who are articulate and have strong views or feelings undoubtedly predominated among the recipients of our written invitations for comments who responded.

The panel carried out a content analysis of the user responses and a few simple tabulations based on the responses of Census Bureau subscribers, covering five general topics: acquisition, processing, and uses of foreign trade data; the specific kinds of data used; evaluation of costs and convenience of data access; evaluation of the quality of the data; and current and anticipated future needs for additional data. Few of the users' responses covered every one of these topics. Each of the responses was reviewed and its contents, if any, relative to each of the above subject categories briefly summarized. Then the summaries of individual user comments for each topic were reviewed and synthesized as part of the findings presented in the body of the report. For topics commented on by many of the Census Bureau subscribers, a few simple tallies were prepared. The rest of this appendix presents some of the individual responses.

MERCHANDISE TRADE DATA

Sources and Kinds of Data

Among the organizations that responded to the survey, the Census Bureau was the most frequently cited source of foreign trade data. However, this could be misleading, since nearly one-half of the responses came from organizations on the list of subscribers to Census Bureau data products. With a few exceptions, commercial firms that rely entirely on secondary sources for their foreign trade data were not covered directly in our canvass of users. We know from our contacts with some of the data retailers that there are a large number of such data users in the private sector.

There is considerable variation in the number of different sources used. Large companies, companies that are primarily in the information business, and government agencies are more likely to use multiple sources. Of 27 Census Bureau subscribers in the manufacturing sector who responded, 10 relied solely on those foreign trade data. Data from the Piers Import/Export Reporting Service (PIERS) were used by 12 of the remaining 17, and for several of these it was the only source used in addition to Census Bureau data.

A few companies, especially those with manufacturing facilities in other countries, are interested in the total international trade picture for specified commodities, not just bilateral trade between the United States and other countries. To obtain information on non-U.S. trade, they must rely on data produced by other countries or by data retailers in the public or private sector.

The kinds of data used are even more variable than their sources, so it is hard to generalize; nevertheless, some patterns do emerge from our user statements.

Except for academic research users, most private sector users of foreign trade data appear to want monthly data. A distinction is drawn between market analysis, which requires monthly data, and strategic planning, which can usually be based on annual data. Some market analysts are aware of the volatility of monthly trade data for specific commodities. Two responses from manufacturers noted that they use rolling 12-month totals for their analyses.

In the public sector, frequency requirements are more varied. Users of monthly data include policy analysts, such as those at the Federal Reserve Board and units of the International Trade Administration and Agricultural Marketing Service of the Department of Agriculture that provide current market analysis for their constituencies. Other researchers in the Federal Reserve System or the Department of Labor's Office of International Labor Affairs rely mostly on annual or quarterly data. State agencies that promote production for export rely on annual data, since no monthly or quarterly data on exports by state of origin are available.

Most users, other than those interested only in broad economic indicators, need data for selected commodities or commodity groups. Users looking only at international trade are generally content with commodities as classified under the Harmonized System (HS), but those who want to look at both domestic and foreign components of production and consumption usually find it necessary to convert the HS data to a system compatible with the U.S. Standard Industrial Classification (SIC), or vice versa.

Finally, there are users in the transportation industry with entirely different needs. Mode of shipment—vessel, air, or other—is their primary interest, along with data on port of entry or exit, point of origin within the exporting country, and final destination in the importing country.

USES

In asking foreign trade data users to tell us how they use the data, we did not try to constrain their uses to any specified set of categories. However, earlier attempts at classification were of some value in organizing the information they gave us (see Committee on National Statistics, 1976). We discuss uses in three broad categories: private sector, excluding research; public sector, excluding research; and research in both the private and public sectors.

In the private sector, nonresearch uses of merchandise trade data that were reported fell into three broad categories: market analysis, strategic planning, and activities intended to influence government policy and administrative decisions. Of these three, market analysis, often called market-share analysis, was by far the most frequently mentioned. Such analysis focuses on past, present, and future (forecasted) supply and demand balances for specific products of interest to the user. Producers want to track their own market shares and those of their competitors, both at the country and individual company level. A business researcher for a chemical manufacturer said that PIERS was a powerful tool and that, in combination with Census Bureau data, it provided a detailed picture of product movement. With these sources and a knowledge of the industry, a user can usually determine "how much of a particular chemical is imported or exported and by which company."

Companies usually do market analysis only for their own use, but research and consulting firms and in some instances even manufacturers share information with their customers or clients. Thus, for example, an aircraft manufacturer reported that it provides information to airlines on international commodity movements by air to help the airlines in planning their freight operations.

Strategic planning is a longer range activity and does not necessarily require up-to-the minute monthly data. It does require the analysis of trend data for specific commodities and country combinations. Such analyses are used to support decisions on investments in new facilities and their location and on the development and marketing of new products.

Companies in the private sector try to influence government decisions in a variety of ways and often use statistics on various aspects of foreign trade to support their cases. Manufacturers who believe that foreign competitors are using unfair trade practices, such as dumping, will marshal the evidence and present it to Congress and the appropriate executive branch agencies. One large corporation stated that the foreign trade data it acquires and processes are useful to company officials who serve on various government committees concerned with trade policies.

Another interesting example of this type of use was described by the manufacturer of a specialized product that requires a particular type of wood that is not widely available. Some countries placed import restrictions on this product in the belief that it could be just as well manufactured domestically, using any available type of wood. The company provided customers in these countries with U.S. export data showing that it was selling its product to countries all over the world, allowing some of the customers to appeal successfully to their governments to remove the import restrictions.

We also heard from some law firms that assist clients in their dealings with government agencies on trade regulatory matters. Understandably, these users did not provide specific information on their clients or the issues they dealt with, but they had some interesting comments on other aspects of the data (covered below).

In the public sector, we identified three main categories for nonresearch uses of foreign trade data: policy guidance, administrative decisions, and trade promotion. Aggregate trends in foreign trade, as presented in the Census Bureau's monthly trade balance series and the Bureau of Economic Analysis's quarterly balance-of-payments trade balance series, are important elements of the economic data that guide broad economic policies at the national and international levels. Detailed information on trade for specific countries and commodities is used to evaluate U.S. international trade policy and to predict the likely effects of new legislation and regulations. Primary concerns are the international competitiveness of U.S. exports and the effects of imports on domestic employment and earnings. Agencies such as the International Trade Administration, the International Trade Commission, and the Labor Department's Office of International Labor Affairs are frequently asked to prepare analyses of these issues for policy makers in the executive branch and Congress.

Administrative decisions that depend on foreign trade data include decisions on which foreign countries are eligible for various trade preference programs and which U.S. companies are eligible for assistance to counteract the effects of import competition. At the federal level, the International Trade Commission is the primary user of data for these purposes. Some of the program eligibility requirements have precise cutoffs for eligibility, with the result that the accuracy of the data can become critical in borderline cases. The ability to develop comparable data for imports and domestic production is also an important consideration.

To promote exports, and in some instances the substitution of domestic products for imports, federal and state agencies monitor foreign trade and conduct market analyses for the benefit of current and potential exporters. At the federal level, the Commerce Department's International Trade Administration and the Agriculture Department's Agricultural Marketing Service are important users of foreign trade data for these purposes. At the state level, departments of commerce or industry and other state agencies assist exporters by providing technical assistance, market information, export financing, and state representatives to foreign countries. To support and monitor the effectiveness of these activities, states have strongly urged the federal government to provide detailed state-by-state data on exports and imports.

Quantitative research on international trade was reported to us by foreign trade data users in executive branch agencies, the Federal Reserve System, international agencies, universities (some supported by federal funding) and commercial and nonprofit research organizations. Most of the research is policy oriented; much is aimed at better understanding the effects of foreign trade on the U.S. economy. Some examples of research topics and studies are the development of models to predict the outcomes of changes in foreign trade policies; analysis of the response of specific industries to global exchange rate disturbances; identification of the determinants of trade patterns, including cost, production, and demand factors, for specific commodities; analysis of the determinants of the commodity composition of trade for various foreign countries; cross-sectional and longitudinal analysis of the economic determinants of variation in the volume of aggregated and disaggregated bilateral trade flows; and the testing of hypotheses that trade enhances cooperation and deters conflict between countries.

The majority of the researchers who work on these topics combine data on foreign trade with data on domestic production and consumption; they therefore tend to use SIC-based classifications for foreign trade data by commodity.

DATA ACQUISITION AND PROCESSING

Most of the Census Bureau subscribers who commented on costs were satisfied with the fees charged for trade data, and some thought they were quite low. Some subscribers who used data from both the Census Bureau and other sources noted that data from private sources (such as the Journal of Commerce, PIERS, or Tradstat) or other countries were more expensive. One respondent observed that the charges for Japanese data on imports and exports were about 20 times the charges for comparable U.S. data. Another, who uses data from the Census Bureau, PIERS, and Tradstat, noted that PIERS data were more expensive than Census data but believed that PIERS was a cost-effective service. The same user noted that Tradstat was twice as expensive as PIERS but still regarded Tradstat as quite affordable. Two Census Bureau subscribers said they would be willing to pay more for data of higher quality.

Most of the comments on costs of acquisition obtained from sources other than the Census Bureau's subscriber list (groups 1, 2, and 4; see Table B-1, above), also indicated satisfaction with Census Bureau charges for foreign trade data. One group of academic users took a strongly contrary view, however, pointing out that the annual costs of obtaining the Census Bureau's import and export tapes, along with the concordance tapes needed to convert the commodity data to other classifications, would total $1,200. Their statements also commented on the high costs of purchasing international bilateral trade data from the United Nations or the Organization for Economic Cooperation and Development (OECD) and expressed their unhappiness that purchasers are not permitted to share these data with other institutions, so that acquisition through data retailers is precluded.

Users had numerous suggestions for making the data more convenient to work with, which in most cases was equivalent to saying that they would like data suppliers to add value to their product in ways that would reduce users' processing costs. These suggestions covered four topics: mode of dissemination, time-series data, seasonal adjustment, and classification.

Most users were aware that the Census Bureau is phasing out

its microfiche releases and shifting to the use of CD-ROM, so comments on the difficulty of working with microfiche are now of limited relevance. For the record, however, an academic respondent said that "microfiche is probably the most 'user-hostile' manner in which this information could be stored," citing the fact its resolution was not sufficient to use it for optical scanning or even to make readable hard-copy prints.

A majority of the users who commented on the Census Bureau's switch to CD-ROM appeared to be looking forward to it, even though some recognized that the costs of acquisition and processing would be higher. However, these views were by no means unanimous. Some users objected to what they anticipated would be substantial increases in costs to acquire and process data in CD-ROM format that were previously available on microfiche. Some mode-related comments came from Census Bureau subscribers who use the microfiche releases who may not have been aware of the impending switch to CD-ROM. Some had been using spreadsheet utilities for their analyses and would have liked to receive the data in a form more directly compatible with that approach.

The development of usable time-series data is complicated by two factors: revisions made to correct reporting and processing errors and changes in commodity classifications and definitions used for key variables. The shift in January of 1989 from the classifications of the Tariff Schedule of the United States Annotated (TSUSA) for imports and the Statistical Classification of Domestic and Foreign Commodities Exported from the United States (Schedule B) for exports to the Harmonized System brought significant advantages in terms of increased international comparability of foreign trade data, but it created difficulties for users attempting to maintain time series for specific commodities.

Some users' comments on revisions to correct errors came from Census Bureau subscribers. Four of them want the Census Bureau to provide more complete information about revisions or expressed unhappiness about the lack of such information. A U.S. agency that uses Census Bureau foreign trade data and also compiles trade data from its own sources compares these data and submits information about suspected errors to the Census Bureau. That statement said that revisions based on their feedback were being made at a slower pace than in the past. The respondent attributed this change to shortage of staff in the Census Bureau's Foreign Trade Division and problems associated with the changeover to the Harmonized System. An international organization expressed concern about the size of revisions in Census Bureau data and questioned whether the same revisions were being applied to all data series.

We received several comments on the shift to the Harmonized System. Most of those who commented approved of the change or at least recognized the need for it, but some raised questions about how best to bridge the break in commodity time-series data. A representative of an international organization, recognizing the cost of providing a bridge between the old and new systems, nevertheless urged that Census Bureau recompile prior years' data in the HS commodity classifications. Users also mentioned other factors that have complicated the development and use of time-series data, such as the substitution of Canadian import data for U.S. export data that took effect at the start of 1990 and the frequent changes in commodity definitions within existing classification systems.

Comments on the seasonal adjustment of foreign trade data came mostly from trade policy and research-oriented users in federal agencies and universities. One agency user believed that the seasonal adjustment factors were not being revised often enough and complained that the older seasonally adjusted data were not being revised to reflect recalculated factors. Other respondents, including a data retailer and a federal agency, wanted seasonally adjusted data at a finer level of detail.

Problems associated with the use of foreign trade and domestic production or employment data in the same analyses were mentioned by several users, including both researchers and persons doing market share analyses for a company, commodity, or industry. A federal agency user called for an improved and automated, current and consistent master concordance that could be used to link trade classifications to domestic output and employment classifications.

It is difficult to identify any consensus from the users' comments on acquisition and processing of data. Federal agency users are in a privileged position and tend to be fairly well satisfied. One of them said: "The availability of the COMPRO data base to federal users greatly facilitates access to trade information; hopefully, the new National Trade Data Bank will perform the same service to the general public." Researchers in universities had varying opinions. For those who are working under government contracts or grants, the acquisition of data is often facilitated by access to COMPRO. One individual researcher who did not use this source said that the U.S. foreign trade data he needed for his project "was easy to find and use." At the other end of the spectrum, a university research group that creates and maintains extensive economic models said that most of the other economic data sets they were using were much less expensive and easier to process than the U.S. merchandise trade data.

It is even more difficult to summarize the experiences and comments of commercial users on data acquisition and processing, and we are limited by the fact that most of our responses in this group came from subscribers to Census Bureau data, rather than those who rely entirely on data retailers or other sources. One thing that did emerge clearly in the comments from Census Bureau subscribers was their concern about the timeliness of the data (see next section).

TIMELINESS

Broadly speaking, timeliness is a component of data quality. Timeliness is measured by the length of time that elapses between the end of the reference period for a particular data set and the time when the data are available to users. Data are considered to be more or less timely depending on whether this elapsed time is short or long. For many kinds of uses, the utility of data for a particular time period declines as time passes.

We asked users of foreign trade data to comment on timeliness, and nearly half of the respondents did say something about it. It seems reasonable to assume that most of those who did not comment are not greatly concerned with the timeliness. However, of those who did comment, few were fully satisfied. Thus, timeliness is clearly a matter of concern for many users.

Concerns about timeliness ranged from mild to severe. It was not always possible to relate the users' comments on timeliness to specific data sources and publications or other data products. However, a substantial number referred specifically to the microfiche versions of the Census Bureau's IM145, IM146, and EM545 monthly reports. Most of these users were tracking specific commodities, and some had arranged to receive data on selected commodities from computer printouts, which are available earlier than the microfiche reports. Some users of the Census data commented that delays in availability of the IM145 and EM545 microfiche reports had been increasing. One user who had tried to circumvent these delays by telephoning the Commerce Department for specific information was finding this increasingly difficult to do. Clearly, some users were more aware than others of the variety of means of access to the Census Bureau data. (As noted, the panel obtained users' comments prior to the change from microfiche to CD-ROM; user comments on this change are discussed above.)

Only a few of the users who complained about lack of timeliness explained, even in general terms, why they thought they needed the data sooner. Those who did mentioned factors such as the seasonality of their business, the need to follow the dynamics of the market closely, and the need for timely data to prevent unfair trade practices such as dumping.

Several users compared the timeliness of the Census Bureau foreign trade data with data from other sources or commented on changes in the timeliness of Census Bureau products. With respect to other countries, their views were somewhat mixed. One user singled out Japan as having a better record, and another said that most developed countries did better than the United States. However, another said, that delays in availability of Canadian data were equal to those experienced for U.S. data. Some users pointed out that data from private sources, such as those from the PIERS system (which, however, covers only vessel trade at selected major ports), were available sooner than the Census Bureau data.

Two consulting and research organizations commented on trade-offs between timeliness and accuracy. The result was a standoff. One was willing to wait a little longer for more accurate data, but the other was willing to sacrifice some accuracy and detail for more timely data. Another user said: "We would pay some premium for prompt information in the areas of our greatest interest."

A review of the comments on timeliness suggests that there are certain categories of users more likely than others to demand quick access to data. Most "impatient" users of foreign trade data are in the private sector, and the majority appear to be doing market analysis, including monitoring of competitors, for themselves, clients, or members of industry associations. Users making short-term decisions involving international financial markets may not have an absolute time requirement, but according to one data retailer, his clients in this category want the data "5 minutes" before anyone else.

Government and university researchers who use foreign trade data for basic economic research tend to be much more patient. Most work with annual or less frequent data and are much less concerned with timeliness than with the availability of extended time-series data and issues of comparability between foreign trade and other economic data series.

Government users who supply inputs to the country's short-term trade, monetary, and fiscal policies belong in the impatient group. A representative of the Federal Reserve System observed: "The issue of timeliness is nearly as important, from the Fed's perspective, as that of accuracy . . . efforts to enhance the timely reporting of monthly trade data should also be given high priority."

A statement prepared in 1986 by the U.S. International Trade Commission, which furnishes Congress and the executive branch information and analysis based on federal economic statistics for use in making trade policy decisions, emphasized problems created by "untimely reporting," including the carryover of data from one reporting period to the next. The scope of the carryover problem was subsequently reduced by shifting the initial release date from 30 to 45 days after the end of each reporting period. The same statement was critical of delays in the availability of reports on domestic output in manufacturing by the Standard Industrial Classification.

Users of foreign trade data at the state level face a somewhat different situation. Most data of interest to them—for example, exports by state of origin—are only published on an annual basis. At present, these users appear more concerned about provision of additional commodity detail and improvements in accuracy than about timeliness. Some commented on the general lack of timeliness of publication of results from the Annual Survey of Manufactures, which are issued with a lag of 2-3 years.

In summary, a substantial minority of users who responded to our invitations for comments, mostly those using monthly data, wanted more timely foreign trade data. Prominent among this group were users who represented manufacturers or economic consulting and research firms and were using the data for market analysis. Only a few said why they wanted more timely data, and the consequences of delayed availability were only hinted at in one or two instances. Government users who analyze current economic data to aid decisions on short-term international and domestic economic policies also wanted more timely data. Researchers, on the other hand, whether in government or in universities, seemed to be satisfied with this aspect of the foreign trade data.

It will be of considerable interest to see whether two recent changes in the procedures for dissemination of foreign trade data— the Census Bureau's phase-out of microfiche and switch to CD-ROM for many of its reports and the development of the National Trade Data Bank by the Commerce Department's Office of Business Analysis—make it possible for private-sector users to get the data they want in a more timely manner.

ACCURACY

It is more difficult for users to evaluate the accuracy of foreign trade data than it is for them to evaluate timeliness. Nevertheless, nearly half of the users who made presentations, wrote, or were interviewed by panel members had something to say about accuracy. Only a few of those were fully satisfied. Some of the concerns about accuracy were expressed in moderate terms, but other users were more critical. Some users said they had no basis for judging the accuracy of foreign trade data, but others mentioned various ways in which they attempt to evaluate the data. Some, especially those who have few competitors for particular products, compare their own data on export shipments with those of the Census Bureau. A manufacturer of a specialized wood product had compared the EM-545 data with his own records of shipments for all of 1989 and submitted a lengthy listing of the errors found. He felt certain that if he had been able to detect so many errors in his firm's shipments, there must have been enough additional errors to make the statistics virtually useless. The nation's other manufacturer of this product had similar comments.

Another method of checking is to calculate unit values and review them for reasonableness. A chemical manufacturer who routinely does this found that exports of a specific commodity were being reported in pounds instead of kilograms. Another chemical manufacturer found the Census Bureau's data on shipments of materials under a particular tariff code showing extraordinarily high values per kilogram for several months. A commodity specialist at the Census Bureau was able to check the records and discovered that the commodity had been misclassified.

Some users have compared Census Bureau data on vessel imports and exports with data from the PIERS system and identified what they believe to be errors in one or the other system. A unit of the U.S. Department of Agriculture (USDA) regularly monitors Census data for specific commodities, countries, ports, and customs districts, using data from other USDA units on grain inspections and export sales of agricultural commodities. Its feedback to the Census Bureau frequently leads to revisions of the merchandise trade data. The Energy Information Administration, which regularly includes Census data on coal imports and exports in its publications, has found it necessary to submit the data received from the Census Bureau to an edit procedure in order to eliminate what it considers to be incorrect or misleading information (Energy Information Administration, 1989).

Comparisons of imports or exports by country with aggregate figures often reveal discrepancies. A representative of the Bureau of Statistics for the International Monetary Fund wrote that his staff had been unable to account for large discrepancies between aggregate trade data and the total of exports to and imports from partner countries that were observed for some years.

In addition, a Minnesota official compared the agricultural exports for the state, as reported in the Census Bureau's country-of-destination series, with estimates published by the Department of Agriculture. The official found that for 1988 the agricultural exports reported for Minnesota in the country-of-destination series were $259 million, compared with $1.8 billion estimated by the Department of Agriculture. For the United States as a whole, the relative difference in agricultural export statistics was smaller but still substantial, with the Census Bureau reporting U.S. agricultural exports of $23.4 billion in 1988, compared with Agriculture's $35.3 billion. Clearly, there was a problem with the allocation of exports to states.

Some users gave their views on the reasons for specific errors or, more broadly, on what they believed to be the main sources of error. We consider first the errors that exist in the official trade documents (or computer records) when they are received by the Census Bureau. The importance of reporting errors, in contrast to processing ones, was highlighted by a chemical manufacturer. He conjectured that most accuracy problems of U.S. trade data occur in data collection rather than in analysis or manipulation of the data by government analysts.

The problem of reporting amounts in pounds instead of kilograms has already been mentioned. Misclassification of commodities is clearly a problem, especially at the more detailed levels of classification. A chemical manufacturer said: "In general I have found the reports to be very helpful for the analysis of major commodity chemicals . . . As the product becomes more specialized . . . the numbers begin to become more and more inaccurate." A statement from the U.S. International Trade Commission (ITC) (written before the changeover to the Harmonized System) pointed out that the Customs Service has little incentive to look beyond the 5-digit level of the TSUSA, the level at which duties are assigned. Consequently, ITC believed that the 7-digit statistical categories were not receiving the attention needed to ensure accurate reporting.

Some users mentioned problems with reports of value. In some instances, it was hard to separate conceptual and operational reporting problems. A university economist, for example, believed that the rising share of intrafirm trade was making present methods for calculating trade values and prices less and less reliable because there is a large arbitrary element in the prices and values reported for such transactions when multinational firms carry out transfer pricing practices.

A more clear-cut reporting problem, undervaluation of trade with Canada due to missing inland freight, was described in a presentation by a representative of the Bureau of Economic Analysis. He explained that the value of U.S. exports is supposed to include all inland transportation costs. Unfortunately, this is not the case, and for some time BEA has included an estimate of this undervaluation in its balance-of-payments series. BEA's estimate is based on a sample survey conducted by the Census Bureau in 1969 for documents filed in July 1968, which remains the only possible basis for the estimate. In 1988 BEA added $1.8 billion to exports to Canada. A statement by an official of the Commerce Department's International Trade Administration expressed doubt as to whether the U.S.-Canada data exchange, which began at the start of 1990, would fully resolve the problem of undocumented exports. He expected that Canadian customs would be likely to take less interest in duty-free imports from the United States.

Information on state of origin for exports is of special interest to state and local officials interested in the promotion of exports and the use of port facilities. A state official reported that state-of-origin information is missing from approximately 25 percent of all shippers' export declarations (SEDs). When the information is reported, it may not be correct. The same official asserted that the Census Bureau's *Origin of Movement* series is of limited use because the series inaccurately assigns exports to a state or region that may not have produced the exported item. The series showed that Louisiana, for example, exported 44 percent of total U.S. crop exports, although it produced only 1.6 percent of the total U.S. crop output. Some users believed that significant numbers of shipments, especially exports, were being missed altogether. A former Commerce Department official noted that Census' recent port audits had found underreporting of air freight to be a significant problem. He believed that seaborne exports, especially those moving out in containers, might also be subject to substantial underreporting. Another user believed that information about small items combined with other items in a single container could easily be lost.

Shifting to the question of how the accuracy of foreign trade data is affected by the Census Bureau's processing operations, we return to the case of the two specialized wood product manufacturers, mentioned above. One of them had sent us a listing of suspected errors in Census's 1989 data for exports of their product, with a copy to Census. Their earlier attempts to notify Census of these problems had apparently gone astray, but this listing reached the appropriate commodity specialist in the Foreign Trade Division, who determined that the main cause of the errors was incorrect or outdated values of the parameters used in the computer edit checks of value-to-quantity ratios. These parameter values can be changed monthly, as needed, but, to a large extent, feedback from users, such as occurred in this instance, seems to be the primary source of information used to keep them current.

The deliberate exclusion of low-value import and export transactions from processing by the Census Bureau is not, in itself, a source of error. However, Census publishes monthly estimates of the total value of these excluded shipments by country, and some users questioned the accuracy of these estimates. A specialist in market development for an aircraft manufacturer felt that the Census Bureau's estimates of low-value shipments were very unrealistic. A member of a group of foreign trade data users commented that the frequent increases in the cutoffs for low-value shipments were making it extremely difficult to monitor changes in the rapidly growing international air freight industry.

Data on exports by state of origin are produced by the Census Bureau in its *Origin of Movement* series, based directly on the SEDs, and its *Exports from Manufacturing Establishments*, based primarily on the Annual Survey of Manufactures (ASM). State users were critical of the quality of data in both series. For the first of these two series, the Massachusetts Institute for Social and Economic Research (MISER), in cooperation with Census, has developed procedures to allocate the state-of-origin information missing from about 25 percent of all SEDs. A representative of the Michigan Department of Commerce criticized the ASM-based series as too dependent on untested assumptions and adjustments.

To some extent, the problems with these series do not arise from reporting or processing errors; they occur simply because the exporter is not asked to report (and would probably not be able to report accurately in many instances) the state where the exported commodity was produced or grown, rather the state from which it started its export journey. In one of our on-site interviews, a representative of a consulting and research firm said he did not think that the state data for imports and exports would be very useful because of such definitional problems. Only a few users addressed the question of how their uses were affected by errors in foreign trade data, and some of those who did merely indicated that the data had to be used with caution. However, more serious consequences were reported by a few.

In the private sector, a chemical manufacturer said that accurate and timely import statistics were necessary to prevent dumping by foreign firms. A law firm concerned with trade regulatory matters provided a very specific example in which a questionable data adjustment by a Census Bureau employee caused one of its clients to lose continuing eligibility for duty-free treatment under the Generalized System of Preferences, which depended on the country's share of total imports in a specified category remaining below 50 percent.

In the public sector, the 1986 statement by a representative of the U.S. International Trade Commission was quite explicit about the effects of errors in foreign trade data. He explained that in the agency's import-injury investigations, inaccuracies in the statistics could mean the difference between an affirmative and a negative determination, thereby affecting the granting or withholding of import relief. In addition, errors in reporting the country of origin of imports have erroneously caused products of some countries to become ineligible for preferential trade programs and, in other instances, have resulted in the misapplication of quota agreements.

As indicated above, some user statements addressed tradeoffs among timeliness, accuracy, and cost. Three statements from consulting and research firms identified quality as their primary concern. One was willing to surrender detail for accuracy and would even be willing to work with quarterly data if they were more accurate. A representative of the International Trade Administration expressed concern that recent efforts to facilitate movement of shipments through ports despite staffing cuts would lead to more errors in commodity classification: "It is clear that Customs' automated programs are designed to promote processing but will do little to overcome problems of misreporting."

Most of the users' recommendations for improving the accuracy of foreign trade data were fairly general. Some chemical manufacturers who had expressed concerns about misclassification of commodities called for more checking of information supplied by exporters, active Census Bureau efforts to solicit users' reactions about the quality of the data, and, in one instance, increasing and enforcing penalties for misclassification or nonreporting.

A user in the Department of Agriculture recommended improved communication "among the various government agencies using and/or contributing to each other's data."

Other users recommended that the Census Bureau make increased efforts to evaluate its merchandise trade data and provide users with more information about its quality. One of them recommended expansion of the recently initiated port audit program. Another called for more information "about how the data are gathered and how the numbers are affected by reporting problems and bottlenecks in the system." One respondent interviewed by panel members believes that current impressions about the quality of the data come primarily from "disaster stories" about substantial anomalies uncovered by users and that lack of systematic information about quality "contributes unnecessarily to the impression that all the data have very substantial errors embedded in them."

The Census Bureau, which tries to detect and correct at least some errors by the application of a series of edit checks, also comes in for its share of criticism. Some users who follow the data for specific commodities told us that they had notified the Census Bureau of apparent errors that they had identified. In some instances the problems had been dealt with adequately; but in others, they believed that Census had been unresponsive or had taken too long to eliminate the problem. A specific problem identified was the lack of any mechanism to systematically update values of parameters, such as acceptable ranges for unit values, for the thousands of commodities that the Census Bureau deals with. There were a few mentions of "disasters," that is, large errors that Census failed to detect or correct prior to publication. What is not clear was what happens when these disasters come to the Census Bureau's attention: To what extent are users notified of the revisions made? Is information about such errors used to develop improvements in the processing system, rather than just to make corrections?

Concerns about the accuracy of the data appear to be strongest in two quarters: agencies such as the U.S. International Trade Commission, which make administrative decisions based on the data, and companies that use the data for up-to-the-minute market share analysis. Both groups work with data for detailed commodity categories and often with monthly data. At this level of detail, well over half of the nonempty data cells are based on only one or two shipments, so that even a single error can have a large impact. Given the Census Bureau's relative lack of control over the quality of the incoming data and its limited resources for detecting and correcting errors, one has to ask whether it is reasonable to expect Census to meet demands for merchandise trade information at the current level of detail with data of acceptable quality.

UNMET USERS' NEEDS

Many users said they would like to have additional foreign trade data, and the kinds of data they would like varied widely. We have not tried to estimate the cost of providing all of the new data that users would like to have, but it would clearly be very high. The more costly data needs identified included: expanded coverage of low-value transactions, especially those shipped by air; substantial expansion of data on state of origin for exports and final state destination for imports; expansion of the samples used in the Bureau of Labor Statistics foreign-trade-price-index program to support more detail by commodity group and trading partner; and a survey to compile information on export orders.

Several users in chemical and other manufacturing industries called for finer commodity detail that would make it possible for them to monitor trade in the specific commodities that they produce and export. For example, one such request was for reporting of horseshoe nails separately from other categories of nails. Many of these users also called for elimination or reduction of the use of "basket categories" that group miscellaneous commodities or transactions that cannot be coded precisely within a broad group. As might be expected, similar comments were received from membership organizations and from consulting and research firms that serve manufacturing industries.

Leaving aside major changes, such as the recent shift to the Harmonized System, commodity classifications and definitions are frequently changed in order to adapt to the development of new products and to meet special needs expressed by users. Some users would like additional assistance in keeping up with these changes and making the necessary adjustments to the time series that they are maintaining. A consulting and research firm asked that the Census Bureau provide not only a list of such changes, but "some explanation of why the category changed and specifically what products are affected."

Two users asked that commodities be classified by the level of technology required to produce them. This might be interpreted as a request for the producer to add value to the basic data, since one way to satisfy this need would be for users to place detailed commodities into "level of technology" categories according to their own classification schemes. In addition, there were several comments about the need to provide better compatibility between merchandise trade and domestic production commodity data. This area is another in which users' needs might be met either by the Census Bureau's producing new data or by users' adding value to existing data. A membership organization suggested that the United States give serious consideration to making the commodity codes used for merchandise trade more directly compatible with those used for domestic production.

Representatives of air carriers and aircraft manufacturers expressed considerable concern about the exclusion of low-value shipments from the regular monthly processing of official trade documents and about the lack of detail provided and questionable accuracy of the estimates provided for this category of shipment. They pointed out that the excluded shipments encompass the whole air express and most of the air cargo industry. They clearly would like to see the Census Bureau resume processing all or a sample of the low-value shipments.

Users also mentioned several other types of data needs that could be met by adding items to the SEDs and import entry summaries or by processing and disseminating existing information on these forms in new ways. Some of these needs might be met by the users themselves through manipulation of data already available from Census, but they are noted here for the sake of completeness. Some chemical manufacturers expressed a desire for additional data on weights or volumes or the use of different units. A user from a company associated with container shipping asked for data that would require the addition of several new items, such as container size and mode of domestic transit, to the import and export documents. A university researcher proposed the use of a new commodity classifier based on the price of individual items. A representative of BEA proposed the addition of an item to the Customs Bureau import entry summary form to indicate whether or not the additional transaction was billed in a foreign currency. Two users called for additional improved data on affiliated trade, that is, intrafirm trade within multinational enterprises. At present, Census does not provide any data on affiliated trade: BEA derives a limited amount of this information from its enterprise-based surveys of U.S. direct investment abroad and foreign direct investment in the United States. The recent inclusion of the exporter's employer identification number on the SED opens up the possibility of distinguishing affiliated and nonaffiliated exports through a linkage process involving the Foreign Trade Division's export file, the Census Bureau's Standard Statistical Establishment List (SSEL), and the BEA surveys. A feasibility study was undertaken in 1986, and recent legislation giving BEA limited access to the SSEL is expected to facilitate the development of this kind of data.

In addition, in a "grab bag" category, several users expressed an interest in obtaining data in a form that identifies individual exporters and importers (or consignees), such as are presently available for vessel shipments from the PIERS system. Some of them recognized that it might not be possible for the Census Bureau to provide data at this level of detail. Included in this group of users was a unit of the Canadian government mainly concerned with the promotion of domestic production to substitute for imports to Canada. The reports published by this unit include lists of importers who are potential buyers of domestically made products. They would like to be able to use U.S. trade data to develop lists of U.S. importers and manufacturers who would be potential customers for Canadian exports.

So far, we have covered user-identified needs that could be met primarily through enhancements of the Census Bureau's foreign trade statistics program on the basis of processing official trade documents. Now we turn to user needs whose satisfaction would require the use of other sources of foreign trade data or, in at least one instance, the creation of a new data source. Two users called for expansion of the Bureau of Labor Statistics' monthly trade price index program to develop bilateral trade price indexes. One of them also proposed a survey of export orders. Such a survey would presumably be based on a sample of manufacturers and wholesalers. In his view, the data from such a survey would be valuable for the analysis and projection of export developments. Another proposal, from a user in the Canadian government, has implications for the censuses and surveys conducted by the Census Bureau's Industry Division. This user recommended that data on the production of U.S. firms be collected or compiled using the Harmonized System, so that it would be possible to estimate apparent domestic consumption for export commodities. This user also noted that Statistics Canada would be reporting production on this basis, beginning in 1990. The chief economist of a large U.S. corporation wants BLS to provide data on productivity for more countries as an aid in understanding international competitiveness and comparative advantage. He specifically mentioned Malaysia and Thailand as countries for which he would like to be able to monitor productivity levels achieved, rather than just growth rates, especially in manufacturing.

Several users want access to more complete and centralized information on tariffs and nontariff trade restrictions. Some wanted the information for operational rather than statistical uses, but others want it in connection with their research. An official of a foreign economic research unit in the Department of Labor called for the development and maintenance of a tariff-rate file, with inclusion of information about product and country eligibility for special tariff rates. With regard to nontariff trade restrictions, a university researcher and an economist in the Federal Reserve System were clearly frustrated by their inability to obtain detailed information. The lack of such information on a historical basis made it difficult, if not impossible, for them to analyze the structural characteristics of protection and its effect on country-specific trade patterns. The user from the Federal Reserve System pointed out that the United Nations and the World Bank maintain extensive sets of data on nontariff barriers but that, because of the political sensitivity of these data, these agencies are reluctant to allow researchers access.

Most of the users who gave us their views focused their attention on current needs for data and did not respond to our invitation to comment on anticipated future needs for additional or different data as the international trade environment changes. There were some notable exceptions, however. The corporate economist and chief statistician of a major data wholesaling corporation recommended that the panel step back from the existing system and take "a more comprehensive look at what is really needed for longer term policy making." He mentioned several ongoing and anticipated changes in the environment for international trade. Among them were the greatly expanded role and flexibility of multinational corporations and the attendant increase in the volume of intracompany transfers, trends toward multilateral reductions in trade barriers and the establishment of regional trading blocs, shifts to market-based economic activities in the Eastern European countries, and the discontinuities in long-standing trade time series created by the recent adoption of the Harmonized System. The corporate economist stated: "A fundamental redesign of information gathering about international transactions is called for . . . ." With respect to merchandise trade, he said: "A redesigned trade data system could be developed by using well-known principles of sampling and devoting the same resources that are currently expended (for 100 percent processing of foreign trade documents) for a much more sophisticated and intensive analysis of the characteristics behind the data."

Others described what are seen as the main challenges facing the present U.S. system of foreign trade statistics: the possibility that starting in 1992 it may no longer be possible to identify country of origin or destination within the European Economic Community; the full implementation of the Canada-United States Free Trade Agreement, which will lead to the end of filing of import documentation on both sides of the border; the increasing commingling of goods and services, making the collection of detailed merchandise trade statistics less meaningful and relatively more costly; and the arbitrary nature of the valuation of commodities in affiliated transactions. In view of these emerging trends, some doubt that the U.S. system of merchandise trade statistics could be maintained indefinitely in its present form and therefore that large investments to make it more efficient would be misdirected. With respect to the scheduled 1992 changes in the European Economic Community, a business analyst for a chemical manufacturer had a specific recommendation, namely, that the U.S. should press the EC to continue reporting exports and imports by individual countries within the EC.

Several users commented on the difficulty of using existing foreign trade statistics to understand the increasingly complex flows involved in production by multinational companies. They noted that parts of final products are often made in several countries and shipped back and forth before final assembly. Lack of information about these processes, they believed, might distort perceptions of U.S. bilateral trade problems and economic and political responses to them. On the marketing side, they wanted better access to data on bilateral trade transactions not involving the United States.

INTERNATIONAL SERVICES TRANSACTIONS AND CAPITAL FLOWS

Only about one-third of the more than 100 respondents to our canvass commented on statistics for international services transactions or financial flows. This was not unexpected because nearly one-half of these organizations were reached through the list of subscribers to the Census Bureau's publications of merchandise trade statistics. Furthermore, data on merchandise trade have historically received the lion's share of attention and interest from the general public, and only a relatively small number of specialists follow trends in other kinds of international economic transactions.

The past decade, however, has seen a rapid growth of the service sector, both domestically and internationally, with a consequent increase in the demand for data needed by the government to establish and evaluate national strategies and priorities and by the private sector to monitor trends and analyze market shares. To ensure that these areas were properly covered in its study, the panel invited several experts on statistics on international services transactions and financial flows, representing both producers and users of data, to make presentations. Primary attention was given to international services transactions.

INTERNATIONAL SERVICES TRANSACTIONS

Some users commented on unresolved problems associated with the concepts and definitions used in the collection and dissemination of data on trade in services. Two users said that the dividing line between goods and services is often not clear. One pointed out that multinational companies have considerable flexibility in valuing services associated with goods and may be expected to use this freedom to change the domestic or foreign content of their products to their own advantage. He believed that there should be a standardized way to allocate such costs.

One official from the Office of the U.S. Trade Representative pointed out that the terms "exports of services" and "invisibles," which are used in analyzing services transactions, are frequently misunderstood. He recommended that total trade in services be labeled as "U.S. sales of services to foreigners," rather than as "exports": the former applies to both cross-border sales and sales through affiliates; the latter bears the connotation of cross-border trade only. Similar recommendations were made by both a staff member of the Senate Subcommittee on Government Information and Regulation of the Committee on Government Affairs and the Coalition of Services Industries.

A representative from the Office of the U.S. Trade Representative (USTR) also commented on the completeness, timeliness, and comparability of U.S. statistics on international service transactions. With respect to completeness, he stated that "several important sectors, particularly financial services and transportation, are underrepresented" and that certain types of financial services are not covered at all. On the subject of timeliness, he noted that the need to obtain the data through establishment surveys precludes the development of monthly data, and he pointed to the fairly substantial lag in obtaining information through such surveys.

On the question of international comparability, the USTR representative said that many countries do not collect balance-of-payments data in the same detail as the United States. To improve comparability for those who do, international agencies are attempting to establish standard classifications and formats for compiling and presenting the data. Two university researchers who are adding services trade to a general equilibrium model covering several industries and countries confirmed the need for such standards; they said they were facing enormous difficulties in putting the data for different countries on a comparable basis.

A former Commerce Department official pointed to several possible sources of error in the statistics on services transactions. He believes that the methods now used in estimating receipts and expenditures related to international travel, including transportation expenditures, should be thoroughly evaluated. U.S. residents are not questioned about how much they spend abroad after they return; rather they are asked when they depart from the United States how much they intend to spend. The sample excludes travelers on chartered planes, and the sample data are processed by a private company subject to relatively limited control.

He also noted that for several types of services, data are now collected that previously had not been available. Yet the minimum amounts of individual transactions for which reports are requested are so high that presumably some types of transactions, for example, legal services, are substantially underreported. For some kinds of transactions, no data are collected or estimated: for instance, receipts and expenditures by news organizations or incomes from the sale of foreign newspapers and magazines that are printed in the country where they are sold but obtain their content from abroad through electronic transmission. On the subject of completeness, a statement from the Coalition of Services Industries noted that BEA surveys have begun to capture information on some service industries previously ignored but that many service industries still are not covered by any survey. The statement also asserted that reporting requirements and the complexity of the surveys have limited company response.

A BEA official alluded to the effects of the U.S.-Canada data exchange agreement on the valuation of U.S. exports to Canada, pointing out that one consequence would be a complete lack of data on cross-border receipts and payments by U.S. and Canadian carriers because Canadian import data are valued on a free-on-board (f.o.b.) basis.

Several users commented in broad terms about needs for more and better data on trade in services. An official of the U.S. Trade Representative noted the need for putting together a good information base on service transactions for use in connection with the Uruguay round of multilateral negotiations on services trade and said that much more detailed data may be needed as the negotiations progress. An official of the Department of Statistics of the International Monetary Fund also alluded to interest in an expanded list of service items in the context of these negotiations.

User statements included recommendations covering several aspects of statistics on international service transactions. A statement from the Coalition of Services Industries expressed substantial dissatisfaction with the data currently available and recommended clarification of concepts, more detail on different types of services, and monthly reporting. Other statements by a rather diverse group of users called for a variety on enhancements and improvements of services trade data, including more data on the educational component, more analyses of the data, development of price indices, more detail by country, and data by state.

CAPITAL FLOWS

Comments about statistics on financial flows were included in 10 of the presentations and statements received by the panel. The majority dealt with perceived deficiencies in the quality of existing data. In contrast to their perceptions of recent advances in the quality of data on international service transactions, the users believe that the quality of data on financial flows has been declining (see also Lipsey, 1990).

Specific problems with the existing reporting systems were discussed by researchers of the Federal Reserve Board and the Department of the Treasury. Both emphasized coverage problems and inaccurate reporting. Concerning the coverage problem, the Treasury International Capital (TIC) system concentrates on large filers and tends to miss the small filers. Given the development of the 24-hour international market, it is believed that the system will have to be modified to encompass the smaller players if they become more prevalent. Concerning inaccurate reporting, respondents said filers are devoting less resources to accurate reporting and do not exercise adequate quality control. In addition, data collection agencies have inadequate quality control. Users believe that the accuracy of the data on U.S. capital flows and investment income cannot be improved without the devotion of additional resources and efforts to convince filers that accuracy in these reports is important.

Others noted that large quantities of physical cash move in suitcases and boxes outside normal banking channels. Electronic transfers among banking institutions have ballooned, and the movement of financial transactions is increasingly difficult to monitor. One proposed solution is for transnational banking authorities and national central banks to undertake a careful review of the types of financial flows occurring inside and outside of current measurement systems. One respondent believes this to be of paramount importance because the current information is woefully inadequate to address the key policy issues that will be important in the 1990s and beyond.

A researcher at the Federal Reserve Bank of New York also recognized increasing difficulties in measuring financial flows. The most important future problem he could foresee was the globalization of financial markets. Noninterest income has been growing in size relative to total services trade, but, it has become increasingly difficult to measure these transactions, even in nominal terms.

Some users called for additional detail on certain kinds of financial transactions and for greater consistency with other kinds of data. A representative of an industry association wanted foreign investment data to be available at finer levels of disaggregation and on a consistent basis with other data series. A bond market specialist from an investment firm was interested in better information on interest income received and paid, portfolio investment incomes, and factors driving foreign direct investment and foreign takeovers in the United States. A Treasury Department representative said that criticisms of the crude breakdown used in the TIC reporting system were common and that users wanted more information on purchaser characteristics and coverage of instruments, such as futures swaps, that could be used as hedges.

Finally, as was the case for merchandise and services trade, users of state data wanted information on some types of financial transactions at the state level. A representative from the Minnesota Department of Trade and Economic Development told the panel that data for the state from the BEA surveys of U.S. affiliates of foreign firms were of limited value due to disclosure problems. No information is provided on the value of Japanese affiliates in Minnesota, for example, because it could potentially reveal proprietary data of a single firm. Yet the Japan External Trade Organization reports two dozen firms in Minnesota owned in part or entirely by Japanese entities. The Minnesota representative also said that a second source of information on foreign investments at the state level is the transactions data produced by the Commerce Department's International Trade Administration, which provides an annual listing of individual foreign investment transactions in the United States. Because the information is collected from secondary sources, it is fully disclosed. But the Minnesota official found the information from this source to be of limited usefulness, because the value was reported for fewer than half of the transactions and because the listing provided only a limited amount of summary information by state.

INVITATION FOR WRITTEN COMMENTS

Reproduced below is the text of the letter sent by panel chair Robert E. Baldwin to solicit comments from users of international trade data.

Accurate, timely and relevant data on U.S. foreign trade are necessary for many purposes, especially in the present era of trade deficits, greater competition from abroad, and increasing globalization of production. Under the auspices of the National Academies of Sciences and Engineering—National Research Council, the Committee on National Statistics is undertaking a two-year panel study to evaluate the quality of U.S. foreign trade statistics and to develop recommendations for improving them. The study, which has been funded by the Bureau of the Census and the Bureau of Economic Analysis of the U.S. Department of Commerce and the Customs Service of the U.S. Department of the Treasury, covers international trade in both merchandise and services.

For our evaluation, it is essential that we obtain the views of a wide spectrum of users of foreign trade data. As part of the panel study we will be interviewing users in several categories, but our resources are insufficient to meet or speak with all of you. Therefore, as Chair of the Panel on Foreign Trade Statistics, I would like to invite you to submit written statements describing what foreign trade data you are using, where you obtain the data, how you use the data, what your views are on the adequacy of the data for your purposes and how it might be improved, and what type of trade data will be most useful to you in the coming years.

Please send your statements to Dr. Anne Kester, the Study Director of the Panel on Foreign Trade Statistics, at the address shown below. Information on any or all of the following subjects will be useful:

• The kinds of data that you are using. (Specify level of detail such as geographic and commodity types for merchandise trade data and services categories for services trade statistics.)
• The sources — governmental or non-governmental — from which you obtain the data?
• How you process and use the data.
• Your views about various aspects of the data you use, including relevance, level of detail provided, frequency of publication, timeliness, accuracy, costs of obtaining the data and compatibility with other kinds of data, such as domestic production, as well as your views on how they might be improved.
• Your anticipated future needs for additional or different data as the international trade environment changes.

To be of maximum benefit to our study, please send your statements to us by April 30, 1990. We look forward to hearing from you.

PROTOCOL FOR INFORMAL INTERVIEWS WITH DATA USERS

Reproduced below is the protocol for panel and staff members in interviews with data users.

A. Introduction
   Review purpose of interview and how the information will be used. If agreed to by respondents, start recording.

B. User/respondent characteristics.
   1. Organization or business.
      Name and address.
      Type of organization.
   2. For each person being interviewed, name, telephone number and position in organization or business.
   3. Are those present answering questions for the entire organization or only part of it? If the latter, may want to identify other important users in the organization.

C. Acquisition of foreign trade data by the organization.
   1. Source agencies/organizations: Census, BEA, BLS, ITA, USDA, EIA, United Nations, OECD, EUROSTAT, private companies, etc.
   2. For each source, modes of acquisition.
      Hard copy publications.
      Electronic (magnetic tape, CD-ROM, on-line, other).

Microform/microfiche.
Other.
3. Specifics. Obtain name, source, frequency and cost of each acquisition. For frequency, is it regular (monthly, quarterly, or annual) or occasional?

D. How are data converted to usable information?
   1. Which of the following are done?
      Extract data items for citation in article or report.
      Extract data items for use in models.
      Calculate indices.
      Create new tables.
      Time series analyses.
Other
   2. If yes to any of the items in C,1, how are the data prepared for input to perform the necessary calculations?
   3. Are data adjusted to conform to concepts or classifications different from those used by the source organization? If yes, what adjustments are made?
   4. Are foreign trade data processed or analyzed in conjunction with other kinds of data, e.g., data on domestic production or sales?

E. Specific data items used.
   1. Are the same items used regularly or do they vary over time. If the latter, what is the nature of the variation?
   2. Broad categories of data used: imports, exports, prices, service trade, others.
   3. Variables, e.g., quantity, value (Customs import value, C.I.F. import value, F.A.S. export value).
   4. Classifiers.
      a. Commodities. Which classification systems are used? What is the finest level of detail and what are the groups or items of interest at that level?
      b. Geography.
         Region/country of origin or destination. What is finest level and which regions or countries are of interest?
         Port or district of entry/exit. Which are of interest?
         State of origin of exports. Which ones?
      c. Mode of transportation.

F. Outputs containing foreign trade data.
   1. Publications of user organization or individual. For each one identified obtain:
      a. Name and type of publication (e.g., newsletter, industry or trade publication, economic report or bulletin, article for scholarly journal, etc.).
      b. How foreign trade data are presented (e.g., tables, charts, cited in text).

    c.   Frequency (periodicity or one-time).

    d.   Size and nature of audience, method of distribution.

  2. Electronic media distributed to other organizations or individuals. Identify specific medium, e.g., magnetic tapes, diskettes, CD-ROM, on-line access.

  3. Internal reports. For each one identified, obtain information on general nature and purpose, frequency, recipients and how the foreign trade data are presented.

G. Intended effects/uses of outputs. Identify and discuss all that apply.

  1. Influence trade policies or negotiations.

  2. Influence legislation or regulation relevant to foreign trade.

  3. Analysis and forecasting of general economic conditions.

  4. International market analysis.

  5. Investment decisions.

  6. Provide general information to secondary users.

  7. Other.

H. Satisfaction with data currently available.

[NOTE: If respondents are unsatisfied with any aspects, probe concerning adverse effects of perceived deficiencies on the uses identified in G. If they express satisfaction with respect to items 1 to 4 below, ask how their uses of the data would be affected if the amount of detail or frequency of publication were reduced, the delays following the end of reference periods were increased, or subscription prices were increased?]

  1. Content. Does it meet all needs? If no, what else is needed? Are there problems of comparability with other kinds of data?

  2. Costs and convenience of acquisition and user processing of foreign trade data. If not satisfied, what improvements are desired?

  3. Frequency and timeliness. Ask how respondents' use of the data would be affected if data are published less frequently (e.g., for merchandise trade statistics, from a monthly to a quarterly or annual basis.) Ask specifically about reactions to February 1987 shift from 30 to 45 days for publication of Census monthly data on merchandise trade.

  4. Are there problems associated with revisions? Describe.

  5. Accuracy. Have respondent's uses been affected by errors in data? How? How were the errors detected? Do they inform source organizations? Have they received satisfactory responses?

  6. Information on data concepts, definitions and methodology. What sources of information do they use and are these adequate for their needs?

  7. What are the other limitations of the data?

I. Future data needs.

Do respondents expect that their needs for foreign trade data will change in the future? If yes, how and why?

J. Access to users of foreign trade data supplied by this organization.

If this organization supplies foreign trade data to other organizations and individuals through publications or other media, inquire about their willingness to allow use of their mailing list for distribution of an invitation for users of their data to submit written statements to the Panel on Foreign Trade Statistics.

C

A Comparison of U.S. Export Statistics With Those of Major Trading Partners

This note compares the accuracy of export statistics across five developed countries: the United States, Japan, West Germany, the United Kingdom, and Canada. The statistics analyzed in this note are those reported in the various issues of the *Direction of Trade Statistics Yearbook* published by the International Monetary Fund (IMF). These countries were selected for two reasons. First, they are the four largest importers of U.S. exports: the four countries' share of the total U.S. exports was 40.7 percent for 1980-1989 (see Table C-1). Second, they are also the important export destinations for other countries: the export shares of the other four countries in each country's total exports were: 42.6 percent for Japan, 18.7 percent for West Germany, 27.9 percent for the United Kingdom, and 79.0 percent for Canada (see Table C-1).

International experiences suggest that import data are in general more accurate (or are more seriously collected by officials) than export data, probably because of taxation and trade restrictions. Based on this observation, this note assumes that each country's import statistics represent true trade flows and treats the difference between an exporting country's export data and the corresponding importing country's data as an inaccurate portion of export statistics.

Most countries report their imports on the cost-insurance-freight (c.i.f.) valuation basis and their exports on the free-on-board (f.o.b.) basis. The c.i.f./f.o.b. ratios are different among countries, mainly due to each country's geographical location and trade contents.

221

TABLE C-1 Export Shares by Destination, 1980-1989 (in billions of dollars)

Export Shares	1980	1981	1982	1983	1984	1985	1986	1987	1988	1989	10-Year Average
U.S. exports (f.o.b.)											
to Japan, West Germany, United Kingdom, and Canada	79.8	84.1	74.6	79.4	91.3	90.2	94.1	113.9	139.8	160.5	
to World	220.7	233.7	212.2	200.5	217.8	213.1	217.2	252.8	319.9	363.8	
4 countries' share (%)	36.2	36.0	35.2	39.6	41.9	42.3	43.3	45.1	43.7	44.1	40.7
Japan's exports (f.o.b.)											
to United States, West Germany, United Kingdom, and Canada	43.9	52.9	49.1	57.8	75.9	83.0	104.7	112.1	123.0	127.2	
to World	130.4	151.5	138.4	146.9	169.7	177.1	210.7	231.3	264.9	274.5	
4 countries' share (%)	33.7	35.0	35.5	39.3	44.8	46.8	49.7	48.5	46.5	46.3	42.6
West Germany's exports (f.o.b.)											
to United States, Japan, United Kingdom, and Canada	27.8	26.4	27.6	30.1	34.6	39.3	52.5	62.1	66.3	67.2	
to World	192.8	176.0	176.4	169.4	171.7	183.9	243.3	294.1	323.3	341.3	
4 countries' share (%)	14.4	15.0	15.7	17.8	20.2	21.4	21.6	21.1	20.5	19.7	18.7
United Kingdom's exports (f.o.b.)											
to United States, Japan, West Germany, and Canada	25.5	26.5	25.1	24.4	26.3	30.1	32.0	39.2	42.5	45.2	
to World	110.0	102.2	96.9	91.6	93.8	101.2	107.0	131.2	145.1	152.3	
4 countries' share (%)	23.2	25.9	26.0	26.7	28.1	29.8	30.0	29.9	29.3	29.7	27.9
Canada's exports (f.o.b.)											
to United States, Japan, West Germany, and United Kingdom	48.9	53.9	53.4	60.7	73.6	75.1	74.2	80.3	93.5	97.2	
to World	67.7	72.7	71.2	76.7	90.2	90.7	89.7	98.1	116.5	120.6	
4 countries' share (%)	72.2	74.2	75.1	79.1	81.5	82.8	82.8	81.9	80.3	80.6	79.0

SOURCE: International Monetary Fund (1986b, 1990b).

This note uses the c.i.f./f.o.b. factors (CFF) shown in the IMF's *International Financial Statistics*. The CFF series originate from the balance-of-payments statistics; a country's total costs for freight and insurance are computed as differences between its imports (c.i.f.) and its trading partner's corresponding exports (f.o.b.). The CFFs are "average" figures for the total imports. Nonetheless, using them is probably better than just using the 1.1 figure usually applied by other researchers for some countries. (The CFF series used in this note can be found in *International Financial Statistics Yearbook, 1989*.)

The yearly data for each country from 1980 to 1989 are examined as follows:

(a) is the country's exports (f.o.b.) to the other four countries (in millions of dollars);

(b) is the other four countries' imports (c.i.f.) from the country concerned (in millions of dollars);

(c) is the other four countries' imports, expressed in (f.o.b.) terms, from the country concerned (in millions of dollars),

$$(c) = \frac{(b)}{CFF} \; ;$$

(d) is the discrepancy on an f.o.b. basis (in millions of dollars),

$$(d) = (a) - (c) \; ;$$

(e) is the discrepancy on an f.o.b. basis, expressed in percentage terms,

$$(e) = \frac{(d)}{(c)} \; .$$

The table below shows the 10-year average discrepancies (in current prices) and discrepancy percentages from 1980 to 1989 for each country. Since the absolute magnitudes of discrepancies vary with the size of each country's exports, the discrepancy percentages are a better measure for international comparisons of the accuracy of countries' statistics than the magnitudes.

Country	Discrepancy	
	$ Millions	Percentages
United States	–7,734	–7.96
Japan	92	0.36
West Germany	30	0.00
United Kingdom	–1,163	–4.04
Canada	689	1.13

The discrepancies and discrepancy percentages of Japan, West Germany, and Canada are close to zero (on average), while those of the United States show large negative figures. This difference suggests that the U.S. export statistics may be less accurate than those of Japan, West Germany, and Canada. If so, trade deficit figures announced by the United States may have been overstated. The U.S. discrepancies and discrepancy percentages appear to be smaller in the recent years, which might indicate the recent improvement of the U.S. export statistics.

The discrepancy percentage of Canada may be biased in the positive direction for several reasons: the main destination of Canada's exports is the United States; Canada and the United States are geographically close, and thus freight and insurance costs are probably lower than those for trade destined for other countries; the U.S. import data are converted from the c.i.f. basis to the f.o.b. basis by using the "aggregate" conversion factors. Therefore, the data on U.S. imports from Canada (f.o.b.) may be understated.

A part of the large discrepancies of the U.S. export statistics might come from their trade contents. If the accuracy of import statistics is positively related to the magnitude of trade restrictions, import data of agricultural trade may be more accurate than those of manufactured goods, because agricultural trade is generally more restricted than manufactured goods trade. If so, the discrepancies of agricultural exports may be biased in the negative direction compared with those of manufactured goods exports.

D

Variability in Month-to-Month Changes in the Seasonally Adjusted Merchandise Trade Balances

The data on the seasonally adjusted trade balance typically fluctuate widely from month to month, as has been noted in the body of this report. Evidence shows that many users of these data, including traders and other participants in financial markets in the United States and elsewhere, sometimes overreact to monthly changes in the data. Such overreaction is sometimes attributed to ignorance concerning the extent of the underlying variability in the month-to-month changes, which can lead to misinterpreting a given month's observation as a large deviation and hence indicative of a shift in trend when it is within a range or band that could be considered reasonable in the light of the history of variability in the data.

But this phenomenon raises the key question: How should the variability in the data be measured? This appendix explores the issue of variability in the month-to-month changes in the seasonally adjusted trade balance, develops a measure of this variability that takes account of the autocorrelation that is present in the data series, and uses this measure to determine a band for the monthly changes from February 1987 through February 1991, thus providing a simple characterization of the variability in the data. Several other features of the data extending back to 1977 are also considered.

This appendix was prepared by panel member W. Allen Spivey.

Figure D-1 displays the seasonally adjusted trade balance (which we denote ATB) from January 1987 through February 1991, and Figure D-2 shows a plot of the month-to-month changes (or first differences, denoted DATB) in the ATB series from February 1987 through February 1991. The DATB series in Figure D-2 displays considerable variability and also shows that the month-to-month changes have a pronounced alternating pattern. If the monthly change is a large and positive number for a given month t, for example, the change for the following month, t+1, tends to be smaller and is often a negative number. Conversely, if the observation for month t is a negative number, the following month's observation tends to be a positive number. Data for the ATB and DATB time series are shown in Table D-1.

PROBLEMS WITH THE DATA

One of the most difficult problems with the monthly trade data is that the seasonally adjusted balance (the difference between the value of merchandise exports and imports) for a given month does not necessarily reflect trade flows in the month: this is called the carryover problem. This problem arises when, for a variety of reasons (see Chapter 4), the data on export or import transactions for a given month include transactions that actually occurred in one or more previous months, so that the value actually reported for a given month can be much larger or smaller than it should be. For example, for several years in the mid-1980s, carryovers for imports were often as high as 50 percent of the reported monthly total and as high as 13 percent for exports, and data for a month sometimes included carryovers from as many as 18 prior months.

These carryovers mean that a plot of the time series of monthly changes in the trade balance could have a large spike for a given month when a substantial portion of the figure did not represent a large change taking place in the month but rather transactions attributable to underreporting in one or more previous months. They also mean that not only is the observation for the given month incorrectly reported, but also that those for one or more prior periods were understated and thus inaccurate. Figure D-3 shows the first differences of the seasonally adjusted trade balance data for the period January 1977 through March 1990, unadjusted for carryovers. Large spikes are shown for various months, particularly July and August of 1984 and September and October of 1985, although the monthly changes between these pairs of months are comparatively small.

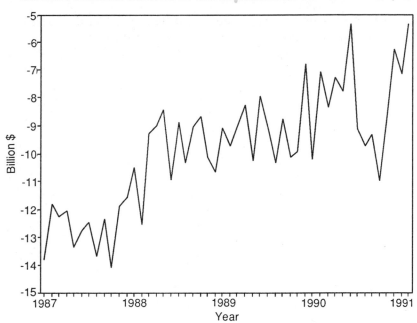

FIGURE D-1   Seasonally adjusted merchandise trade balance: January 1987-February 1991.

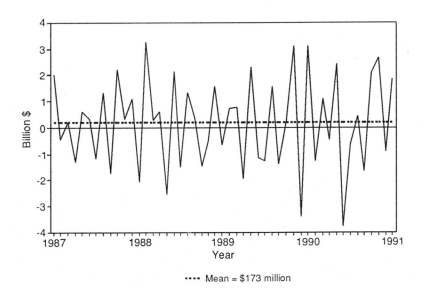

FIGURE D-2   Seasonally adjusted merchandise trade balance, first differences: February 1987-February 1991.

TABLE D-1   Seasonally Adjusted Trade Balance (ATB) and First Differences (DATB), 1987-1991 (in millions of dollars)

Year and Month	ATB	DATB
1987		
1	−13,810.2	—
2	−11,813.8	1,996.4
3	−12,264.8	−451.0
4	−12,055.4	209.4
5	−13,370.3	−1,314.9
6	−12,759.6	610.7
7	−12,451.2	308.4
8	−13,659.9	−1,208.7
9	−12,345.3	1,314.6
10	−14,116.6	−1,771.3
11	−11,890.6	2,226.0
12	−11,570.4	320.2
1988		
1	−10,495.6	1,074.8
2	−12,555.6	−2,060.0
3	−9,300.7	3,254.9
4	−9,027.4	273.3
5	−8,414.8	612.6
6	−10,969.0	−2,554.2
7	−8,859.6	2,109.4
8	−10,365.4	−1,505.8
9	−9,042.6	1,322.8
10	−8,682.4	360.2
11	−10,157.2	−1,474.8
12	−10,655.4	−498.2
1989		
1	−9,085.2	1,570.2
2	−9,750.8	−665.6

continued

By early 1988 carryovers had been reduced to about 5 percent for both exports and imports, and efforts to reduce carryover problems have been continuing. Unfortunately, it is not possible for the Census Bureau to make adjustments for carryover errors in the data prior to January 1987. The data in Figures D-1 and D-2 and in Table D-1, however, have been adjusted by Census Bureau personnel for carryover problems. Some carryovers still exist in these data, but Census personnel believe that they do not exceed 5 percent for either exports or imports in this period.

TABLE D-1 *Continued*

Year and Month	ATB	DATB
1989—*continued*		
3	−9,032.0	718.8
4	−8,280.4	751.6
5	−10,260.6	−1,980.2
6	−7,952.0	2,308.6
7	−9,081.0	−1,129.0
8	−10,328.1	−1,247.1
9	−8,768.7	1,559.4
10	−10,152.3	−1,383.6
11	−9,912.7	239.6
12	−6,795.5	3,117.2
1990		
1	−10,197.8	−3,402.3
2	−7,096.1	3,101.7
3	−8,369.8	−1,273.7
4	−7,305.8	1,064.0
5	−7,769.5	−463.7
6	−5,339.6	2,429.9
7	−9,118.9	−3,779.3
8	−9,734.1	−615.2
9	−9,326.3	407.8
10	−10,987.6	−1,661.3
11	−8,911.7	2,075.9
12	−6,277.0	2,634.7
1991		
1	−7,163.8	−886.8
2	−5,333.8	1,830.0

NOTES: ATB, seasonally adjusted trade balance with data corrected for carryovers; DATB, first differences of ATB. For DATB, the mean is 172.9878.

SOURCE: Data derived from various monthly trade statistics published by the Bureau of the Census.

Our analysis and measurement of the variability of the DATB time series is therefore based on the 49 observations for February 1987 to February 1991 (see Table B-1)—a relatively small number of observations that restrict the choice of methods and models available for modeling and measuring data variability.

Largely because of this small number we have used autoregressive, integrated, moving-average models, often referred to as ARIMA models, to model the autocorrelation in the DATB time series and to measure data variability. We also experimented with mod-

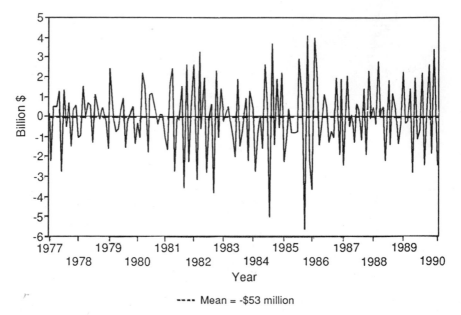

FIGURE D-3 Seasonally adjusted merchandise trade balance, first differences not adjusted for carryovers: January 1977-March 1990.

els from several other model classes, including ARCH (autoregressive conditional heteroskedastic), GARCH (generalized ARCH), and spectral models, but results were inconclusive, primarily because of the small sample size.

MEASURING THE VARIABILITY OF MONTH-TO-MONTH CHANGES

We applied the usual ARIMA modeling procedures (see Box and Jenkins, 1976:Chapters 6-8). Figure D-1 suggests that the levels of the seasonally adjusted trade data are nonstationary; however, the month-to-month changes or first differences DATB appear to be stationary (see Figure D-2) so ARIMA methods can be applied to them. Moreover, a perusal of discussions of the U.S. trade deficits appearing in the business media strongly suggests that data users appear to be much more interested in the month-to-month changes than in the levels of the trade deficit.[1]

---

[1] A similar situation exists with other major economic variables. Data users typically are more concerned about monthly changes in employment and in unemployment rates than with levels; changes in GNP often command greater

Proceeding to the modeling of the DATB series, Figure D-4 displays plots of the sample autocorrelation (ACF) and partial autocorrelations (PACF) and related estimates for these data. The dots in the ACF and PACF plots denote approximately 2 standard errors. Figures D-4, D-5, and D-6 were developed by using Version 6.03 of the SAS computer program.

One interpretation of the ACF and PACF is that the former dies down towards zero and the PACF has a spike at lag 1. This interpretation suggests that the stochastic process generating the DATB time series is an autoregressive process of order 1, or an AR(1) process. A reasonable alternative interpretation is that the ACF cuts off after lag 1 and that the PACF dies down towards zero, so that an alternative identification is that the process is a moving average of order 1, or an MA(1) process.[2] Both of these models were estimated, and the results were subjected to the usual model diagnostic procedures. Both models produced similar and satisfactory diagnostic results, but the AR(1) model was chosen because it is easier to interpret in the context of the problem being addressed. Several other ARIMA models were examined, including an ARMA(1,1) in the first differences, but one or more coefficients were insignificant, and model diagnostics were poor.

Figure D-5 shows properties of the estimated or fitted model. The fitted model is

$$\hat{y}_t = -0.56076 y_{t-1} ,$$

where for any t, y_t denotes the first difference or the change in the seasonally adjusted trade balance from time t–1 to time t. The model is estimated by means of a nonlinear maximum likelihood

---

interest than its levels, particularly when it is believed that the economy may be approaching a turning point; and money and capital markets typically direct more attention to changes, and to percentage changes, in the money supply than to the levels of the money supply.

[2]A finite, stationary AR process can be expressed as an infinite-order MA process and a finite, invertible MA process can be expressed as an infinite-order AR process. A stationary AR(1) process, when expressed as an infinite-order MA process, can have an autocorrelation with a large spike or value at lag 1 and have a sequence of small spikes for longer lags (the autocorrelations at longer lags can be buried in the noise of the process). A similar result can occur when an MA(1) process can be expressed as an infinite–order AR process. Moreover, in applied ARIMA modeling it is not unusual to encounter a time series that can be reasonably interpreted as being generated by either and AR(1) process or an MA(1) process—as is the case here.

The SAS System

ARIMA Procedure

Name of variable = DATB.

Mean of working series = 172.9878
Standard deviation   = 1711.725
Number of observations =   49

Autocorrelations

Lag	Covariance	Correlation	-1 9 8 7 6 5 4 3 2 1 0 1 2 3 4 5 6 7 8 9 1	Std
0	2930002	1.00000	|********************|	0
1	-1626917	-0.55526	*********** | .	0.142857
2	575820	0.19653	. |**** .	0.181638
3	-28642.362	-0.00978	. | .	0.185927
4	-137857	-0.04705	. *| .	0.185938
5	-486438	-0.16602	. ***| .	0.186180
6	898349	0.30660	. |****** .	0.189178
7	-1048414	-0.35782	.*******| .	0.199061
8	252469	0.08617	. |** .	0.211781
9	207594	0.07085	. |* .	0.212495
10	-148982	-0.05085	. *| .	0.212976
11	9524.907	0.00325	. | .	0.213224
12	271820	0.09277	. |** .	0.213225

"." marks two standard errors

Partial Autocorrelations

Lag	Correlation	-1 9 8 7 6 5 4 3 2 1 0 1 2 3 4 5 6 7 8 9 1
1	-0.55526	***********| .
2	-0.16162	. ***| .
3	0.04044	. |* .
4	-0.00624	. | .
5	-0.30932	******| .
6	0.10303	. |** .
7	-0.14240	. ***| .
8	-0.31023	******| .
9	-0.09420	. **| .
10	0.03994	. |* .
11	-0.02221	. | .
12	-0.11952	. **| .

Autocorrelation Check for White Noise

To Lag	Chi Square	DF	Prob	Autocorrelations					
6	25.26	6	0.000	-0.555	0.197	-0.010	-0.047	-0.166	0.307
12	34.39	12	0.001	-0.358	0.086	0.071	-0.051	0.003	0.093

FIGURE D-4 Autocorrelations and partial autocorrelations for first differences of seasonally adjusted merchandise trade balance.

procedure as indicated in the SAS output in Figure D-5. The autocorrelation coefficient is significant at the conventional levels. The negative autocorrelation estimate, $\hat{\phi}_1 = -0.56076$, suggests that the process generating the time series tends to produce observations that alternate in sign. Thus, one would expect a large and positive observation in a given period to be followed in the next period by an observation having a negative value.

An analysis of the residuals of the fitted model was performed.

```
                          The SAS System

                        ARIMA Procedure

                 Maximum Likelihood Estimation

                                    Approx.
           Parameter    Estimate    Std Error    T Ratio   Lag
           AR1,1        -0.56076     0.11996      -4.67      1

           Variance Estimate = 2080549.15
           Std Error Estimate = 1442.41088
           AIC                = 853.282143
           SBC                = 855.173964
           Number of Residuals=         49

                  Correlations of the Estimates

                     Parameter          AR1,1

                     AR1,1              1.000

                Autocorrelation Check of Residuals

   To    Chi                    Autocorrelations
   Lag  Square DF    Prob
    6     5.96   5   0.310 -0.075 -0.067  0.085 -0.227 -0.076  0.178
   12    14.45  11   0.209 -0.309 -0.008  0.168 -0.016  0.055  0.111
   18    22.44  17   0.168 -0.048  0.214  0.041 -0.203  0.051 -0.118
   24    26.57  23   0.275  0.009  0.117  0.023 -0.076  0.149 -0.047
```

FIGURE D-5   Properties of maximum likelihood estimated model for seasonally adjusted merchandise trade data.

The autocorrelations and partial autocorrelations of the residuals (see Figure D-6) support the view that the residuals are from a white-noise process, with the possible exception of lag 7—which might indicate some residual seasonality at this lag. Joint or "portmanteau" tests for 6, 12, 18, and 24 lags (see Figure D-5) also suggest white noise (the portmanteau test is discussed in Ljung and Box [1978]). Further analysis of model residuals using a Kolmogorov-Smirnov test, a test of skewness and of kurtosis, and a p-plot of the residuals against a normal distribution all supported the adequacy of the AR(1) model.

Figure D-5 indicates that the standard error of the AR(1) model is $1.442 billion (rounded). The mean of the residuals is $249.049 million (rounded). Thus, the standard error of the month-to-month changes in the seasonally adjusted trade balance is approximately six times larger than the mean. The parameters of the AR(1) model are estimated by the SAS program using a nonlinear maximum likelihood procedure. The mean of the residuals is not necessarily zero because the sum of the model residuals is not

The SAS System

ARIMA Procedure

Autocorrelation Plot of Residuals

```
Lag Covariance Correlation -1 9 8 7 6 5 4 3 2 1 0 1 2 3 4 5 6 7 8 9 1          Std
  0   2080549   1.00000     |                    |********************|         0
  1   -156675  -0.07530     |                .   **|   .               |  0.142857
  2   -140217  -0.06739     |                .    *|   .               |  0.143665
  3    175992   0.08459     |                .     |**  .              |  0.144309
  4   -472739  -0.22722     |                .*****|   .               |  0.145317
  5   -157247  -0.07558     |                .   **|   .               |  0.152395
  6    370990   0.17831     |                .     |****  .            |  0.153158
  7   -642327  -0.30873     |                ******|   .               |  0.157338
  8 -16141.980 -0.00776     |                .     |   .               |  0.169250
  9    349746   0.16810     |                .     |***  .             |  0.169258
 10 -33484.472 -0.01609     |                .     |*  .               |  0.172631
 11    114649   0.05511     |                .     |*  .               |  0.172662
 12    230624   0.11085     |                .     |**  .              |  0.173020
                                                       "." marks two standard errors
```

Partial Autocorrelations

```
Lag Correlation -1 9 8 7 6 5 4 3 2 1 0 1 2 3 4 5 6 7 8 9 1
  1   -0.07530     |              .   **|   .            |
  2   -0.07348     |              .    *|   .            |
  3    0.07443     |              .     |*  .            |
  4   -0.22348     |              .****  |   .           |
  5   -0.10156     |              .   **|   .            |
  6    0.13784     |              .     |***  .          |
  7   -0.29506     |              ******|   .            |
  8   -0.06919     |              .    *|   .            |
  9    0.09463     |              .     |**  .           |
 10    0.07710     |              .     |**  .           |
 11   -0.03989     |              .    *|   .            |
 12    0.03249     |              .     |*  .            |
```

The SAS System

Variable	Label	N	Mean	Sum
DATB		49	172.9877551	8476.40
FORECAST	Forecast for DATB	49	-76.0616740	-3727.02
RESIDUAL	Residual: Actual-Forecast	49	249.0494291	12203.42

FIGURE D-6 Autocorrelations and partial autocorrelations of residuals (see Figure D-5).

constrained by the estimation to be zero, as is the case when an AR(1) model is estimated by an ordinary least-squares (OLS) algorithm. Estimation of an AR(1) model by OLS produces biased parameter estimates in finite samples. (The statistical properties of ARIMA model estimates under various nonlinear estimation procedures are examined extensively in Box and Jenkins [1976]).

The standard error of the AR(1) model estimated by SAS and used here provides an estimate of the standard deviation of the conditional distribution of y_t for time t. This is an appropriate estimator to use for the standard deviation of the process generating the month-to-month changes and so is used to measure the variability of these changes.

A SIMPLE CHARACTERIZATION OF VARIABILITY

We now use the values of the mean and standard error of the residuals to develop a control chart display for the monthly changes in the seasonally adjusted trade balance data. Figure D-7 shows the first differences DATB, with a zero line, a dashed line denoting the mean of 249.0494291, and dashed lines plotted at 3 standard errors (3 × 1442.41088 = 4327.23264) above and below the mean, which can be interpreted as upper and lower control or specification limits, respectively. In other words, this is a control chart for the observations y_t on the month-to-month changes. In quality-control applications, a process is typically regarded as being "out of control" when an observation exceeds a control limit, when there are aberrant sequences of observations or "runs" above and below a given level, or when a "run up" of observations alter-

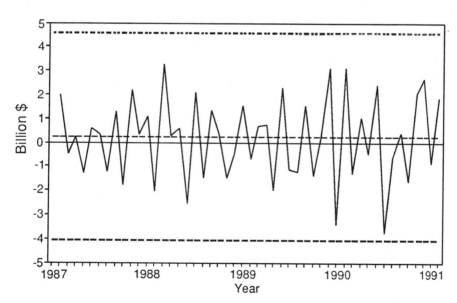

Mean of the Residuals From the AR(1) Model = $249 million

− − Mean of First Diff.   ···· Upper Control Limit   − − Lower Control Limit

FIGURE D-7 Control chart for data on monthly changes, seasonally adjusted merchandise trade balance.

nates with a "run down" (Alwan and Roberts, 1988:87). When one or more of these conditions is displayed, one takes action in some operational sense to respond to the process.

Figure D-7 does not show an observation exceeding the specification limits, nor does it display runs. Thus, if one were to have used this approach from control charts for the period from February 1987 through February 1991, one would not have taken action because of extreme values or aberrant observations at any time. Stated another way, none of the monthly changes over this period would have been regarded as sufficiently unusual to lead one to believe that the process generating the data had shifted its mean or changed in any other important way.

To sum up: the key issue here, as noted at the beginning of this appendix, is the large variability in the month-to-month changes in merchandise trade balance data. Such variability is measured by the standard error, which is about six times larger than the mean for the data. A conventional 3-standard error band is very wide and is probably much wider than would be expected on an intuitive basis by many data users. Therefore, the month-to-month changes are not outside expectations for the characteristics of the data.

E

An Alternative Seasonal Adjustment Procedure for Merchandise Trade Data

Some experts claim that the high volatility of the U.S. monthly trade balance is due to the fact that the trade balance, which is usually close to zero, is derived from the difference of two large figures, imports and exports. However, our analysis shows that the data do not support this claim. For example, the mean monthly merchandise trade balance for 1985-1990 is about –$10.5 billion, the mean monthly export figure for the period is $23.5 billion, and the mean monthly import figure is $34.0 billion: the difference is a substantial proportion of the means.

We have considered alternative methods of seasonally adjusting the data because an initial analysis of the data leads us to believe that the X-11 seasonal adjustment procedure currently used by Census Bureau not only fails to remove much of the seasonal noise from the data, but also adds more noise to the data.[1] Figure E-1 shows that the seasonally unadjusted series has a clear seasonal pattern. The X-11 adjusted trade balance, shown in Figure E-2, displays only slightly less volatility than the original series, and a seasonal pattern is still discernible. The standard deviation

This appendix was prepared by panel member Jerry A. Hausman; Mark Watson, professor, Northwestern University; and Ruth Judson, a graduate student at the Massachusetts Institute of Technology.
[1]In this paper we concentrate on the customs valuation of imports; however, use of c.i.f. value of imports leads to very similar conclusions.

of the unadjusted series over the 1985-1990 period is \$2.1 billion, and the standard deviation of the adjusted series is \$1.9 billion.

We propose an alternative method of seasonal adjustment that uses a time-series model with unobserved components—the Kalman filter model. We assume that each seasonally unadjusted trade balance figure is actually the sum of three components that are not observed individually: a nonseasonal term, representing the component of trade that varies due to economic conditions unrelated to the time of year; a seasonal term, representing the component of trade that varies due to the season; and an error or noise term.[2] This can be written as

$$(1) \quad Y_t = N_t + S_t + e_t .$$

We then assume a time-series structure for each term. We model the first two terms, N_t and S_t, as 1-period and 12-period random walks and e_t as white noise to yield the following ARIMA process for the observed trade balance:

$$(2a) \quad (1 - L)N_t = e^n_t , \text{ and}$$
$$(2b) \quad (1 + L + L^2 + \ldots + L^{11})S_t = e^s_t .$$

With this model, the process is then characterized by a variance parameter for each error component. For each combination of variance parameters, the Kalman filter algorithm finds the optimal decomposition of the process into the three unobserved components given in equation (1), assuming the structure from equations (2a) and (2b). The Kalman filter also yields a likelihood value for each decomposition so that we can choose the variance components to maximize the likelihood. Once we have the optimal decomposition at the optimal variance parameter values, the model-based seasonally adjusted estimate is simply the nonseasonal component.[3]

The first model-based seasonally adjusted trade balance is given in Figure E-3. The graph is considerably smoother than the X-11 output. Only data available at the time t, when the trade balance was announced, were used to produce the series shown in Figure

---

[2]See Hausman and Watson (1985) and Hausman and Watson (1990); note that the 1985 paper uses a basic ARIMA model, and the 1990 paper allows for heterogeneity in the seasonal component.

[3]This approach is analogous to doing a regression with seasonal dummies and then defining the adjusted estimate as the data minus the fitted seasonal components from the regression.

E-3.[4] The standard deviation of the model-based adjusted series is $1.5 billion, which is considerably lower than that of the X-11 series.

Figure E-4 uses historical data to seasonally adjust the data. That is, to estimate the seasonally adjusted trade balance at time t, we used data that became available after time t. This figure is probably the "best" to use for comparison with data from Census Bureau procedures since the Census Bureau uses historical data when it applies the X-11 procedure. The series shown in Figure E-4 is significantly smoother than that in Figure E-3, for which only concurrent data were used for seasonal adjustment. The standard deviation of the optimally seasonally adjusted trade balance shown in Figure E-4 is $1.4 billion. Although some improvement is evident, it is interesting to note that the method that uses only concurrent data does about 95 percent as well as the method that uses historical data.

We obtained similar results for the monthly and yearly changes in the trade balance. The standard deviation of the monthly change in the trade balance is $2.6 billion for the series adjusted with X-11; for the series adjusted with the model-based procedure, the standard deviation of the monthly change is $1.9 billion. For yearly change, the X-11 procedure yields a series with a standard deviation of $2.7 billion; the model-based procedure yields a series with a standard deviation of 2.1 billion. The standard deviation of the first difference and yearly difference fall by about $0.1 billion each when historical data are used. Thus, the standard deviation of the seasonally adjusted series from the model-based procedure is usually about 20 percent smaller than that obtained by the X-11 procedure.

An even more appropriate comparison uses the basic underlying series (n_t in Hausman and Watson, 1985, 1990) after the seasonal component has been removed. The historic filter comparison is probably the most relevant since it uses the same data used by the Census Bureau to report its seasonally adjusted series. In Table E-1, we present data on three series: the monthly trade balance (N_t), the change in the monthly trade balance ($N_t - N_{(t-1)}$), and the annual change in the monthly trade balance ($N_t - N_{(t-12)}$). All three numbers are used in announcements and subsequent analyses. The ratios of the root mean square errors demonstrate

---

[4]We refer to these data as concurrent data; however, the description is only approximately correct since the data are subsequently revised by the Census Bureau. We have only had access to the final revised data.

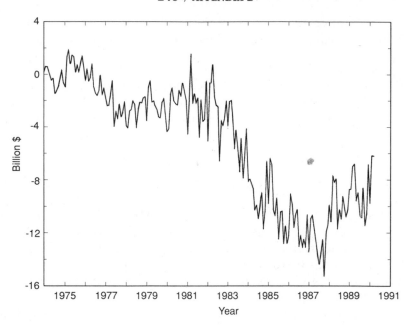

FIGURE E-1   Merchandise trade balance, not seasonally adjusted.

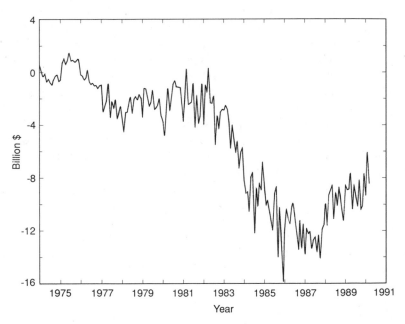

FIGURE E-2   Merchandise trade balance with X-11 seasonal adjustment.

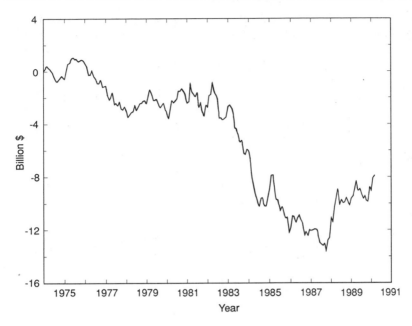

FIGURE E-3 Merchandise trade balance with proposed new seasonal adjustment. NOTE: See text for method of adjustment.

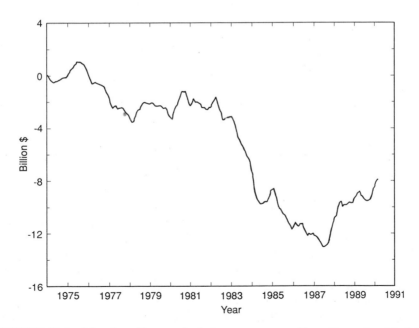

FIGURE E-4 Merchandise trade balance, seasonally adjusted with historical data. NOTE: See text for method of adjustment.

TABLE E-1 Trade Balance (Exports Minus Imports), Seasonally Adjusted Data, Root Mean Square Error (in millions of dollars)

A. Homoskedastic Model			
Model	N_t	$N_t - N_{(t-1)}$	$N_t - N_{(t-12)}$
Historical Filter			
Optimal	351.0	543.7	240.0
X-11	822.9	1,144.4	1,270.6
Ratio: optimal/X-11	0.426	0.475	0.189
Concurrent Filter			
Optimal	462.9	709.7	254.0
X-11	895.4	1,153.9	1,275.8
Ratio: optimal/X-11	0.517	0.615	0.199
Comparison			
Our concurrent	462.9	709.7	254.0
Government historical	822.9	1,144.4	1,270.6
Ratio: government historical/			
our concurrent	0.563	0.620	0.200
B. Heteroskedastic Model			
Model	N_t	$N_t - N_{(t-1)}$	$N_t - N_{(t-12)}$
Historical Filter			
Optimal	355.0	552.5	265.6
X-11	801.0	1,120.7	1,229.2
Ratio: optimal/X-11	0.443	0.493	0.216
Concurrent Filter			
Optimal	460.7	703.5	287.0
X-11	901.4	1,191.1	1,258.6
Ratio: optimal/X-11	0.511	0.591	0.228

continued

that the optimal model-based filter does significantly better than the X-11 procedure: for the homoskedastic model-based procedure using monthly figures, the root mean square error of the model is just 0.43 as large as that for the X-11 procedure; for the monthly change figures, the model-based procedure is 0.48 as large; finally, using yearly change data, the model-based procedure is 0.19 as large. Evidently, much of the variability in the trade balance data is created by an adjustment procedure that is extremely nonoptimal.

Even if we compare the optimal seasonally adjusted series using only concurrent data with the Census Bureau series, which uses historical data, the improvement is still large. The monthly

TABLE E-1   *Continued*

C. Heteroskedastic Model,
RMSE of Estimated N_t,
Monthly Values

| Month | Historical Filter | |
	Optimal	X-11
January	446.5	852.1
February	335.4	838.3
March	258.4	788.4
April	278.1	775.4
May	342.2	777.6
June	324.4	791.2
July	379.7	787.2
August	379.7	808.6
September	338.1	808.6
October	338.4	791.6
November	374.6	791.7
December	464.3	801.3

series has a root mean square error about 0.56 as large; the monthly change ratio is 0.62 as large; and the yearly change ratio is 0.20 as large. Thus, using only data available at the time of the initial announcement of the trade balance produces a seasonally adjusted series that has considerably less variation than the Census Bureau's X-11 procedure, which uses historical data. Considerable room for improvement thus exists in the X-11 procedure used for trade balance data.

This research is suggestive of one of the serious problems with the trade balance data reported by the Census Bureau, although it cannot be taken to be definitive. We have used the revised trade data rather than the initial announcement data.[5] Substantial adjustments are often made in the initially announced trade data, which is another source of variability. Hausman and Watson (1990) use a model that accounts for data revision. However, we were unable to obtain from the Census Bureau a consistent series for the unadjusted trade data, which would allow us to control for this additional source of variability. (The data were not available

---

[5]Since government statisticians also use revised data, the comparison of the two methods is valid.

so we could not extend our method.) A model-based procedure would permit a significant reduction in the additional variability contained in the initial announcement data since the Kalman filter model permits a forecast of the unadjusted data that would be averaged in an optimal way with the announced data. We expect that the resulting weighted average would eliminate much of the variability before the revisions are made.

F
Options for the Use of Sampling to Collect Merchandise Trade Data

This appendix discusses three major options for using sampling techniques for the compilation of U.S. merchandise trade data: cutoff sampling of low-value trade documents, probability sampling of documents, and collection of data from a sample of enterprises or establishments. The three options are not necessarily mutually exclusive: it would be possible, for example, to use a combination of cutoff and probability sampling of trade documents; another possibility would be to use an establishment sample to produce preliminary estimates of a few monthly aggregates, while continuing to rely on the present system for detailed data.

The first two options relate solely to the production of merchandise trade data based on the official import and export documents. The third option, collection of data from enterprises, has broader implications. This method could either supplement or replace the production of merchandise trade data based on the official documents. It also has the potential for collecting not only merchandise trade data, but also some kinds of services trade data from the same sample of enterprises.

CUTOFF SAMPLING OF LOW-VALUE TRADE DOCUMENTS

Cutoff sampling of low-value trade documents is currently used by the Census Bureau in compiling monthly merchandise trade data. The method consists of capturing the desired information from all import and export transactions for which the value equals or exceeds specified dollar cutoffs. However, the Census Bureau publishes monthly estimates of the total value of the excluded low-valued shipments by country (although not by commodity), using multiplicative estimation factors based on historical data.

For exports, the cutoff is $2,500 (raised from $1,500 as of October 1989 data) and shippers' export declarations (SEDs) are no longer required for transactions of less than that amount. For exports to Canada, the SED filing requirement has recently been eliminated for all except a few regulated transactions because, under the U.S.-Canada data exchange agreement, the United States is now relying on Canadian import data to report U.S. exports to Canada, just as Canada is using U.S. import data to report Canada's exports to the United States.

For imports, the current cutoffs are $250 for selected commodities for which there are import quotas and $1,250 for all others. (The latter value was raised from $1,000 as of October 1989.)

ADVANTAGES OF CUTOFF SAMPLING

An obvious advantage of cutoff sampling is that it is the present system: it does not require any resources for testing and development. The sampling process for the documents that are processed manually is straightforward: documents with only low-value transactions are set aside; if a document has both types of transaction, data are keyed only for those above the cutoffs. Since the main costs are for keying, savings are roughly proportional to the number of transactions below the cutoff figures. Significant savings in manual processing costs can be realized by raising the cutoff point, especially for exports, for which about 60 percent of the total value of exports comes from transactions that are not being reported electronically. (Data exchange with Canada covers about 20 percent of total value of exports; the other 20 percent is reported electronically.) For import and export transactions reported electronically, the "sampling" is even simpler: it consists of computer instructions to omit any transactions below the cutoffs from all tabulations. For exporters, the cutoff system reduces the reporting burden because they are not required to file SEDs for transactions below the cutoff (except for certain controlled commodities).

Last, but not least, for transactions above the cutoff figures, there are no limits on the amount of detail that can be tabulated (except as required by the confidentiality policy that groups together export data for detailed commodities if publication of data might reveal individual company activities). This advantage is somewhat illusory because for some cells the excluded (below cutoff) transactions constitute a substantial part or even all of the true total.

DISADVANTAGES OF CUTOFF SAMPLING

The use of cutoff sampling means that there is no direct information available on transactions below the cutoff point (except for exports to Canada, for which some information on transactions of as low as about $770 in value is available as a result of the U.S.-Canada data exchange). As of October 1989, the Census Bureau estimated that low-value shipments accounted for about 0.7 percent of the value of imports and 2.9 percent of the value of exports. The effect of their omission on highly aggregated data is fairly small, but some of the thousands of cells of data published monthly are subject to much larger effects. Adams (1989) stated that the increase in the export cutoff (from $1,500 to $2,500) would lose data for approximately 15,000 (11 percent) of the commodity by country by method of transportation data cells. At the individual country level, the increase would lose 50 percent or more detail for six of our smallest trading partners. The proportion of the value of air shipments lost by raising the cutoff was about 5 times the proportion lost for vessel shipments (Dickerson, 1989).

Except for exports to Canada, the monthly estimates of low-value shipments by country are obtained by multiplying the current cutoff figures by factors derived from earlier data. For exports, at least, there is no reliable way to evaluate the accuracy of these estimates because no documents are available for the transactions they include. (Theoretically, it would be possible to require exporters to periodically file SEDs for low-value shipments, but this would be operationally complex and could absorb much of the savings from using cutoff sampling.) A Census Bureau memorandum (Huang, 1987) states that "the validity of the estimated low value factors is in doubt."

The use of cutoff sampling provides exporters with an opportunity to escape the SED filing requirement. For example, an exporter with a shipment valued at $6,000 could treat it as three separate shipments valued at $2,000 each. We have seen no evidence, however, that this is a common practice.

FUTURE PROSPECTS

The potential and actual savings from the use of cutoff sampling are much greater for transactions reported on paper documents than they are for those reported electronically. Future costs of compiling merchandise trade data based on cutoff samples are difficult to predict because they are subject to opposing trends. Expected increases in the number of foreign trade transactions could lead to substantial increases in the cost of processing the documents if there were no change in the proportion of transactions covered by electronic reporting. However, there are three factors that can limit such cost increases or even lead to reductions: the substitution of foreign import data for U.S. export data; increases in the proportion of transactions reported electronically; and increases in the cutoff point.

• Substitution of Canadian data on imports from the United States for U.S. data on exports to Canada began in January 1990. As a result, there is now no need to process paper documents for transactions covering about 20 percent of the value of U.S. exports. Similar substitution arrangements with other trading partners, including the European Community, are under consideration but the prospects of implementation within the next 5 years appear slight. The arrangement with Canada resulted from several years of negotiation and development work, and arrangements with other countries would require solutions to problems that did not exist for U.S. exports to Canada, such as shipments through intervening countries and elapsed time between date of export and date of import.

• According to the Census Bureau, as of early 1991 electronic reporting covered about 78 percent of the total value of imports and about 40 percent of total value of exports. The prospects for increasing the proportion for imports are said to be good: there are some effective incentives for importers to shift to electronic reporting. For exports, the prospects will be good if exporters are provided incentives to shift to electronic reporting.

• As has happened from time to time in the past, the cutoffs can be increased again in the future. Although there have been many studies to determine the effects on the data of proposed increases in cutoffs, there are no firm criteria used to determine how far the cutoffs can be raised. Decisions seem to be driven more by budgetary considerations.

PROBABILITY SAMPLING OF TRADE DOCUMENTS

In general terms, probability sampling requires that all units belonging to a defined universe have a known, nonzero chance of selection. Large units, if desired, can be given a selection probability of one. Probability sampling of foreign trade documents or transactions could be applied to all official documents submitted by U.S. importers and exporters or it could be applied to some subset, such as all transactions valued at or above specified cutoffs. The latter approach would be a combination of probability and cutoff sampling.

Starting in 1953 and continuing until 1982 for imports and 1985 for exports, the Census Bureau selected probability samples of low-value import and export transactions, processed these transactions, and used the data in its monthly estimates. Cutoffs and sampling fractions were changed frequently during this period. These sampling procedures were dropped and replaced by cutoff sampling primarily because funds available for processing paper documents were insufficient to process the increasing number of documents received each month.

ADVANTAGES OF PROBABILITY SAMPLING

As is the case for cutoff sampling, savings can be realized by processing only a probability sample of documents. If the sample selection and estimation procedures are simple, the savings can be roughly proportional to the reduction in the number of documents processed; if they are complex, the savings will be less. The size of the samples required to obtain sufficiently reliable estimates is a key determinant of cost savings. Sample size requirements are primarily a function of how many distinct data cells must be estimated for each month or other time period.

The use of sampling may permit more timely publication of data and reduction of nonsampling error through more thorough review of the data for sample transactions. However, these results are not guaranteed: they depend on the particular sampling plan and operational procedures used. The sampling errors resulting from the use of sampling can be estimated directly from the sample data, unlike the errors of estimates for transactions below the cutoff, which are difficult to determine with any degree of confidence.

DISADVANTAGES OF PROBABILITY SAMPLING

Probability sampling introduces some requirements that do not exist when cutoff sampling is used. An estimation procedure must be used, which usually involves weighting the data for transactions in the sampled portion of the universe. To comply with

Census Bureau standards and generally accepted procedures, sampling errors must be estimated periodically and the estimates of sampling error included in publications or made available to data users by other means.

The main disadvantage, however, is the introduction of sampling error. For data cells or estimates based on large samples, this is a minor problem, and nonsampling errors are often much larger than sampling errors. About 90 percent of the detailed data cells for exports, however, are based on five or fewer transactions (Bureau of the Census, 1983). For these cells, any use of sampling would introduce high and probably unacceptable levels of sampling error. Many nonzero cells would have no sample transactions and would have to be shown in publications as estimated zero cells.

OPTIONS FOR PROBABILITY SAMPLING OF TRANSACTIONS

There are many different ways in which probability sampling could be introduced (or reintroduced) into the compilation of merchandise trade statistics. To narrow the possibilities, we eliminate several options:

• Sampling of transactions that are reported electronically. Although some savings might accrue from sampling these transactions, the savings are likely to be quite small in relation to what could be saved by reducing the number of paper documents to be processed.

• Sampling of import transactions not reported electronically. The Census Bureau has set a target for raising the level of automated reporting of imports to 90 percent of total value by 1991 (Adams, 1989). The costs of setting up and operating a sampling procedure for the remaining 10 percent would probably use up a substantial part of the potential cost savings.

• Reintroduction of sampling of export transactions below the present cutoff without any sampling of transactions above the cutoff. This option would increase the reporting burden on exporters and would increase overall processing costs. Even if funds were available, they might better be used for other purposes.

• Sampling paper export documents to produce more timely preliminary estimates of the key merchandise trade statistics, but processing all documents, possibly on a delayed schedule, to eventually produce the present level of detail. This option would add substantially to the present cost of the program.

Elimination of these options leaves the possibility of processing only a sample of the paper documents for export transactions, including some that are valued at or above the present $2,500 cutoff. If the goal of the program is to continue to produce monthly data by commodity, country, and U.S. customs district at the present level of detail, this is not a viable option. With about 90 percent of the nonzero data cells having five or fewer shipments and about 75 percent having only one or two shipments (Bureau of the Census, 1983), the sampling errors for any kind of sample would clearly be unacceptable. Therefore, in the following discussion it is assumed that the data requirements can be changed to reduce the amount of detail produced on a monthly basis for exports. Such a reduction would not require any change in the current statute, which requires substantial monthly detail on imports but only one overall figure for exports.

There are two ways of changing the data requirements so that estimates of acceptable precision could be produced by sampling. One is to reduce the number of data cells estimated for a given month or other reference period. The other is to reduce the frequency with which estimates are published—to change the frequency from monthly to quarterly or annual for some cells. Some combination of these changes is possible. During a budget crisis in the early 1980s, Census explored the possibility of using a 50 percent sample of export documents for transactions valued at or above the then cutoff of $500 and below a series of upper limits ranging from $5,000 to $100,000 (Puzzilla, 1983). At that time, the proposed sampling scheme would have reduced the number of documents to be processed by more than 40 percent, even with an upper limit of $5,000. The only data cells evaluated in that study were totals for nine broad commodity groups and three methods of transportation. The differences between the universe totals and the sample estimates for these 12 cells were all acceptably small.

We can conclude at this point only that sampling non-Canadian paper export documents at a rate that would lead to a significant reduction in processing costs would provide monthly estimates of acceptable reliability for an unknown number, x, of data cells, with x lying somewhere between 12 and the more than 200,000 export data cells for which data are published (or made available in CD-ROM format) monthly. This is, of course, a wide range of uncertainty. To narrow it would require a more comprehensive version of the 1983 study undertaken by the Census Bureau. Such a study would not be unduly expensive and might be carried out with assistance from the Census Bureau's Statistical Research Division. There are several general considerations for designing such a study:

• The study should provide information on the reliability of monthly, quarterly, and annual estimates for the same data cells. With fixed sampling fractions, the accumulation of sample data over more than one month can provide estimates of acceptable reliability for longer periods.

• The study should be designed to provide data for several alternative sample designs with varying stratum definitions and sampling fractions. It is likely that any acceptable design would include a "certainty stratum," that is, a category of large transactions that would be included in the sample with a probability of one.

• One would expect a new study to be somewhat better than the 1983 study because all Canadian and automated transactions would not be included in the estimates. Sampling would apply only to the approximately two-thirds of transactions not in those categories.

• There are two different approaches to undertaking a study of this kind. The 1983 study compared estimates from one particular sample with corresponding data items tabulated from all transactions. An alternative would be to develop estimates of within-stratum variances for several variables for all of the potential design strata. These estimated variance components could then be used to evaluate the expected levels of reliability for several alternative sample designs. The latter approach would be more flexible for examining several alternatives.

• The evaluation of alternative designs should take into account the actual selection process that would be required for each. If a design is too complex, a substantial part of the cost savings could be used up in selecting the sample.

• It might be desirable to undertake the study with a database for a period prior to October 1989, so that export transactions in the $1,500-$2,500 range could be included. The additional cost of sampling documents in this range at a low rate could be quite small, and including these documents in the sampled universe would eliminate some of the uncertainty associated with estimates based on historical factors for low-value shipments.

• On the basis of such a study, the Census Bureau could develop for discussion with data users one or more options for sampling non-Canadian paper export documents. For each option, the description would identify the levels of detail that could be published monthly, quarterly, and annually, the expected levels of reliability for each type of estimate, and the expected cost savings.

Processing Considerations

Panel members were somewhat surprised at the amount of manual handling required by the present system for processing paper documents and noted that there may be document processing technology available that could be applied to reduce the volume and cost of manual operations. There are at least two possibilities directly relevant to a decision on whether to use extensive probability sampling of non-Canadian paper export documents.

The first would be to redesign the SED to incorporate machine-readable codes to allow fully or partly automated sorting and batching of incoming documents consistent with the different kinds of treatment they require in the sample selection procedures, and the data entry procedures. If this could be done, the next step, sample selection, could be at least partially automated. A more difficult problem, but one which would certainly justify some systems development effort, can be considered: If more extensive sampling of paper documents is adopted, is there some relatively low-cost method by which the nonsample documents could be stored and indexed to permit on-demand special 100 percent tabulations of documents in small cells identified by variables such as country, detailed commodity, method of transportation? If this type of system could be developed, special needs not covered by the sample-based routine tabulations could be provided at a reasonable cost on a reimbursable basis.

SAMPLING OF ENTERPRISES AND ESTABLISHMENTS

Some kinds of data on merchandise trade can be collected from business enterprises or establishments. For about 30 years, establishments included in the Census Bureau's Annual Survey of Manufactures (ASM) have been asked to report what proportion of their total production (plant value) has been exported. The 1987 economic censuses included a question about total value of exports for all establishments, and the 1987 ASM included a question on what percentage of the cost of materials was accounted for by materials of foreign origin. The information reported by establishments has been used for various purposes, including estimation of the number of jobs in manufacturing accounted for by exports, by state, and, more recently, as one of the inputs to an exporter data base being developed by the Foreign Trade Division.

Until now, only annual data on total exports have been collected from establishments. Could detailed monthly data on merchandise imports and exports be collected from a sample of enterprises or establishments to supplement or replace the data currently being compiled from official foreign trade documents? If this is technically possible, would it be desirable in the short run or in the long run? How would the costs of the trade statistics program be affected? These are difficult questions. The remainder of this section attempts to identify the main issues that must be considered in arriving at answers and to eliminate some of the less realistic options.

Data Requirements

What kinds of information would one want to obtain from monthly samples of importers and exporters? Would one want to collect data from importers and exporters as defined in the present system based on official trade documents or from the ultimate consumers of imports and the original producers of exports? Preliminary information from linkages of SEDs with data from the 1987 economic censuses shows that most exporters of record are manufacturers or wholesalers; only about 2 percent are freight forwarders. Less is known about the characteristics of importers, but it is likely that a substantial proportion of the importers of record are customs brokers who complete the entry forms and pay the duties but do not necessarily know the ultimate destination of the goods. Thus, the kind of information that could be collected would depend on how importers and exporters were defined for enterprise surveys. From some points of view, it might be preferable not to define them exactly as they are in the present system.

How much detail could be collected from enterprises? To reproduce the full detail available from the present system of official trade documents, it would be necessary to ask a large sample of enterprises to report full data for each of their import and export transactions or, at best, to report combined data for transactions during the reference period for the same country, commodity, and method of transportation. Alternatively, establishments with large numbers of transactions could be asked to report data for only a sample of their transactions.

On the basis of these considerations, we can readily conclude that it would not be possible, with collection of data from a sample of enterprises, to produce monthly merchandise trade data at the present level of detail, largely for the same reasons that it would not be possible to do this with more extensive probability sampling of official trade documents. In addition, the reporting burden on the enterprises must be considered. Even to provide summary data on a monthly basis might turn out to be a costly and time-consuming effort for the sample enterprises and one they would be unwilling to undertake. (Under current law, Census Bureau establishment surveys that require more frequent than annual reporting cannot be made mandatory.)

What kinds of merchandise trade data could reasonably be produced by collecting data from a sample of enterprises? There are at least three possibilities. One would be the production of preliminary estimates of a few summary values significantly in advance of the release of the detailed data, which occurs about 45 working days after the end of the reference month. A second would be the production of final estimates with much less detail than is provided by the current system. If this is the only source of merchandise trade information, however, a change in the law might be necessary, at least with respect to the requirements for monthly data on imports. A third possibility would be the collection of information not readily available from the present system, such as information on the characteristics of importing and exporting establishments (such as size and industry classification) and on ultimate destination of imports. In addition, some information on trade in services is currently being collected by the Bureau of Economic Analysis in enterprise surveys: to the extent that the same enterprises engage in both merchandise and service trade, both kinds of data could be collected from the same sample units.

A long-range consideration is that the structure of international trade may change in ways that eliminate the need, for administrative purposes, for much of the information presently captured from official documents. If this happens, collection of data from enterprises may be the only way to obtain certain kinds of data.

TECHNICAL CONSIDERATIONS

Given preliminary agreement on the data requirements for surveys of importers and exporters, the next steps would include development of a sampling frame, design of a sample of enterprises and establishments to meet the survey goals, and the development and testing of suitable data collection instruments and procedures.

The development and maintenance of a sampling frame of importers and exporters is made easier by the addition of employer identification numbers (EINs) to the official trade documents starting in 1985. Computer files of import and export records can be matched to EIN records from the economic censuses and the Census Bureau's Standard Statistical Establishment List to produce listings of importers and exporters—with their names and addresses, establishment detail, and characteristics, such as industry classification and volume of imports and exports—that could be used to design an efficient sample. Such a matching process, based on 1987 trade documents and the 1987 economic censuses is, in fact, under way for exporters (Farrell, 1989). (However, no matching is being performed for importers.) For intercensal use as a sampling frame, the resulting exporter database would have to be updated annually on the basis of the ASM and the Annual Company Organization Survey. (The latter updates the information on establishments for multiestablishment companies.) The annual cost of updating is estimated to be $500,000 (Farrell, 1989). One problem with this procedure is incomplete reporting of EINs on the SEDs, which exceeded 20 percent for the 1987 trade records. This problem could be dealt with in various ways if the exporter data base were funded as an ongoing activity.

To determine the optimum design for a sample of enterprises for any purpose, it is necessary to have information about their distribution by some measure of size, such as total value of imports and exports, that is related to the variables of interest. If the distribution is highly skewed—that is, if a few units account for a large part of the volume of imports and exports—reliable estimates for some variables could be developed using a fairly small sample of enterprises. Nonetheless, no reliable data on the distribution of imports and exports by company or establishment are presently available. For exports, such data will become available when the exporter database linkages have been completed; no comparable data sources for imports are under development.

Data collection procedures would require extensive testing. The survey objectives and data requirements would have to be specified in detail. A series of feasibility tests and pretests would be needed to find out whether respondents are able and willing to report the desired information.

Important policy issues would have to be confronted. Would response to the planned surveys be mandatory and, if so, would new legislation be needed? What limits would have to be imposed on the release of survey results in order to preserve the confidentiality of responses for individual enterprises and establishments? How would new surveys conducted by the Census Bureau be coordinated or integrated with surveys presently conducted by the Bureau of Economic Analysis on related topics?

CONCLUSIONS

A new establishment sample is clearly not a viable option in the short term to replace the present system of compiling merchandise trade data from official trade documents, even if the amount of detailed data required monthly could be reduced somewhat. Substantial time and resources would be needed to decide what kind of information and how much detail could and would be reported on a monthly basis by importers and exporters. In addition, since all other countries presently compile their foreign trade statistics from official documents, shifting to an establishment basis for U.S. foreign trade statistics would complicate data exchange arrangements (such as the one between the United States and Canada) and might make U.S. data less comparable with those of other countries.

There are some kinds of data relevant to foreign trade, however, for which enterprises and establishments are the logical source of information. Examples are the data on exports by manufacturers and wholesalers and costs of imported materials being collected in the economic censuses and the ASM and the data on import and export prices collected from a sample of establishments by the Bureau of Labor Statistics. There are other kinds of useful information that might best be collected in new establishment surveys. For example, most low-value international shipments by air are carried by a relatively small number of shippers. In view of the interest that has been expressed by specialized user groups for more complete coverage of air shipments, the Census Bureau might want to investigate the possibility of collecting some information about air shipments in sample surveys of shipping companies, which would include all of the large shippers. Because of the specialized user groups involved, it would be appropriate for the Census Bureau to make such an activity contingent on receipt of at least partial funding from users.

G

Biographical Sketches of Panel Members and Staff

ROBERT E. BALDWIN is Hilldale professor of economics at the University of Wisconsin and a research associate at the National Bureau of Economic Research (NBER) and director of NBER's project on U.S. trade relations. He received a Ph.D. in economics from Harvard University and taught at Harvard and the University of California at Los Angeles before moving to Wisconsin. He previously served as the chief economist in the Office of the U.S. Trade Representative and the Shelby Cullon and Katheryn Davis visiting professor of international economics at the Graduate Institute of International Studies in Geneva. He has published numerous articles in various professional journals in the fields of international trade and economic development and is the author of several books, including *The Political Economy of U.S. Import Policy* (1985) and *Trade Policy in a Changing World Economy* (1988). He has served as a consultant on trade matters for numerous national and international organizations including the United Nations, the World Bank, and the Organization for Economic Cooperation and Development. He is also a member of the Council on Foreign Relations and the Advisory Committee of the Institute for International Economics.

ANDREW F. BRIMMER is the president of Brimmer & Company, Inc., and Wilmer D. Barrett professor of economics at the University of Massachusetts. He received a Ph.D. in economics from Harvard University. Previously, he was a member of the Board of

Governors of the Federal Reserve System and the Thomas Henry Carroll visiting professor at the Graduate School of Business Administration of Harvard University. He currently serves on the board of directors of numerous corporations and is a member of numerous professional organizations. He holds 22 honorary degrees from universities and colleges.

ROSANNE COLE is the Director of Economic Research and Forecasting at IBM Corporation. She holds an A.B. in mathematics from Miami University and a Ph.D. in economics from Columbia University. Prior to joining IBM, she served on the staff of the National Bureau of Economic Research. She is a member of a number of advisory committees to federal statistical agencies. At IBM, she is responsible for economic studies of the information industry, tracking industry developments, and for forecasts of the impact of changes in general economic conditions and government policies on industry growth.

RICHARD N. COOPER is the Maurits C. Boas professor of international economics at Harvard University. He previously served as Under Secretary for Economic Affairs in the U.S. State Department (1977-1981), Deputy Assistant Secretary of State for International Monetary Affairs (1965-1966), and senior staff economist for the Council of Economic Advisers (1961-1963). He was also provost and professor of international economics at Yale University. He currently serves as chair, Federal Reserve Bank of Boston; chair, advisory committee, and director, Institute for International Economics; and chair, Executive Panel to Chief of Naval Operations. He also serves on the board of directors of a number of corporations and is a member of the Trilateral Commission and the Council on Foreign Relations. He received an A.B. from Oberlin College, an M.Sc. (Econ.) from the London School of Economics, and a Ph.D. from Harvard University. He has published over 300 articles and books, including *The International Monetary System* and *Economic Policy in an Interdependent World.*

JACOB DEUTCH is a consultant on quality control and statistical surveys and an adjunct faculty member in economics at the Johns Hopkins University and the University of Maryland (Baltimore County). He holds master's degrees from the Johns Hopkins University in management science, liberal arts, and education. He entered government service as a policy analyst with the Social Security Administration and retired as chief of Evaluation and Measurement Systems.

DAVID T. DEVLIN is a vice president of Citibank and Deputy Senior Adviser for International Operations, which is responsible for setting limits on Citibank cross-border exposure in some 100 countries. He has also been involved with organizing Citibank businesses with foreign financial institutions and central banks, as well as foreign governments. Previously, he served as chief of operations in setting up the Institute of International Finance in Washington, which monitors economic developments in some 50 countries for major international banks. Prior to joining Citibank, he was associate director for international economics at the Bureau of Economic Analysis of the Department of Commerce and chief of the Balance of Payments Division of the Federal Reserve Bank of New York. He has a Ph.D. in economics from Columbia University.

EDWIN D. GOLDFIELD is a senior associate on the staff of the Committee on National Statistics. He was director of the committee from 1978 to 1987. His earlier career at the Bureau of the Census included serving as program coordinator of the decennial census, chief of the Statistical Reports Division, assistant director of the Bureau, and head of the Bureau's International Statistics Program Center. His other positions included staff director of the U.S. House of Representatives Subcommittee on Census and Statistics, consultant to the Social Science Research Council and Mutual Security Agency, and a member of the Editorial Advisory Board of the International Encyclopedia of the Social Sciences. He is a past president of the Washington Statistical Society and a fellow of the American Statistical Association and a past member of its board of directors.

A. BLANTON GODFREY is chair and chief executive officer of Juran Institute, Inc. Prior to joining Juran Institute, he was with AT&T Bell Laboratories, where he headed the quality theory and technology department, which is responsible for applied research in the areas of quality, reliability, and productivity. He holds a B.S. in physics from Virginia Polytechnic Institute and State University and an M.S. and a Ph.D. in statistics from Florida State University. He is an adjunct associate professor in the School of Engineering at Columbia University. He is a fellow of the American Statistical Association, a fellow of the American Society for Quality Control, a member of Sigma Xi, an academician of the International Academy for Quality, and a member of the American Association for the Advancement of Science. He contributed to the creation of the Malcolm Baldrige National Quality Award and served as a judge for the first 3 years of the award.

JERRY A. HAUSMAN is professor of economics at Massachusetts Institute of Technology. His research specialties are econometrics and applied microeconomics. He was an undergraduate at Brown University and did his graduate work at Oxford University, where he was a Marshall Scholar. He has served as a consultant to numerous government agencies, and he was a member of the Committee on National Statistics from 1985 to 1989. He received the John Bates Clark Award of the American Economic Association in 1985 and the Frisch Medal of the Econometrics Society in 1985.

THOMAS B. JABINE is a statistical consultant who specializes in sampling, survey research methods, and statistical policy. He was formerly a statistical policy expert for the Energy Information Administration, chief mathematical statistician for the Social Security Administration, and chief of the Statistical Research Division of the Census Bureau. He has a B.S. in mathematics and an M.S. in economics and science from the Massachusetts Institute of Technology. He is a member of the International Statistical Institute and a fellow of the American Statistical Association.

HELEN B. JUNZ is Special Trade Representative and director of the Geneva Office of the International Monetary Fund (IMF). She joined the IMF as a senior adviser in the European Department and served as deputy director of the Exchange and Trade Relations Department prior to her present appointment. She received an M.A. in economics from the New School for Social Research. Before joining the IMF, she held the positions of economic adviser, Organization for Economic Cooperation and Development (OECD); adviser, Division of International Finance, Board of Governors of the Federal Reserve System; senior international economist, U.S. Council of Economic Advisers; Deputy Assistant Secretary for Commodities and Natural Resources, U.S. Department of the Treasury; vice president, First National Bank of Chicago; and vice president, Townsend-Greenspan and Company, Inc., New York.

ANNE Y. KESTER served as study director of the Panel on Foreign Trade Statistics and is currently directing a study on U.S. international capital flows at the National Research Council. While serving at the National Research Council, she has been on leave from the U.S. General Accounting Office (GAO), where she holds a position of assistant director. Before joining GAO, she was a research associate at the Graduate School of Business Administration at Harvard University and a senior management consultant at a Harvard-affiliated consulting firm. Prior to that, she served as an economic consultant to the U.S. Department of Agriculture, several research institutions, and various corporations. She received an M.A. in public policy and administration and a Ph.D. in economics from the University of Wisconsin.

ROBERT Z. LAWRENCE is Albert L. Williams professor of international trade and investment at the John F. Kennedy School of Government, Harvard University. He received a B.A. in economics from the University of Witwatersrand, South Africa, and an M.A. in international relations and a Ph.D. in economics from Yale University. He was a research associate and senior fellow in the Economic Studies Program at the Brookings Institution, an instructor at Yale University, and a professorial lecturer at the Johns Hopkins School of Advanced International Studies. He has served as a consultant to the Federal Reserve Bank of New York, the World Bank, the Organization for Economic Cooperation and Development, and the United Nations Conference on Trade and Development. He is a nonresident senior fellow at the Brookings Institution. He is the author of several books.

EDWARD E. LEAMER is Chauncey Medberry professor of management at the Anderson School of Management, University of California, Los Angeles. Previously, he was professor and chair in the Department of Economics at UCLA. Prior to that he taught at Harvard University. He is a fellow of the American Academy of Arts and Sciences and a fellow of the Econometric Society. He is a research associate of the National Bureau of Economic Research and coeditor of the *Journal of International Economics*. He received an M.A. in mathematics and a Ph.D. in economics from the University of Michigan.

SAMUEL PIZER has been a consultant to the International Monetary Fund for a number of years, serving at various times as the director of the technical staff and member of the Working Party on the Discrepancy in the World Current Account, consultant to the Managing Director, and consultant to the Working Party on the Measurement of International Capital Flows. Previously, he was senior adviser, associate adviser, and senior economist for the Division of International Finance at the Federal Reserve Board.

Earlier, he worked at the Department of Commerce and served as assistant chief of the Balance of Payments Division. He has a B.A. and an M.A. from the George Washington University.

S. JAMES PRESS is professor of statistics at the University of California, Riverside. He served as a member of the Committee on National Statistics for 6 years and has served on four of its scientific study panels. He received a Ph.D. from Stanford University in statistics. He has taught at Yale University, the University of Chicago, the University of British Columbia, and the London School of Economics and Political Science.

W. ALLEN SPIVEY is C.E. Griffin distinguished professor of business administration and professor of statistics at the University of Michigan, Ann Arbor. His previous appointments include teaching at the London School of Economics, Harvard University, and at the Kyoto American Studies Seminar in Japan as a Fulbright professor. He has also lectured at the European Business School (INSEAD) in Fontainebleau, France, and at the London Business School. He has served as an associate editor of the *Journal of Business and Economic Statistics* and of *Management Science* and as a consultant and proposal referee for the Ford Foundation and the National Science Foundation. He is a Fellow of the American Statistical Association and of the Royal Statistical Society (Great Britain).

ELLEN TENENBAUM is a public policy analyst at Westat, Inc. While at the National Research Council, in addition to this study, she served as a consultant to the Committee on Mandatory Retirement in Higher Education and the Panel on Statistics on Supply and Demand for Precollege Science and Mathematics Teachers. She holds an M.A. in public policy from the University of California, Berkeley.

MARTIN B. WILK is an adjunct professor at Carleton University, Ottawa, Ontario, Canada. He was previously consultant to Deputy Minister, Revenue Canada, and chief statistician of Statistics Canada. He previously taught at Rutgers University. He received a Ph.D. in statistics from Iowa State University. He is a member of many other professional associations, an elected member of the International Statistical Institute, an honorary fellow of the Royal Statistical Society, and an honorary member of the Statistical Society of Canada.

Acronyms

ORGANIZATIONS

BEA Bureau of Economic Analysis (U.S. Department of Commerce)

BIS Bank for International Settlements

BLS Bureau of Labor Statistics (U.S. Department of Labor)

EC European Communities

EIA Energy Information Administration

EUROSTAT Statistical Office of the European Communities

FTD Foreign Trade Division (Bureau of the Census, U.S. Department of Commerce)

GAO U.S. General Accounting Office

GATT General Agreement on Tariffs and Trade

IMF International Monetary Fund

IRS Internal Revenue Service (U.S. Department of the Treasury)

ITA International Trade Administration (U.S. Department of Commerce)

NBER National Bureau of Economic Research

NIH National Institutes of Health (U.S. Department of Health and Human Services)

OECD Organization for Economic Cooperation and Development

OMB U.S. Office of Management and Budget

| USDA | U.S. Department of Agriculture |
| USTTA | U.S. Travel and Tourism Administration (U.S. Department of Commerce) |

STATISTICAL TERMS AND SYSTEMS

ABI	Automated Broker Interface (Customs Service, U.S. Department of the Treasury)
AERP	Automatic Export Reporting Program (Bureau of the Census, U.S. Department of Commerce)
ARCH	autoregressive conditional heteroskedastic models
ARIMA	autoregressive, integrated, moving average models
AES	Automated Export System
ASM	Annual Survey of Manufactures (Bureau of the Census, U.S. Department of Commerce)
CMIR	Currency and Monetary Investments Report (U.S. Department of the Treasury)
COMPRO	Computerized Data Program on Foreign Trade (maintained by ITA)
CPC	central product classification
EIN	employer identification number
GARCH	generalized ARCH
HS	Harmonized Commodity Description and Coding System
IBF	international banking facility
NIPA	national income and products accounts (U.S. Department of Commerce)
NTDB	National Trade Data Bank (U.S. Department of Commerce)
OLS	ordinary least squares
SED	shipper's export declaration
SIC	standard industrial classification
SITC	standard international trade classification
SNA	system of national accounts (developed under the auspices of the United Nations)
SOI	*Statistics of Income* (U.S. Department of the Treasury)
SSEL	Standard Statistical Establishment List (Bureau of the Census, U.S. Department of Commerce)
TCMP	Taxpayer Compliance Measurement Program (IRS, U.S. Department of the Treasury)
TIC	Treasury International Capital (U.S. Department of the Treasury)
TSUSA	Tariff Schedule of the United States Annotated

OTHER

AOQL	average outgoing quality limit
CD-ROM	compact disk-read only memory
c.i.f.	cost-insurance-freight
CIRS	continuous independent review system
f.a.s.	free-along-side
FDI	foreign direct investment
f.o.b.	free-on-board
GNP	gross national product
JASA	*Journal of the American Statistical Association*
MOT	mode of transportation
NVOCC	non-vessel operating commercial carrier
PIERS	Piers Import/Export Reporting Service
SCB	*Survey of Current Business*
TRIMS	trade-related investment measures

References and Bibliography

Adams, D.
   1989   Priority Issues: Improving Foreign Trade Statistics—Quality Is-
          sues. Paper prepared for the Panel on Foreign Trade Statistics,
          Committee on National Statistics, National Research Council.
          Bureau of the Census, U.S. Department of Commerce, Washing-
          ton, D.C.
Alterman, W.
   1990   U.S. import and export price indexes—second quarter 1990. *Bu-
          reau of Labor Statistics News* (July):1-28.
   1992   Price trends in U.S. trade: new data, new insights. In P. Hooper
          and J.D. Richardson, eds., *International Economic Transactions:
          Issues in Measurement and Empirical Research.* Chicago: Uni-
          versity of Chicago Press.
Alwan, L.C., and H.V. Roberts
   1988   Time series modelling for statistical process control. *Journal of
          Business and Economic Statistics* (6):87-96.
Arndt, H.
   1984   Measuring trade in financial services. *Banca Nazionale del Lavoro
          Quarterly Review* 149(June):197-213.
Ascher, B., and O. Whichard
   1992   Developing a data system for international sales of services:
          progress, problems, and prospects. In P. Hooper and J.D. Richardson,
          eds., *International Economic Transactions: Issues in Measure-
          ment and Empirical Research.* Chicago: University of Chicago
          Press.
Auerbach, S.
   1987   Trade deficit report rocks stocks, bonds. *The Washington Post*
          (October 15):A1.

Bailey, V., and S. Bowden
  1985   *Understanding United States Foreign Trade Data.* International
          Trade Administration. Washington, D.C.: U.S. Department of
          Commerce.
Bailey, V., and J. Tucker
  1989   *Harmonized Trade Data Time Series.* SITC Rev.3 3-Digit Com-
          modities 1986—First Half 1989. International Trade Adminis-
          tration. Washington, D.C.: U.S. Department of Commerce.
Bank for International Settlements
  1991   *International Banking and Financial Market Developments.* Basle:
          Bank for International Settlements.
Bezirganian, S.D.
  1991   Affiliates of foreign companies: operations in 1989. *Survey of
          Current Business* 71(7):72-93.
Boskin, M.
  1990   Testimony before the Joint Economic Committee, U.S. Con-
          gress. (March) Council of Economic Advisers, Washington, D.C.
  1991   Testimony before the Subcommittee on Government Informa-
          tion and Regulation, Senate Committee on Governmental Af-
          fairs. (May) Council of Economic Advisers, Washington, D.C.
Bowerman, B.L., and R.T. O'Connell
  1987   *Time Series Forecasting,* 2nd ed. Boston: Duxbury Press.
Box, G.E.P., and G.M. Jenkins
  1976   *Time Series Analysis: Forecasting and Control,* rev. edition.
          San Francisco: Holden-Day.
Bureau of the Census
  1974   *Standards for Discussion and Presentation of Error in Data.*
          Technical Paper 32. Washington, D.C.: U.S. Department of
          Commerce.
  1980   *U.S. Foreign Trade Statistics: Classifications and Cross-Clas-
          sifications, Section 1.* Schedule B Export Classifications Corre-
          lated with Schedule E, Agricultural, Nonagricultural, End-Use,
          and SIC-Based Product Codes. Washington, D.C.: U.S. Depart-
          ment of Commerce.
  1983   Unpublished report of an intra-agency committee established
          by the Associate Director for Economic Fields to review confi-
          dentiality issues in the foreign trade statistics program.
  1986a *Automated Reporting Program for Exporting Companies.* Wash-
          ington, D.C.: U.S. Department of Commerce.
  1986b *U.S. Commodity Exports and Imports as Related to Output:
          1982 and 1981.* Washington, D.C.: U.S. Department of Com-
          merce.
  1987   *Highlights of U.S. Export and Import Trade.* FT990 April 1987.
          August. Washington, D.C.: U.S. Department of Commerce.
  1988a *Form 7525-V-ALT-(Intermodal): Shipper's Export Declaration.*
          Primarily for vessel shipments. Washington, D.C.: U.S. De-
          partment of Commerce.

1988b *1986 Annual Survey of Manufactures. Geographic Area Statistics.* M86(AS)-3. Washington, D.C.: U.S. Department of Commerce.

1988c *1986 Annual Survey of Manufactures: Statistics for Industry Groups and Industries.* (Including Capital Expenditures, Inventories, and Supplemental Labor, Fuel, and Electric Energy Costs). M86(AS)-1. Washington, D.C.: U.S. Department of Commerce.

1988d *1986 Annual Survey of Manufactures. Value of Product Shipments.* M86(AS)-2. Washington, D.C.: U.S. Department of Commerce.

1989a *Analytical Report Series: Manufacturing. Exports from Manufacturing Establishments: 1985 and 1986.* AR86-1. Washington, D.C.: U.S. Department of Commerce.

1989b *1987 Census of Manufactures and Census of Mineral Industries. Numerical List of Manufactured and Mineral Products.* Reference Series, MC87-R-1. Washington, D.C.: U.S. Department of Commerce.

1989c *1987 Census of Manufactures: Preliminary Report Industry Series.* Miscellaneous Fabricated Metal Products, Industries 3491, 3492, 3493, 3494, 3495, 3496, 3497, 3498, and 3499. MC87-1-34F(P). Washington, D.C.: U.S. Department of Commerce.

1989d *1987 Industry and Product Classification Manual (1987 SIC Basis).* EC87-R-3. Washington, D.C.: U.S. Department of Commerce.

1989e "Paperless" Foreign Trade Statistics, FY 1991 Budget Initiative. (May) Foreign Trade Division, Bureau of the Census. U.S. Department of Commerce, Washington, D.C.

1990a Adjustment of U.S. Merchandise Trade Data for Seasonality and Price Change. (March) Foreign Trade Division, Bureau of the Census, U.S. Department of Commerce, Washington, D.C.

1990b *Foreign Trade Statistics.* CFF No. 14. (March) Washington, D.C.: U.S. Department of Commerce.

Bureau of Economic Analysis

1990a *U.S. Direct Investment Abroad: Operations of U.S. Parent Companies and Their Foreign Affiliates, Revised 1987 Estimates.* Washington, D.C.: U.S. Department of Commerce.

1990b *Foreign Direct Investment in the United States: 1987 Benchmark Survey, Final Results.* Washington, D.C.: U.S. Department of Commerce.

1990c *The Balance of Payments of the United States—Concepts, Data Sources and Estimating Procedures.* Washington, D.C.: U.S. Department of Commerce.

1991a Revaluation of the U.S. Net International Investment Position. BEA 91-25. U.S. Department of Commerce, Washington, D.C.

1991b Summary of U.S. International Transactions. BEA 91-26. U.S. Department of Commerce, Washington, D.C.

Bureau of Labor Statistics
1988   *LABSTAT Users Guide.* NIH/BOEING Version, Including LABSTAT Browse. Washington, D.C.: U.S. Department of Labor.

Carson, C., and J. Honsa
1990   The United Nations system of national accounts: an introduction. *Survey of Current Business* June 70(6):20-30.

Cole, R.
1990   Revising the federal statistical system: a view from industry. *American Economic Association Papers and Proceedings* 80(2):333-336.

Committee on Engineering as an International Enterprise
1990   *National Interests in an Age of Global Technology.* A report of the National Academy of Engineering, Washington, D.C.: National Academy Press.

Committee on National Statistics
1976   *Setting Statistical Priorities: Report of the Panel on Methodology for Statistical Priorities of the Committee on National Statistics* Assembly of Mathematical and Physical Sciences, National Research Council. Washington, D.C.: National Academy of Sciences.

1986   *Statistics About Service Industries: Report of a Conference.* Commission on Behavioral and Social Sciences and Education, National Research Council. Washington, D.C.: National Academy Press.

Committee on Very Large Databases
1990   Very Large Databases: Major Issues-Managing Growth for Maximum Use. Numerical Data Advisory Board, Commission on Physical Sciences, Mathematics, and Resources, National Research Council, Washington, D.C.

Cooper, R.N.
1968   *The Economics of Interdependence.* New York: Council on Foreign Relations and McGraw-Hill Book Company.

1986   *Economic Policy in an Interdependent World: Essays in World Economics.* Cambridge, Mass.: MIT Press.

1988   Survey of issues and review. Pp. 247-262 in L. Castle and C. Findlay, eds., *Pacific Trade in Services.* Boston: Allen & Unwin.

Corrigan, G. E.
1990   Reforming the U.S. financial system: an international perspective. *Quarterly Review* (Federal Reserve Bank of New York) 15(Spring):1-14.

Council of Economic Advisers
1990   *Economic Report of the President.* Annual Report. Washington, D.C.: U.S. Government Printing Office.

1991   *Economic Report of the President.* Annual Report. Washington, D.C.: U.S. Government Printing Office.

Cremeans, J.
  1989   *Progress Report on the National Trade Data Bank (NTDB)*. December. Washington, D.C.: U.S. Department of Commerce.
Customs Service
  1985   *U.S. Customs Service Automated Broker Interface*. Washington, D.C.: U.S. Department of the Treasury.
  1986   *Harmonized System Handbook: A Guide to the New U.S. Tariffs*. HB 3600-06. Washington, D.C.: U.S. Department of the Treasury.
  1987   *ACS Overview*. Office of Automated Commercial System Operations. Washington, D.C.: U.S. Department of the Treasury.
  1988   *ABI Information Package*. Office of Automated Commercial System Operations. Washington, D.C.: U.S. Department of the Treasury.
  1989a   Census Interface—Processing Procedures. Customs Directive 3560-01. U.S. Department of the Treasury, Washington, D.C.
  1989b   Export Commodity System, FY 1991. U.S. Department of the Treasury, Washington, D.C.
Customs Service and Bureau of the Census
  1988   *Memorandum of Understanding—Continued Cooperation, Automated Broker/Census Interface*. Washington, D.C.: U.S Department of the Treasury and U.S. Department of Commerce.
Deardorff, A., and R. Stern
  1990   Computational Analysis of Global Trading Arrangements. Department of Economics, University of Michigan, Ann Arbor.
Devlin, D.
  1988   The balance of payments. Pp. 3-22, Section 3, in I. Walter and T. Murray, eds., *Handbook of International Business*. New York: John Wiley & Sons.
Dickerson, D.
  1989   Impact of Raising the Export Exemption Level from $1,500 to $2,000 and $2,500. Internal memorandum to B. Walter, through K. Puzzilla, June 5. Bureau of the Census, U.S. Department of Commerce, Washington, D.C.
DiLullo, A.
  1980   Service transactions in the U.S. international accounts, 1970-1980. *Survey of Current Business* 61(November):29-46.
DiLullo, A., and O. Whichard
  1990   U.S. international sales and purchases of services. *Survey of Current Business* September 70(9):37-72.
Du Bois, M.
  1989   EC ministers agree to end border checks. *The Wall Street Journal* (October 10):A16.
The Economist
  1988   In a maze of numbers. *The Economist* (August 20):61-62.

Energy Information Administration
1989 *Quarterly Coal Report: April-June 1989.* Publication DOE/EIA-012 (89/2Q). Washington, D.C.: U.S. Department of Energy.

Farrell, M.
1989 Creating the Exporter Data Base (EDB)—Rev. 1. October. Memorandum to Don Adams, Chief, Foreign Trade Division. Bureau of the Census, Department of Commerce, Washington, D.C.

Farrell, M., and A. Radspieler
1988 Origin of Merchandise Exports Data. Foreign Trade Division, Bureau of the Census, U.S. Department of Commerce, Washington, D.C.
1989 Census Bureau State-By-State Foreign Trade Data: Historical Perspectives; Current Situation; Future Outlook. Paper presented to the National Governors' Association, Committee on International Trade and Foreign Relations. (May) Bureau of the Census, U.S. Department of Commerce, Washington, D.C.

Farrell, M., and M. Risha
1989 More than 100,000 exporters ship U.S. manufactured goods, Census Bureau reports. *U.S. Department of Commerce News.* Bureau of the Census. CB89-92. (June) Washington, D.C.: U.S. Department of Commerce.

Federal Reserve Bulletin
1990 The Federal Reserve in the payments system. *Federal Reserve Bulletin* (May):293-298.

Feketekuty, G.
1988 *International Trade in Services.* Washington, D.C.: American Enterprise Institute.

Fouch, G., and S. Bezirganian
1990 Growth in foreign direct investment in the United States outpaced that of U.S. direct investment abroad in 1989. *U.S. Department of Commerce News.* Bureau of Economic Analysis, U.S. BEA 90-30. (July) Washington, D.C.: U.S. Department of Commerce.

Fuerbringer, J.
1989 For collectors of U.S. data, a close call last month. *The New York Times* (November 3):C1.
1990 A rusty statistical compass for U.S. policy mappers. *Chance* 3(1):36-39.

Fusfeld, H.
1989 Proceedings of an International Conference on Changing Global Patterns of Industrial Research and Development. Sponsored by the Center for Science and Technology Policy, Rensselaer Polytechnic Institute School of Management, and Trygghetsradet SAF-PTK, Swedish Employment Security Council.

Gardner, B., and J. Ashcroft
1988 Letter to Mr. James C. Miller, Director, Office of Management

and Budget. State-by-State Data on Exports and Imports. Washington, D.C.: National Governors' Association.

Gbur, E.
1986 Memorandum: Feasibility of Sampling SED's under $2,500. Bureau of the Census, Department of Commerce, Washington, D.C.
1987 Effect of Increasing the Reporting Exemption Level for Exports. Bureau of the Census, U.S. Department of Commerce, Washington, D.C.

Gibbs, M.
1985 Continuing the international debate on services. *Journal of World Trade Law* 19(May-June):199-218.

Gonenc, R.
1988 Changing economics of international trade in services. Pp. 167-186 in B.R. Guile and J.B. Quinn, eds., *Technology in Services, Policies for Growth, Trade, and Employment*. National Academy of Engineering. Washington, D.C.: National Academy Press.

Gonzalez, M., J. Ogus, G. Shapiro, and B. Tepping
1975 Standards for discussion and presentation of errors in survey and census data. *Journal of the American Statistical Association* 70(351):1-23.

Greenwell, J.
1988 Census computer applications: can frequent exporters afford not to participate in the Automated Export Reporting Program? *The Exporter* (July):1-3.

Hausman, J., and M. Watson
1985 Seasonal adjustment with measurement error present. *Journal of the American Statistical Association* 80:531-540.
1990 Seasonal adjustment of preliminary data. *Journal of the American Statistical Association* 90:640-648.

Helfand, S., V. Natrella, and A. Pisarski
1984 *Statistics for Transportation, Communication, and Finance and Insurance: Data Availability and Needs*. Committee on National Statistics, Commission on Behavioral and Social Sciences and Education, National Research Council. Washington, D.C.: National Academy Press.

Hershey, R.
1988 Making trade data more precise. *The New York Times* (May 17):D1.

Hoekman, B., and R. Stern
1992 Evolving patterns of trade and investment in services. P. Hooper and J.D. Richardson, eds., *International Economic Transactions: Issues in Measurement and Empirical Research*. Chicago: University of Chicago Press.

Howenstine, N.
1989 U.S. affiliates of foreign companies: 1987 benchmark survey results. *Survey of Current Business* (July):116-139.

Huang, E.
1987   Report on low value ratio using Automated Broker Interface data. Internal Census Bureau Memorandum to B. Walter, December 17.

Interagency Committee on Measurement of Real Output, Subcommittee on Prices
1973   Report on criteria for choice of unit values or wholesale prices as deflators (the Searle Committee Report). Originally mimeographed June 17, 1960; reprinted with changes and a brief summary of the appendices. *Review of Income and Wealth* 19(3)(September):253-266.

International Monetary Fund
1986a   *Final Report of the Working Party on the Statistical Discrepancy in World Current Account Balances.* Washington, D.C.: International Monetary Fund.
1986b   *Direction of Trade Statistics Yearbook.* Washington, D.C.: International Monetary Fund.
1990a   *International Capital Markets, Developments and Prospects.* Washington, D.C.: International Monetary Fund.
1990b   *Direction of Trade Statistics Yearbook.* Washington, D.C.: International Monetary Fund.
1991   *International Capital Markets, Developments and Prospects.* Washington, D.C.: International Monetary Fund.
1992   *Final Report of the Working Party on the Study of the Measurement of International Capital Flows.*

International Trade Administration
1988   *International Direct Investment: Global Trends and the U.S. Role.* Washington, D.C.: U.S. Department of Commerce.
1989   COMPRO: General Overview. (June 30) U.S. Department of Commerce, Washington, D.C.

Inter-Secretariat Working Group on National Accounts
1990   System of National Accounts (SNA) Review Issues: Discussion paper for 1990 Regional Commission Meetings on SNA. Provisional Future ST/ESA/STAT/SER.F/2/Rev.4. February. Statistical Office, United Nations, New York.

Jabine, T.
1984   *The Comparability and Accuracy of Industry Codes in Different Data Systems.* Committee on National Statistics, Commission on Behavioral and Social Sciences and Education, National Research Council. Washington, D.C.: National Academy Press.

Jackson, J.
1988   *International Competition in Services: A Constitutional Framework.* Washington, D.C.: American Enterprise Institute.

Jones, S.
1990   Thoughts on Longer-Range Improvements in the Federal Statistical Program. Paper presented to the meeting of the Commit-

tee on National Statistics, National Research Council, February 9-10. U.S. Department of the Treasury, Washington, D.C.

Julius, D.
1990   *Global Companies and Public Policy: The Growing Challenge of Foreign Direct Investment.* The Royal Institute of International Affairs. New York: Council on Foreign Relations Press.
1991   *Foreign Direct Investment: The Neglected Twin of Trade.* Group of Thirty, occasional papers, #33. Washington, D.C.: Group of Thirty.

Juster, T. F.
1988   The State of U.S. Economic Statistics: Current and Prospective Quality, Policy Needs, and Resources. Paper presented at the 50th National Bureau of Economic Research Anniversary Conference on Research in Income and Wealth. (May) Washington, D.C.

Kamalich, R. and J. Kwiecinski
1989   CPI User Survey Internal Report. Division of Consumer Prices and Price Indexes. November 20. Washington, D.C.: Bureau of Labor Statistics.

Keane, J.
1987   Exporters: automate your census reports and save time, money, and hassle. Public Information Office, Bureau of the Census. *U.S. Department of Commerce News.* (June) Washington, D.C.: U.S. Department of Commerce.

Kelly, H., and A. Wyckoff
1989   Missing link: the need for better data on purchased services. *The Service Economy* 3(4):1-6.

Knight, P.
1989   Document image processing: fast route to efficient filing. *Financial Times* (November 24).
1990   U.S. merchandise trade: May, seasonally adjusted imports and exports. *U.S. Department of Commerce News.* Public Information Office, Bureau of the Census. FT900 (90-05) CB-90-130. Washington, D.C.: U.S. Department of Commerce.

Kotwas, G. and H. Mearkle
1990   U.S. merchandise trade: May 1990: seasonally adjusted imports and exports. *U.S. Department of Commerce News.* Bureau of the Census. FT900 (90-05) CB-90-130. Washington, D.C.: U.S. Department of Commerce.

Kravis, I., and R. Lipsey
1988   *Production and Trade in Services by U.S. Multinational Firms.* National Bureau of Economic Research. Working Paper No. 2615. Cambridge, Mass.: National Bureau of Economic Research.
1992   The international comparison program: current status and problems. In P. Hooper and J.D. Richardson, eds., *International Economic*

Transactions: Issues in Measurement and Empirical Research. Chicago: University of Chicago Press.

Kravis, I., R. Lipsey, and L. Molinari
1992　Measures of prices and price competitiveness in international trade in manufactured goods. In P. Hooper and J.D. Richardson, eds., *International Economic Transactions: Issues in Measurement and Empirical Research.* Chicago: University of Chicago Press.

Landefeld, J.S., and A. Lawson
1991　Valuation of U.S. net international investment position. *Survey of Current Business* (May)40-49.

Lederer, E.P., W. Lederer, and R. Sammons
1982　International Services Transactions of the United States: Proposals for Improvement in Data Collection. Paper prepared for the U.S. Departments of State and Commerce and the Office of the United States Trade Representatives (January), Washington, D.C.

Lipscomb, E., and B. Walter
1978　Impacts of Reporting Burden Reduction on the Quality of Export Statistics. Bureau of the Census, U.S. Department of Commerce.

Lipsey, R.
1990　Reviving the Federal Statistical System: International Aspects. *American Economic Association Papers and Proceedings* 80(May)(2):337-340.

Lipsey, R., and I. Kravis
1985　The competitive position of U.S. manufacturing firms. *Banca Nazionale del Lavoro Quarterly Review* 153(June):127-154.
1987　The competitiveness and comparative advantage of U.S. multinationals, 1957-1984. *Banca Nazionale del Lavoro Quarterly Review* 161(June):147-165.
1989　Technological Characteristics of Industries and the Competitiveness of the U.S. and its Multinational Firms. Working Paper No. 2933. (April.) National Bureau of Economic Research.

Livingston, S.
1982　Observations on the role of services in international trade. *Fletcher Forum* 6(Winter):91-110.

Ljung, G.M., and G.E.P. Box
1978　On a measure of lack of fit in time series models. *Biometrika* (65):297-303.

Lowe, J.H.
1990　Gross product of U.S. affiliates of foreign companies, 1977-87. *Survey of Current Business* 70(6):45-53.

Lux, M.
1984　The Harmonized Commodity Description and Coding System: Current Situation and Consideration. Statistical Office of the European Communities, Paris, France.

Mackay, E.
1982   The accuracy of international trade data. *Intereconomics* 5(Sept.-Oct.):251-255.

Mangaroo, R.
1986   Census Bureau Automated Data Reporting System Helps Exporters Streamline Their Customs Paperwork. *U.S. Department of Commerce News*. Public Information Office, Bureau of the Census. CB86-181. Washington, D.C.: U.S. Department of Commerce.

Markoff, J.
1988   American Express goes high-tech. *The New York Times* (July 31):3:1.

Marquez, J.
1990   Table of Mean and Standard Deviation of the U.S. Trade Balance for Several Periods. (May) Board of Governors of the Federal Reserve System, Washington, D.C.

Marquez, J., and N. Ericsson
1990   Evaluating the Predictive Performance of Trade-Account Models. International Finance Discussion Papers, Number 377. Board of Governors of the Federal Reserve System, Washington, D.C.

Marsh, B.
1989   Small businesses aren't so little when it comes to role in exports. *The Wall Street Journal* (August 18):B2.

Maskus, K.
1992   Comparing international trade data and product and national characteristics data for the analysis of trade models. In P. Hooper and J.D. Richardson, eds., *International Economic Transactions: Issues in Measurement and Empirical Research*. Chicago: University of Chicago Press.

Mearkle, H., and R. Preuss
1990   U.S. Merchandise Trade: January 1990. *U.S. Department of Commerce News*. Public Information Office, Bureau of the Census. FT900 (90-01). CB-90-51. Washington, D.C.: U.S. Department of Commerce.

Monk, H.
1985   Memorandum: Specifications for Developing Standard Industrial Classification (SIC)-Based Tariff Schedules of the United States Annotated (TSUSA) Classification System. Bureau of the Census, U.S. Department of Commerce, Washington, D.C.

Neece, W.
1984   Statistical Classification Systems. Bureau of the Census, U.S. Department of Commerce, Washington, D.C.

Norwood, J.
1989a What is Quality? Paper presented at the annual research conference of the Bureau of the Census. U.S. Department of Commerce, Washington, D.C.
1989b Data Quality for Public Policy. Paper presented at the Joint

Session of Society of Government Economists and the American Economic Association. (December) Atlanta, Georgia.

Office of Business Analysis
1990   *National Trade Data Bank: Interim Report to Congress as Required by Section 5413, Omnibus Trade and Competitiveness Act of 1988.* Actions taken pursuant to Subtitle E, Title V of the Omnibus Trade and Competitiveness Act of 1988. Washington, D.C.: U.S. Department of Commerce.

Official Journal of the European Communities
1989   Proposal for a Council Regulation (EEC) on the statistics relating to the trading of goods between member states. *Official Journal of the European Communities* C(41):5-13.

Organization for Economic Cooperation and Development
1990   *OECD Countries' International Trade in Services.* Economics and Statistics Department. (January.) Paris: Organization for Economic Cooperation and Development.

Ott, M.
1988   Have U.S. exports been larger than reported? *Federal Reserve Bank of St. Louis Review* 70(Sept.-Oct.):3-23.

Park, J.
1990   America's 50 biggest exporters: overseas sales take off at last. *Fortune* (July 16):76-77.

Puzzilla, K.
1983   Impact of using a fifty percent sample of records at various value cut-offs to compile monthly export statistics. Internal Census Bureau memorandum to B. Walter, December 1.
1985   Memorandum: Pilot Study Audit of the Seattle-Tacoma Airport. Bureau of the Census, U.S. Department of Commerce, Washington, D.C.
1988   Memorandum: Audit of Export Shipments at Miami International Airport. Bureau of the Census, U.S. Department of Commerce, Washington, D.C.
1989   Memorandum: Final Report on the Results of Air Audits. Bureau of the Census, U.S. Department of Commerce.

Quinn, J., and T. Doorley, eds.
1988   Key policy issues posed by services. Pp. 211-234 in *Technology in Services: Policies for Growth, Trade, and Employment.* National Academy of Engineering. Washington, D.C.: National Academy Press.

Richards, E.
1989   The data deluge. *The Washington Post* (September 24):H1.

Risha, M.
1991   A Comparison of the "Origin of Movement" Series and the "Exports from Manufacturing Establishments" Series. Industry Division Working Papers Series. Bureau of the Census, U.S. Department of Commerce, Washington, D.C.

Rosengarden, E.
  1986   Memorandum to the President's Economic Policy Council, on
          the Request by the Council's Working Group for Comments on
          the Quality of Federal Economic Statistics. (August.) U.S. In-
          ternational Trade Commission, Washington, D.C.
Roth, J.A., J.T. Scholz, and A. Dryden-Witte
  1989   *Taxpayer Compliance: An Agenda for Research.* Panel on Law
          and Justice, National Research Council. Philadelphia: Univer-
          sity of Pennsylvania Press.
Rutter, J.
  1989   Direct Investment Update: Trends in International Direct In-
          vestment. Staff report. International Trade Administration,
          U.S. Department of Commerce, Washington, D.C.
  1988   Global Trends and the U.S. Role. International Trade Adminis-
          tration, U.S. Department of Commerce, Washington, D.C.
Ryten, J.
  1988   Errors in foreign trade statistics. *Survey Methodology* 14(1):3-
          18.
Scholl, R.
  1990   International Investment Position: Component Detail for U.S.
          Assets Abroad and Foreign Assets in the United States for 1989.
          U.S. Department of Commerce News. Office of Public Infor-
          mation, Bureau of Economic Analysis. BEA 90-31. Washing-
          ton, D.C.: U.S. Department of Commerce.
Schott, J., ed.
  1990   *Completing the Uruguay Round, A Results-Oriented Approach
          to the GATT Trade Negotiations.* (September) Washington,
          D.C.: Institute for International Economics.
Schultz, S.
  1984   Trade in services: its treatment in international forums and the
          problems ahead. *Intereconomics* 6(Nov.-Dec.):267-273.
Schultze, C.
  1988   Policy Users Panel. Paper prepared for the National Bureau of
          Economic Research 50th Anniversary Conference on Research
          in Income and Wealth, (May) Washington, D.C.
Sinai, H., and Z. Sofianou, eds.
  1989   International trade in services: how do major countries fare?
          The Service Economy 3(April):13-19.
Statistical Office of the European Communites
  1989a   Classification of International Trade in Services. Working Document
          for the Eurostat-OECD Joint Meeting, September 18-29, Paris,
          France.
  1989b   Improving the System of Collecting Data on International Trade
          in Services. Report by the Balance of Payments Working Party,
          April 17-19, Paris, France.
Statistics Canada
  1987   *Quality Guidelines.* Ottawa, Ontario: Statistics Canada.

Stekler, L.
  1989   *Adequacy of International Transactions and Position Data for Policy Coordination.* NBER Working Paper No. 2844. Washington, D.C.: National Bureau of Economic Research.
  1990   Accuracy of U.S. Data on International Capital Flows. (February) Board of Governors of the Federal Reserve System, Washington, D.C.
  1991a U.S. International Transactions in 1990. Federal Reserve Bulletin. (May) Board of Governors of the Federal Reserve System, Washington, D.C.
  1991b The Statistical Discrepancy in the U.S. International Transactions Accounts: Sources and Suggested Remedies. International Finance Discussion Papers, Number 401, Board of Governors of the Federal Reserve System, Washington, D.C.

Stekler, L., and G.V.G. Stevens
  1992   The adequacy of U.S. direct investment data. In P. Hooper and J.D. Richardson, eds., *International Economic Transactions: Issues in Measurement and Empirical Research.* Chicago: University of Chicago Press.

Stern, R., and B. Hoekman
  1987   Issues and data needs for GATT negotiations on services. *World Economy* 10(March):39-60.

Stout, H.
  1989   Shaky numbers: U.S. statistics mills grind out more data that are then revised. *The Wall Street Journal* (August 31).

Sullivan, W.
  1990   The 1987 Standard Industrial Classification (SIC), the Harmonized System (HS) and Cross Classification HS to SIC. International Trade Administration, U.S. Department of Commerce, Washington, D.C.

Summers, B.J.
  1991   Clearing and payments system: the role of the Central Bank. *Federal Reserve Bulletin* (February):81-91.

Triplett, J.
  1989   Reviving the statistical system: a view from within. *American Economic Association Papers and Proceedings* 80(2):341-344, May.
  1990   The Federal Statistical System's Response to Emerging Data Needs. Bureau of Economic Analysis, U.S. Department of Commerce, Washington, D.C.

Turner, P.
  1991   *Capital Flows in the 1980's, A Survey of Major Trends.* BIS Economic Papers. (April.) Basle, Switzerland: Bank for International Settlements.

Ulan, M., and W. Dewald
  1989   The U.S. net international investment position: misstated and misunderstood. In J. Dorn and W. Niskanen, eds., *Dollars, Deficits, and Trade.* Boston: Kluwer Academic Publishers.

United Nations
1986   Standard International Trade Classification Revision 3. Statistical Papers Series M, No. 34/Rev.3. Department of International Economic and Social Affairs, United Nations, New York.
U.N. Statistical Office
1988a   Draft of the Central Product Classification (CPC). Working Paper. ESA/STAT/AC.32/5. Department of International Economic and Social Affairs, United Nations, New York.
1988b   Draft of the Revised International Standard Industrial Classification of All Economic Activities. Working Paper. ESA/STAT/AC.32/4. Department of International Economic and Social Affairs, United Nations, New York.
1989   *Handbook of International Trade and Development Statistics.* Conference on Trade and Development. Geneva, Switzerland: United Nations.
1990a   System of National Accounts (SNA) Review Issues: Discussion Paper for 1990 Regional Commissions Meetings on SNA. Inter-Secretariat Working Group on National Accounts. Provisional Future ST/ESA/STAT/SER.F/2/Rev. 4. (February) United Nations Statistical Office, New York.
1990b   *UNCTAD Commodity Yearbook.* Conference on Trade and Development, Geneva, Switzerland: United Nations.
U.S. Congress
1988   *Omnibus Trade and Competitiveness Act of 1988.* Subtitle E—Trade Data and Studies, Sections 5401-5413. U.S. Congress. Washington, D.C.: U.S. Government Printing Office.
1990   *JEC to Review Proposals to Improve Federal Economic Statistics.* Joint Economic Committee Press Release. 101st Congress. Washington, D.C.: U.S. Government Printing Office.
U.S. Congress, House of Representatives
1989   Statement of Rep. John J. LaFalce, chairman, Committee on Small Business. Hearing on U.S. International Competitiveness: How to Create an Export Culture. Washington, D.C.: U.S. Government Printing Office.
1990a   *Customs Informed Compliance and Automation Act of 1990.* H.R. 4689. 101st Congress, 2nd Session. Washington, D.C.: U.S. Government Printing Office.
1990b   *Foreign Investment Policy Improvements Act.* HR 4520. 101st Congress, 2nd Session. Washington, D.C.: U.S. Government Printing Office.
1990c   *Report on Abuses and Mismanagement in U.S. Customs Service Commercial Operations.* Subcommittee on Oversight of the Committee on Ways and Means, U.S. House of Representatives. 101st Congress, 2nd Session. Washington, D.C.: U.S. Government Printing Office.
U.S. Congress, Senate
1980   *Protecting the Confidentiality of Shipper's Export Declarations,*

and to Standardize Export Data Submission and Disclosure Requirements. Committee on Governmental Affairs. Report to accompany S.2419. 96th Congress, 2nd Session, Report No. 96-796. Washington, D.C.: U.S. Government Printing Office.

1990 *International Data Improvement Act of 1990.* S2516. 101st Congress, 2nd Session. Washington, D.C.: U.S. Government Printing Office.

U.S. Department of Commerce

1989a Legislative Background—Publication Requirements, Section 301, Title 13, U.S.C. (Foreign Trade Statistics Program). Washington, D.C.

1989b U.S. Code, Title 13—Chapter 9, Collection and Publication of Foreign Commerce and Trade Statistics. Washington, D.C.

1990 *National Trade Data Bank: Interim Report to Congress as Required by Sec.5413, Omnibus Trade and Competitiveness Act of 1988.* Actions Taken Pursuant to Subtitle E, Title V of the Omnibus Trade and Competitiveness Act of 1988. Office of Business Analysis. Washington, D.C.: U.S. Department of Commerce.

U.S. Department of the Treasury

1989a *Report on Foreign Portfolio Investment in the United States as of December 31, 1984.* Office of the Assistant Secretary, International Affairs. Washington, D.C.: U.S. Department of the Treasury.

1989b *Treasury Bulletin* (Winter Issue, March). Washington, D.C.: U.S. Department of the Treasury.

1989c *Customs Regulations of the United States.* Part152.1(c)—Part 152.12, and Part 159.31-159.43. Washington, D.C.: Office of Regulations and Rulings, U.S. Customs Service. Washington, D.C.: U.S. Department of the Treasury.

U.S. General Accounting Office

1987 *System Integrity: Stronger Controls Needed for Customs' Automated Commercial System.* Report to the Commissioner of the U.S. Customs Service. GAO/IMTEC-87-10. Washington, D.C.: U.S. Government Printing Office.

1988 *Customs Automation: Observations on Selected Automated Commercial System Modules.* Briefing Report to Congressional Requesters. GAO/IMTEC-89-4BR. Washington, D.C.: U.S. Government Printing Office.

1989 *Federal Statistics: Merchandise Trade Statistics: Some Observations.* Briefing report to the chair, Panel on Foreign Trade Statistics, Committee on National Statistics, National Research Council. GAO/OCE-89-1BR. Washington, D.C.: U.S. Government Printing Office.

1991 *Customs Automation: Progress Made, More Expected in Revenue Reconciliation Process.* Report to the Chairman, Subcommittee on Oversight, Committee on Ways and Means, House of Representatives. GAO/IMTEC-91-27. Washington, D.C.: U.S. Government Printing Office.

U.S. Office of Management and Budget
1986 *Federal Statistics: A Special Report on the Statistical Programs and Activities of the United States Government Fiscal Year 1987.* Office of Information and Regulatory Affairs. Washington, D.C.: U.S. Government Printing Office.
1987 *Standard Industrial Classification Manual.* U.S. Office of Management and Budget. Washington, D.C.: U.S. Government Printing Office.

U.S. Office of Technology Assessment
1986 *Trade in Services: Exports and Foreign Revenues; Special Report.* OTA-ITE-316. Washington, D.C.: U.S. Government Printing Office.
1989 *Statistical Needs for a Changing U.S. Economy.* Background paper, OTA-BP-E-58. Washington, D.C.: U.S. Government Printing Office.

U.S. Travel and Tourism Administration
Survey of International Air Travelers Departing the United States. OMB Clearance No. 0605-007. Washington, D.C.: U.S. Department of Commerce.

Waite, C.
1987 Memorandum: Developing Sampling Approaches for Export Statistics. Bureau of the Census, U.S. Department of Commerce, Washington, D.C.
1988 Census Bureau Merchandise Trade Data—Program Overview, Developments and Direction. Briefing presented to the Washington Export Council, April 28. Bureau of the Census, U.S. Department of Commerce, Washington, D.C.
1989 Perspectives and Issues—Merchandise Trade Data. Paper submitted to the Panel on Foreign Trade Statistics, Committee on National Statistics, National Research Council. (June.) Washington, D.C.

Wall Street Journal
1988 A wider trade deficit jolts a fragile market; shares off 101 points. *The Wall Street Journal* (April 15):1W.

Walter, B.
1992 Quality issues affecting the compilation of the U.S. merchandise trade statistics. In P. Hooper and J.D. Richardson, eds., *International Economic Transactions: Issues in Measurement and Empirical Research.* Chicago: University of Chicago Press.

Walter, I.
1988 *Global Competition in Financial Services: Market Structure, Protection, and Trade Liberalization.* Washington, D.C.: American Enterprise Institute.

Whichard, O.

1987   U.S. sales of services to foreigners. *Survey of Current Business*
        (January):22-41.

1988   International services: new information on U.S. transactions
        with unaffiliated foreigners. *Survey of Current Business* (Octo-
        ber):27-34.

1989   U.S. multinational companies: operations since 1987. *Survey
        of Current Business* (June):27-39.

Working Group on the Quality of Economic Statistics

1987   Report of the Working Group on the Quality of Economic Sta-
        tistics to the Economic Policy Council. Economic Policy Council,
        Washington, D.C.

Wright, R., and G. Pauli

1988   International trade in financial services: the Japanese challenge.
        Pp. 187-210 in B.R. Guile and J.B. Quinn, eds., *Technology in
        Services, Growth, Trade, and Employment*. National Academy
        of Engineering. Washington, D.C.: National Academy Press.

Wyckoff, A.

1988   Sources and Assumptions of OTA's Input/Output Model. Paper
        presented at the OECD Workshop on Input/Output Techniques,
        Paris, France. (December 14.) Office of Technology Assess-
        ment, Washington, D.C.

Wysocki, B., Jr.

1990   The outlook: U.S. firms increase overseas investments. *The
        Wall Street Journal* (April 9):A1.

Index

149, 157, 162–164, 167, 169, 170, 171, 172, 215
see also Capital flows; Federal Reserve System; Financial services
Bank of Mexico, 146
Basle Committee on Banking Supervision, 169
Bilateral trade and trade agreements, 3, 4, 41, 68, 79, 247, 248
with Canada, 8, 21, 85, 93–94, 104, 211, 213–214, 215, 247, 248
export/import data, 8, 21, 85, 93–94, 95, 100, 104, 111
intermediate inputs, 49
with Japan, 64, 94–95, 100
price indexes, 209
Bills of lading, 84
Budgets of statistical agencies, 2, 24, 25, 26–27
Bureau of Economic Analysis, 12, 35, 72–73
budget of, 26–27, 165
capital flows, 9, 16, 33–34, 65, 157, 159–168, 171, 215–216
computer use, 142
confidentiality restrictions, 117, 215–216
coordination with Census Bureau, 9, 12, 16, 112, 116, 155, 161, 208–209
coordination with other agencies, 146, 164, 173
foreign affiliates, 12–13, 115, 118, 120–125, 134, 154–155, 164–166, 179, 181
foreign direct investments, other, 34, 36, 43, 58, 66, 115, 118, 120–125, 134, 154–155, 157, 159–162, 164–166
input-output tables, 6, 7, 42, 48–49, 56
merchandise trade, 16, 53, 61, 98, 112, 193, 208
NIPA, 35, 59
service sector trade, 12, 33, 57, 65, 66, 114, 115–116, 120–155, 213–214
Bureau of Export Administration, 82
Bureau of Labor Statistics (BLS)
employment data, 55, 59
merchandise sector, 53, 55
price data, 53, 59, 68, 79, 209
service sector, 57

Business, professional, and technical services, 57, 116, 117, 126, 127, 128, 129, 130, 131, 133–134, 135, 152, 159, 170
Business Council on the Reduction of Paperwork, 125, 132

C

Canada, 209, 211, 251
bilateral agreements with, *see under* Bilateral trade and trade agreements
Census Bureau data, 85, 93–94, 104, 145, 209, 247
export statistics, compared with U.S., 221–224
freight and pipeline transport, 139–140, 203, 213–214
service trade, 213–214
statistics exchange, 85, 93–94, 145, 199, 213–214, 224, 246, 247, 248
travel and tourism, 145–146
Canvass of data users
international services transactions and capital flows, 211–216
interview protocol, 217–220
invitation for written comments, 216–217
merchandise trade data, 190–211
methods used in, 187–190
Capital accounts, 20, 25, 159
Capital flows, 16, 65, 156–173, 193
Bureau of Economic Analysis, 9, 16, 33–34, 65, 157, 159–168, 171, 215–216
data collection, general, 2, 5, 13–14, 33–34, 65, 156, 158–164, 171, 215–216
data user evaluations, 211, 214–216
Department of the Treasury, 9–10, 16–17, 65, 157, 158, 159, 164, 167, 168–170, 214, 215
errors and error analysis, 20, 156, 170–171, 214–215
Federal Reserve System, 16–17, 34, 157–158, 162–164, 215
flow-of-funds accounts, 16–17, 73, 157
foreign affiliates, state-level data, 215–216